Study Guide

to accompany

Microeconomics: Principles & Policy

Twelfth Edition

William J. Baumol
New York University and Princeton University

Alan S. Blinder
Princeton University

Prepared by

Kenneth Slaysman
York College of Pennsylvania

SOUTH-WESTERN
CENGAGE Learning

Australia • Brazil • Japan • Korea • Mexico • Singapore • Spain • United Kingdom • United States

For product information and technology assistance, contact us at
**Cengage Learning Academic Resource Center,
1-800-423-0563**.

For permission to use material from this text or product, submit all requests online at **www.cengage.com/permissions**.
Further permissions questions can be emailed to
permissionrequest@cengage.com.

ISBN-13: 978-1-111-97000-0
ISBN-10: 1-111-97000-9

South-Western Cengage Learning
2640 Eagan Woods Drive Suite 220
Eagan, MN 55121

Cengage Learning is a leading provider of customized learning solutions with office locations around the globe, including Singapore, the United Kingdom, Australia, Mexico, Brazil, and Japan. Locate your local office at: **international.cengage.com/region**.

Cengage Learning products are represented in Canada by Nelson Education, Ltd.

For your course and learning solutions, visit **www.cengage.com**.

Purchase any of our products at your local college store or at our preferred online store **www.CengageBrain.com**.

Printed in the United States of America
1 2 3 4 5 6 7   15 14 13 12 11

TABLE OF CONTENTS

PREFACE

INTRODUCTION

This study guide is designed to be used with *Microeconomics: Principles and Policy,* Twelfth Edition, by William J. Baumol and Alan S. Blinder. This guide is not a substitute for the basic textbook; rather, experience has shown that conscientious use of a supplement such as this guide can lead to greater learning and understanding of the course material. It might also improve your grade.

The chapters in this book parallel those in *Microeconomics: Principles and Policy,* Twelfth Edition. Each chapter in the study guide is a review of the material covered in the textbook chapters. You should first read and study each chapter in the textbook and then use the corresponding chapter in this book. "Use" is the correct verb, as chapters in this book are designed for your active participation.

The material with which you will be working is organized into the following elements.

LEARNING OBJECTIVES

Each chapter starts with a set of behavioral learning objectives. These objectives indicate the things you should be able to do upon completing each chapter.

IMPORTANT TERMS AND CONCEPTS

As one of the learning objectives for each chapter states, you should be able to define, understand, and use correctly the terms and concepts that are listed in this section. They parallel the important terms and concepts listed at the end of the text chapter. Being able to define these terms is likely to be important for your grade. But to really understand what they mean, rather than to temporarily memorize their definition, is even better. The ultimate test of your understanding will be your ability to use correctly the terms and concepts in real life situations.

CHAPTER REVIEW

Each chapter review is a summary discussion of the major points for that chapter. The reviews are designed to be used actively. Frequently, you will need to supply the appropriate missing term or to choose between pairs of alternate words. Some of the missing terms are quite specific and can be found in the list of important terms and concepts. At other times, the answers are less clear-cut, as the following hypothetical example illustrates: "If people expect inflation at higher rates than before, nominal interest rates are likely to _____." Any of the following would be correct answers: increase, rise, go up. In cases like this, do not get concerned if the answer you choose is different from the one in the back of the book.

IMPORTANT TERMS AND CONCEPTS QUIZ

Each chapter contains a quiz to help you review important terms and concepts. Match each term with the most appropriate definition.

BASIC EXERCISES

Most chapters have one or more exercises that are designed for you to use as a check on your understanding of a basic principle discussed in the chapter. Many of the exercises use simple arithmetic or geometry. While getting the correct answers is one measure of understanding, do not mistake the arithmetic manipulations for the economic content of the problems. A hand calculator or spreadsheet program may make the arithmetic less burdensome.

SELF-TEST FOR UNDERSTANDING

Each chapter has a set of multiple choice and true-false questions for you to use as a further check on your understanding. It is important to know not only the correct answers but also why the other alternatives are wrong. Answers for the Self-Tests are in the back of this guide.

APPENDIX

A number of chapters in the text contain an appendix, which generally is designed to supplement the chapter content with material that is either a bit more difficult or offers further exposition of a particular economic concept. In some cases, the review material for the appendix parallels that for the chapter, including learning objectives, important terms and concepts, and so forth. On other cases, the appendix material is reviewed here in the form of an additional exercise designed to illustrate the material discussed in the appendix.

SUPPLEMENTARY EXERCISE

Many chapters end with a supplementary exercise, which may be either an additional mathematical exercise or some suggestions that allow you to use what you have learned in real-world situations. Some exercises use more advanced mathematics. Since many of these exercises review Basic Exercise material, they illustrate how economists use mathematics and are included for students with an appropriate background in mathematics. The mathematics are a means to an end and not an end in themselves. It is most important to understand the economic principles that underlie the Basic Exercise, something that does not depend upon advanced mathematics.

ECONOMICS IN ACTION

Most chapters include a brief example, often from recent newspapers or magazines. Each example has been chosen to show how economic concepts and ideas can help one understand real world problems and issues.

ECONOMICS ONLINE

Many chapters include one or more World Wide Web addresses that you can use to access current information or for additional information.

There is also a homepage for the textbook:

http://www.cengage.com/economics/baumol

STUDY QUESTIONS

Each chapter ends with a short list of study questions. Working with friends on these questions is a useful way to review chapter material and should help on examinations.

Being introduced to economics for the first time should be exciting and fun. For many, it is likely to be hard work, but hard work does not have to be dull and uninteresting. Do not look for a pat set of answers with universal applicability. Economics does not offer answers but rather a way of looking at the world and thinking systematically about issues. As the English economist John Maynard Keynes said:

> The theory of economics does not furnish a body of settled conclusions immediately applicable to policy. It is a method rather than a doctrine, an apparatus of the mind, a technique of thinking, which helps its possessor to draw correct conclusions.

IMPORTANT TERMS AND CONCEPTS QUIZ

Choose the best definition for each of the following terms.

1. _____ Opportunity cost
2. _____ Abstraction
3. _____ Theory
4. _____ Correlation
5. _____ Economic model

a. Ignoring many details to focus on essential parts of a problem
b. Two variables change simultaneously, whether or not a causal relationship exists
c. Effects on third parties that are not part of an economic transaction
d. Deliberate simplification of relationships to explain how those relationships work
e. Value of the next best alternative
f. Simplified version of some aspect of the economy

BASIC EXERCISES

Each statement or vignette below illustrates one of the 10 important Ideas for Beyond the Final Exam. Which statement goes with which idea?

_____ 1. Opportunity cost is the correct measure of cost.

_____ 2. Attempts to fight market forces often backfire or have unintended consequences.

_____ 3. Nations can gain from trade by exploiting their comparative advantage.

_____ 4. Both parties gain in a voluntary exchange.

_____ 5. Good decisions typically require marginal analysis.

_____ 6. The adverse impact of externalities can often be repaired by market methods.

_____ 7. There is a trade-off between efficiency and equality. Many policies that promote one damage the other.

_____ 8. The government's tools to even out booms and busts are imperfect.

_____ 9. In the short run, policy makers face a trade-off between inflation and unemployment.

_____ 10. In the long run, productivity is almost the only thing that matters for a society's material well-being.

A. In June 2008, Northwest Airlines offered a last-minute roundtrip cybersaver fare between Los Angeles and New York City for $274. This fare required travelers to fly on Saturday and return the following Monday or Tuesday. At the same time, a regular unrestricted fare was more than $1,422, and the ten-day, advance purchase Saturday stay-over fare was around $315. Economists would argue that, properly counted, Northwest was more than covering costs on the $274 passengers.

B. "We trade because we can get more of the goods and services we value by devoting our energies to what we can do well and using the proceeds to purchase what others are good at making (or doing)." I.M. Destler, "Trade Policy at a Crossroads," *Brookings Review,* Winter 1999.

C. In New York, individuals who need a passport at the last minute have to pay a $35 fee for rush service and often spend most of a day waiting in line. Others pay up to $150 extra for someone else to stand in line for them. "If six hours of your time is worth more than $150, you're going to be prepared to use one of these services," said George Brokaw, a New York investment banker. "Speeding Up a Passport," *The New York Times,* June 6, 1999.

D. Commenting on the economy in July 1998, Alan Greenspan, Chairman of the Board of Governors of the Federal Reserve System, said, ". . . the extent to which strong growth and high labor force utilization have been joined with low inflation over an extended period is . . . exceptional . . . With labor markets very tight and domestic final demand retaining considerable momentum, the risks of a pickup in inflation remain significant . . . [T]he impending constraint from domestic labor markets could bind more abruptly than it has to date, intensifying inflation pressures." Testimony of Alan Greenspan, Chairman of the Federal Reserve Board of Governors Before the Committee on Banking, Housing, and Urban Affairs, U.S. Senate, July 21, 1998.

E. Third–graders Jennifer and Jolene trade sandwiches at lunch because each prefers what the other's mother fixed.

F. Robert Arnold and Robert Dennis argue that the impact of the growth in labor productivity since the beginning of this century has been astounding. Not only has output per worker increased more than sevenfold, but "the typical workday and typical workweek shrank . . . the share of family income required to meet the bare necessities was cut in half . . . and goods that were once considered luxuries came within reach of the middle class." "Perspectives on productivity growth," *Business Economics*, April 1, 1999.

G. A study of 16 American cities found that advertised rents for vacant units were higher in cities with rent control than cities without rent control. In cities without rent control, advertised rents are distributed almost evenly above and below median rents as measured by the U.S. Bureau of the Census. In cities with rent control, "most available units are priced well above the median. In other words, inhabitants in cities without rent control have a far easier time finding moderately priced rental units than do inhabitants in rent-controlled cities." William Tucker, "Rent control drives out affordable housing," *USA Today* (Magazine), July 1998.

H. "There is great comprehension today that ambitious redistribution policies will reduce either economic efficiency or economic growth, or both, because of undesired behavioral adjustment of work, savings, investment, and entrepreneurship." Assar Lindbeck, "How Can Economic Policy Strike a Balance Between Economic Efficiency and Income Equality," in *Income Inequality: Issues and Policy Options*, a symposium sponsored by the Federal Reserve Bank of Kansas City, August 27–28, 1998.

I. Under the EPA's Acid Rain Program, fossil fuel–fired power plants are allotted SO_2 (sulphur dioxide) emission allowances that allow them to emit one ton of SO_2. Utilities with surplus allowances may sell them to utilities whose emissions levels exceed their allowances.

J. "If we knew precisely where we were, understood precisely the relationship between our instruments and macroeconomic performance, had a single objective, and could instantly affect the variable or variables associated with our target(s), implementing [monetary] policy would be easy... It is precisely because none of these preconditions hold that monetary policy is so difficult and principles are needed to guide its implementation." Remarks by former Federal Reserve Governor Laurence H. Meyer. The Alan R. Holmes Lecture, Middlebury College, Middlebury, Vermont, March 16, 1998.

SELF-TESTS FOR UNDERSTANDING

TEST A
Circle the most appropriate answer.

1. Economists define opportunity cost as
   a. the money price of goods and services.
   b. the lowest price you can bargain for.
   c. the value of the next best alternative.
   d. retail prices including sales taxes.

2. Most economists believe that attempts to set prices by decree
   a. will work best in the long run.
   b. are likely to create significant new problems.
   c. are the only way to establish fair prices.
   d. have a history of practical effectiveness.

3. With respect to international trade,
   a. a country can gain only if its neighbors lose.
   b. countries should try to be self-sufficient of all goods.
   c. only those countries with the highest productivity levels will gain.
   d. a country can gain by producing those goods in which it has a comparative advantage and then trading for those things in which other countries have a comparative advantage.

4. Most economists believe that exchange
   a. is likely to be mutually advantageous to both parties when it is voluntary.
   b. only takes place when one side can extract a profit from the other.
   c. usually makes both parties worse off.
   d. is best when strictly regulated by the government.

5. Marginal analysis is concerned with the study of
   a. buying stocks and bonds on credit.
   b. those groups that operate on the fringes of the market economy.
   c. changes, such as the increase in cost when output increases.
   d. an engineer's fudge factor for possible errors.

6. When the actions of some economic agents impose cost on others, for example, the polluting smoke of a factory or power plant,
   a. market mechanisms may exist that can help remedy the situation.
   b. the only answer is government regulation.
   c. there is very little one can do; such is the price of progress.
   d. it is always best to close down the offending action.

7. Economic analysis suggests that
    a. policies that promote the highest rate of economic growth unambiguously improve the distribution of income.
    b. policies to increase equality may reduce output.
    c. incentives for work and savings have almost no impact on people's behavior.
    d. there is no trade-off between the size of the economic pie and how the pie is divided.

8. Monetary and fiscal policy
    a. can eliminate booms and busts if used appropriately.
    b. have no power to influence the economy.
    c. are too complicated to be of practical use.
    d. are powerful but imperfect tools to limit the swings of the business cycle.

9. Most economists believe that policies to reduce inflation
    a. have never been successful.
    b. will never be adopted in democracies.
    c. normally require a higher rate of unemployment.
    d. have an immediate and lasting impact.

10. Small differences in the productivity growth rate
    a. make little difference, even over periods as long as a century.
    b. can compound into significant differences.
    c. can be safely ignored by citizens and politicians.
    d. will lead only to small differences in the standard of living between countries.

TEST B

Circle T or F for true or false.

T F 1. Economic models are no good unless they include all of the details that characterize the real world.

T F 2. Material in this text will reveal the true answer to many important social problems.

T F 3. Economic theory deliberately simplifies relationships to concentrate on their essential casual elements.

T F 4. Economists' policy prescriptions differ because of incomplete information and different value judgments.

T F 5. Theory and practical policy have nothing to do with each other.

T F 6. If two variables are correlated, we can be certain that one causes the other.

T F 7. The best economic models all use the same degree of abstraction.

T F 8. An economist tests a hypothesis when she deliberately simplifies the nature of relationships in order to explain cause and effect.

T F 9. The dollars one must pay is the best measure of the cost of any decision.

T F 10. We would all be better off if the government regulated more markets.

T F 11. The most productive economies would be better off if they did not trade with other nations and tried to produce everything they need by themselves.

T F 12. In any transaction, one party must always gain at the expense of the other.

T F 13. No business should ever sell its output at a price that does not cover its full cost.

T F 14. Because pollution problems are often seen as a market shortcoming, market methods cannot help correct the problem.

T F 15. There is no trade-off between policies that increase output and those that equalize income.

T F 16. The government has all the tools it needs to keep the economy out of recessions.

T F 17. Policies to lower unemployment usually reduce the rate of inflation at the same time.

T F 18. Over the long run, it makes little difference whether productivity grows at 1 percent or 2 percent per year.

| APPENDIX | *Using Graphs*

Important Terms and Concepts

Variable

Origin (of a graph)

Slope of a straight (or curved) line

Tangent to a curve

Y-intercept

Ray through the origin, or ray

45-degree line

Production indifference map

Learning Objectives

After completing this chapter, you should be able to:

* interpret various graphs.

* use a two-variable graph to determine what combinations of variables go together.

* compute the slope of a straight line and explain what it measures.

* explain how to compute the slope of a curved line.

* explain how a 45-degree line can divide a graph into two regions, one in which the Y variable exceeds the X variable, and another in which the X variable exceeds the Y variable.

* construct two-variable and three-variable graphs.

* use a three-variable graph to determine what combinations of the X and Y variables are consistent with the same value for the Z variable.

APPENDIX REVIEW

Economists like to draw pictures, primarily *graphs*. Your textbook and this study guide will make extensive use of graphs. There is nothing very difficult about graphs, but understanding them from the beginning will help you avoid mistakes later on.

All the graphs we will use start with two straight lines, one on the bottom and one on the left side. These edges of the graph will usually have labels to indicate what is being measured in both the vertical and

(1) horizontal directions. The line on the bottom is called the [horizontal/vertical] axis, and the line running up the side is called the _____ axis. The point at which the two lines meet is called the _____. The variable measured along the horizontal axis is often called the *X* variable, whereas the term *Y* variable is often used to refer to the variable measured along the vertical axis.

Figure 1-1 is a two-variable diagram plotting expenditures on alcoholic beverages and ministers' salaries. Does this graph imply that wealthier clergymen drink more, or does it suggest that more drinking in general is increasing the demand for, and hence the salaries of, clergymen? Most likely neither interpretation is correct; just because you can plot two variables does not mean that one caused the other.

Many two-variable diagrams encountered in introductory economics use straight lines, primarily for sim-

(2) plicity. An important characteristic of a straight line is its *slope*, measured by comparing differences between two points. To calculate the slope of a straight line, divide the [horizontal/vertical] change by the corresponding _____ change as you move to the right along the line. The change between any two points can be used to compute the slope because the slope of a straight line is _____. If the straight line shows that both the horizontal and vertical variables increase together, then the line is said to have a [positive/negative] slope; that is, as we move to the right, the line slopes [up/down]. If one variable decreases as the other variable increases, the line is said to have a _____ slope. A line with a zero slope shows _____ change in the *Y* variable as the *X* variable changes.

─ *Figure 1-1* ───────────────────────────

Ministers' Salaries and Expenditures on Alcohol

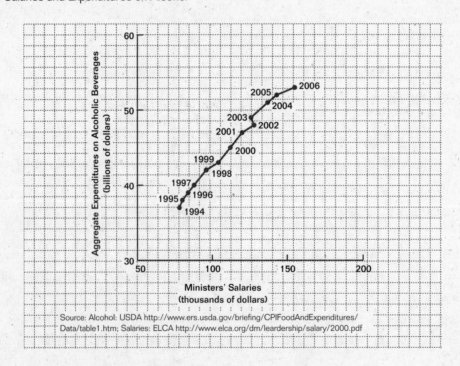

Source: Alcohol: USDA http://www.ers.usda.gov/briefing/CPIFoodAndExpenditures/ Data/table1.htm; Salaries: ELCA http://www.elca.org/dm/leardership/salary/2000.pdf

A special type of straight line passes through the origin of a graph. This is called a _____ through the (3) origin. Its slope is measured the same as the slope of any other straight line. A special type of ray is one that connects all points where the vertical and horizontal variables are equal. If the vertical and horizontal variables are measured in the same units, then this line has a slope of +1 and is called the _____ line.

Like straight lines, curved lines also have slopes, but the slope of a curved line is not constant. We measure the slope of a curved line at any point by the slope of the one straight line that just touches, or is _____ to, the line at that point. (4)

A special type of graph is used by economists as well as cartographers. Such a graph can represent three dimensions on a diagram with only two axes by the use of _____ lines. A traditional application (5) of such a graph in economics is a diagram that measures inputs along the horizontal and vertical axes and then uses contour lines to show what different combinations of inputs can be used to produce the same amount of output. This graph is called a _____ _____ map.

IMPORTANT TERMS AND CONCEPTS QUIZ

Choose the best definition for each of the following terms.

1. _____ Variable
2. _____ Origin
3. _____ Slope
4. _____ Tangent to a curve
5. _____ Y-intercept
6. _____ Ray
7. _____ 45-degree line
8. _____ Production indifference map

a. Graph of how a variable changes over time
b. Straight line, touching a curve at a point without cutting the curve
c. Straight line emanating from the origin
d. Object whose magnitude is measured by a number
e. Straight line through the origin with a slope of +1
f. Point at which a straight line cuts the vertical axis
g. Ratio of vertical change to corresponding horizontal change
h. Point where both axes meet and where both variables are zero
i. A graph showing different combinations of two inputs necessary to produce a given level of output

9

BASIC EXERCISES

READING GRAPHS

These exercises are designed to give you practice working with two–variable diagrams.

1. **UNDERSTANDING A DEMAND CURVE**

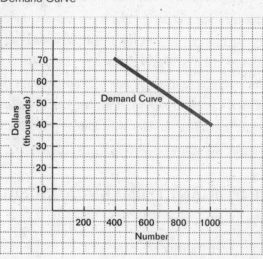
Demand Curve

The demand curve in **Figure 1-2** represents the demand for new Ph.D. economists.

a. What quantity would colleges and universities demand if they have to pay a salary of $70,000?

_____

b. What does the graph indicate would happen to the quantity demanded if salaries fall to $50,000? The quantity demanded would [increase/decrease] to _____.

c. If salaries were $60,000 the quantity demanded would be _____.

d. What is the slope of the demand curve?

_____

e. Explain how the slope of the demand curve provides information about the change in the number of new Ph.D. economists demanded as salary changes.

2. **UNDERSTANDING A 45-DEGREE LINE**

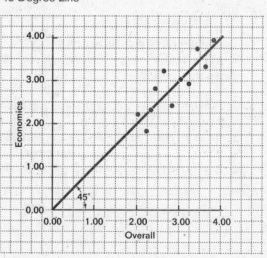
45-Degree Line

Figure 1-3 shows data on grade point averages (GPA) for Valerie and her friends. Overall averages are measured along the horizontal axis while GPAs for courses in economics are measured along the vertical axis. Figure 1-3 also includes a 45-degree line.

a. How many individuals have higher overall GPAs than economics GPAs? _____

b. How many individuals do better in economics courses than in their other courses? _____

c. If all of Valerie's friends had their best grades in economics courses, all of the points in Figure 1-3 would lie [above/below] the 45-degree line.

d. If all of the points in Figure 1-3 were below the 45-degree line, we could conclude that Valerie and her friends did better in [economics/non-economics] courses.

SELF-TESTS FOR UNDERSTANDING

TEST A

Circle the most appropriate answer.

1. The vertical line on the left side of a two-variable diagram is called the
   a. ray through the origin.
   b. vertical axis.
   c. *X* axis.
   d. slope of the graph.

2. A two-variable diagram
   a. can only be drawn when one variable causes another.
   b. is a useful way to show how two variables change simultaneously.
   c. is a useful way of summarizing the influence of all factors that affect the *Y* variable.
   d. can only be used when relationships between variables can be represented by straight lines.

3. The origin of a two-variable graph is
   a. found in the lower right corner of a graph.
   b. the same as the *Y*-intercept.
   c. the intersection of the vertical and horizontal axes where both variables are equal to zero.
   d. found by following the slope to the point where it equals zero.

4. The slope of a straight line is found by dividing the
   a. *Y* variable by the *X* variable.
   b. vertical axis by the horizontal axis.
   c. largest value of the *Y* variable by the smallest value of the *X* variable.
   d. vertical change by the corresponding horizontal change.

5. The slope of a straight line
   a. is the same at all points along the line.
   b. increases moving to the right.
   c. will be zero when the *X* variable equals zero.
   d. is always positive.

6. If a straight line has a positive slope, then we know that
   a. it runs uphill, moving to the right.
   b. the slope of the line will be greater than that of a 45-degree line.
   c. it must also have a positive *Y*-intercept.
   d. it will reach its maximum value when its slope is zero.

Figure 1-4

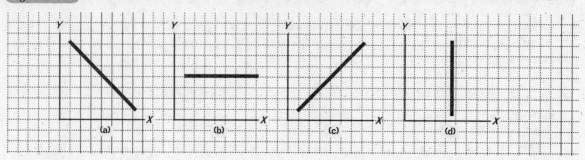

7. Referring to parts (a), (b), (c), and (d) of **Figure 1-4,** determine which line has a(n)

   a. positive slope _____

   b. negative slope _____

   c. zero slope _____

   d. infinite slope _____

Figure 1-5

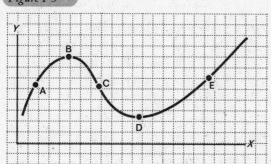

8. Referring to **Figure 1-5,** determine at which point(s) the curved line has a(n)

   a.   positive slope   _____ _____ _____

   b.   negative slope   _____ _____ _____

   c.   zero slope   _____ _____ _____

   d.   infinite slope   _____ _____ _____

9. If when $X = 5$, $Y = 16$ and when $X = 8$, $Y = 10$, then the

   a. line connecting X and Y has a positive slope.

   b. line connecting X and Y is a ray through the origin.

   c. slope of the line connecting X and Y is +6.

   d. slope of the line connecting X and Y is −2.

10. The slope of a curved line is
    a. the same at all points on the line.
    b. found by dividing the Y variable by the X variable.
    c. found by determining the slope of a straight line tangent to the curved line at the point of interest.
    d. always positive.

11. If a curved line is in the shape of a hill, then the point of zero slope will occur at the
    a. origin of the line.
    b. highest point of the line.
    c. Y-intercept of the line.
    d. point where a ray from the origin intercepts the line.

12. The Y-intercept is
    a. the same as the origin of a graph.
    b. the point where a line cuts the Y axis.
    c. usually equal to the X-intercept.
    d. equal to the reciprocal of the slope of a straight line.

13. If the Y-intercept of a straight line is equal to zero, then this line is called
    a. the opportunity cost of a graph.
    b. a ray through the origin.
    c. the 45-degree line.
    d. the X axis.

14. A ray is
    a. any straight line with a slope of +1.
    b. any line, straight or curved, that passes through the origin of a graph.
    c. a straight line with a positive Y-intercept.
    d. a straight line that passes through the origin.

15. If the X and Y variables are measured in the same units, a 45-degree line will
    a. have a positive Y-intercept.
    b. have a negative slope.
    c. show all points where X and Y are equal.
    d. be steeper than the Y axis.

16. If X and Y are measured in the same units, and we consider a point that lies below a 45-degree line, then we know that for the X and Y combination associated with this point,
    a. the X variable is greater than the Y variable.
    b. a line from the origin through this point will be a ray with a slope greater than +1.
    c. the Y variable is greater than the X variable.
    d. the slope of the point is less than 1.

Figure 1-6

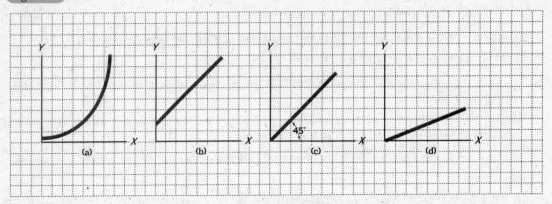

17. Referring to parts (a), (b), (c), and (d) of **Figure 1-6,** which part(s) show a ray through the origin?
    a. (b)
    b. (a) and (c)
    c. (a) and (d)
    d. (c) and (d)

18. If in part (d) of Figure 1-6, the Y variable changes by 2 units when the X variable changes by 5 units, then the slope of the line is
    a. (2/5) = 0.4.
    b. (5/2) = 2.5.
    c. (2 + 5) = 7.
    d. Insufficient information is available to compute.

19. If two straight lines have the same slope, then they
    a. must also have the same Y-intercept.
    b. will show the same change in Y for similar changes in X.
    c. will both pass through the origin.
    d. are said to be complements.

20. A contour map
    a. is always better than a two-variable diagram.
    b. is a way of collapsing three variables into a two-variable diagram.
    c. shows how the Y variable changes when the X variable is held constant.
    d. is only of relevance to cartographers.

TEST B

Circle T or F for true or false.

T   F   1. The line along the bottom of a two-variable graph is called the vertical axis.

T   F   2. The slope of a line measures the value of the Y variable when the X variable is equal to zero.

T   F   3. The slope of a straight line is the same at all points on the line.

T   F   4. A negative slope means that the *Y* variable decreases when the *X* variable increases.

T   F   5. The slope of a curved line cannot be measured.

T   F   6. A straight line that has a *Y*-intercept of zero is also called a ray through the origin.

T   F   7. All rays through the origin have the same slope.

T   F   8. If *X* and *Y* are measured in the same units, then a 45-degree line is a ray through the origin with a slope of +1.

T   F   9. If *X* and *Y* are measured in the same units, then any point above a 45-degree line is a point at which the *Y* variable is greater than the *X* variable.

T   F   10. A contour map is a way to show the relationship between two variables in three dimensions.

SUPPLEMENTARY EXERCISE

The following suggested readings offer an excellent introduction to the ideas and lives of economists past and present:

1. *The Worldly Philosophers: The Lives, Times & Ideas of the Great Economic Thinkers,* 7th ed., by Robert L. Heilbroner (Touchstone Books, 1999).

2. *Lives of the Laureates,* 4th edition, edited by William Breit and Barry Hirsch (MIT Press, 2004). This is a collection of recollections by 18 winners of the Nobel Prize in Economics.

ECONOMICS IN ACTION

PLAY BALL

Are baseball players overpaid? Does it make sense to pay someone more than $10 million to play what is, after all, just a game? Does it seem like baseball salaries have gotten out of hand? Even after adjusting for inflation, Babe Ruth's highest salary is estimated to have been slightly more than $700,000. Why are players today paid so much, and does it make economic sense?

Writing in *Scientific American*, Paul Wallich and Elizabeth Corcoran explain the difference in salaries using the concepts of opportunity cost and marginal analysis, ideas used extensively by economists. Under the reserve clause, in effect from 1903 until the mid-1970s, a baseball player who did not like his contract had little choice other than retiring from baseball. Players were not free to bargain with other teams. After the introduction of free agency, baseball players could sell their services to the team with the best offer.

Gerald Scully, in his book *The Business of Major League Baseball*, used statistical techniques to see how hitting and pitching help determine a team's winning percentage and how a team's revenue relates to its record and the size of the market in which it plays. He then estimated how adding a particular player might add to a team's performance and hence its revenue.

Using data from the late 1980s, Scully found that the performance of selected superstars increased team revenues by $2 million to $3 million, numbers consistent with the highest salaries at the time. Using data from the late 1960s, he estimates that superstars increased team revenues by $600,000 to $1 million and noted that the highest salaries were only $100,000 to $125,000.

15

1. How would marginal analysis help a team determine how much it should offer a free agent?

2. How does the concept of opportunity cost help explain baseball salaries? What was the opportunity cost of a baseball player's time under the reserve clause? How did free agency change the opportunity cost for a player deciding whether to stay with a team or move to a new team?

Sources: Paul Wallich and Elizabeth Corcoran, "The MBAs of Summer," *Scientific American* (June 1992): p. 120. Gerald W. Scully, *The Business of Major League Baseball* (Chicago: University of Chicago Press, 1989).

STUDY QUESTIONS

1. Explain the relationships among theories, models, and hypotheses.

2. Why are theories necessary for understanding the causal links between economic variables? Why can't the facts speak for themselves?

3. Many trace the establishment of economics as a formal field of study to the publication of Adam Smith's *Wealth of Nations* in 1776. Why, after more than 200 years, do so many questions remain?

ECONOMICS ONLINE

Find out about the current and former Nobel Prize winners in Economics at this site maintained by the Nobel Prize committee. There are easy links to the Nobel Prize in Economics from this site:

http://nobelprize.org

The Minneapolis Federal Reserve Bank regularly publishes interviews with economists in its quarterly publication, *The Region.* The December 1994 interview is with Alan Blinder. You can read these interviews online at:

http://minneapolisfed.org/pubs/region/int.cfm

The Economy: Myth and Reality

2

Important Terms and Concepts

Factors of production, or Inputs

Outputs

Gross domestic product (GDP)

Open economy

Closed economy

Recession

Transfer payments

Progressive tax

Mixed economy

Learning Objectives

After completing this chapter, you should be able to:

- explain the difference between inputs and outputs.

- explain why total output of the American economy is larger than that of other nations.

- explain the difference between a closed and an open economy.

- describe the broad changes in American work experience: Who goes to work outside the home? What sorts of jobs do they hold? What sorts of goods and services do they produce?

- describe who gets what proportion of national income.

- describe the central role of business firms.

- describe the role of government in the American economy.

CHAPTER REVIEW

This chapter offers an introduction to and overview of the American economy. The money value of total output of the American economy is usually measured by something called gross

(1) _____ _____ or _____ for short. American GDP is so large because of the size of the work force and the _____ of American workers. Other countries, for example China and India, have larger populations, but the productivity of their workers does not compare with that of American workers.

Why is the American economy so productive? It is useful to view an economic system as a social mecha-

(2) nism that organizes [inputs/outputs] to produce _____. Many believe that the productivity of the American economy is a reflection of business competition fostered by the extensive use of _____ markets and _____ enterprise.

No economy is self-sufficient. All economies trade with each other, although their reliance on trade varies. The average of exports and imports as a percentage of GDP is often used as a measure of the degree to which

(3) an economy can be called _____ or _____. Compared to other industrialized countries, the United States would look like a(n) [closed/open] economy. Both exports and imports have increased substantially since World War II and are now about 14 percent of American GDP.

The term *real GDP* is used to refer to measures of GDP that have been corrected for inflation. Although the time series graph of real GDP for the United States shows significant growth since World War II, it has not been continual growth. There have been periods when total output declined. These periods are called

(4) _____. How the government should respond during or in anticipation of a period of recession continues to spark controversy.

(5) Organizing inputs, also called _____ of production, is a central issue that any economy must address. For the most part, output in the United States is produced by private firms that compete in free markets. Most economists believe that having to meet the competition is an important reason why the American economy is so productive. Inputs include labor, capital (e.g., machinery and buildings), and natural resources. It is the revenue from selling output that creates income for these factors of production.

In the United States, the largest share of income accrues to which factor of production?

(6) _____. The income earned by those who put up the money to buy buildings and machinery comes in the form of interest and profits. Profits account for about _____ cents of each sales dollar. Most Americans work in [manufacturing/service] industries.

The discussion in the text lists five roles for government:

1) To enforce the rules of business and society, including property rights

2) To regulate business

3) To provide certain goods and services, e.g., national defense

4) To raise taxes to finance its operations

5) To redistribute income.

The size of government in the United States relative to GDP is [small/large] compared to most other (7)
industrialized countries. This comparison and any others listed do not say whether particular actions are
best done by the government or by the private economy. Are there legitimate unmet needs that should be
addressed by government, or is government already too big? Much of the material in subsequent chapters
is designed to help you understand what markets do well and what they do poorly. It is hoped that a better
understanding of the insights from economic analysis will help you decide where you would draw the line
between markets and government.

IMPORTANT TERMS AND CONCEPTS QUIZ

Choose the best definition for each of the following terms.

1. _____ Factors of production or Inputs

2. _____ Outputs

3. _____ Gross domestic product (GDP)

4. _____ Open economy

5. _____ Closed economy

6. _____ Recession

7. _____ Transfer payments

8. _____ Progressive tax

9. _____ Mixed economy

a. Money value of final goods and services produced in a year

b. Economy with public influence over the workings of free markets

c. A sustained increase in the average level of prices

d. Money that individuals receive from the government as grants

e. Economy in which exports and imports are small relative to GDP

f. International trade is a large proportion of GDP

g. A period when real GDP declines

h. Labor, machinery, buildings, and natural resources used in production

i. Goods and services desired by consumers

j. The proportion of income paid as taxes increase as income increases

CHAPTER 2

BASIC EXERCISES

THE MORE THINGS CHANGE, THE MORE THEY ARE THE SAME—OR NOT?

Chapter 2 is a quick introduction to the structure of the American economy. These questions ask you to consider how some things may have changed since 1960.

1. What do Americans buy? Complete the missing columns in **Table 2-1** to see how consumption spending has changed. Do these changes surprise you? What do you think explains them? You can find more detail about consumption spending at http://www.bea.doc.gov/National/Index.htm.

Table 2-1

Composition of Consumption Spending

	1960 Spending ($ billions)	Proportion	2010 Spending ($ billions)	Proportion
Durables[a]	45.6	_____	1,089.4	_____
Non-Durables[b]	131.4	_____	2,336.3	_____
Services[c]	154.8	_____	6,923.4	_____
Total	331.8		10,349.1	

[a] e.g., automobiles, furniture
[b] e.g., food, clothing, gasoline
[c] e.g., housing, medical care, entertainment, education

2. How has the spending of the federal government changed? Complete the missing columns in **Table 2-2** to see. Do these changes surprise you? What do you think explains them?

Table 2-2

Composition of Federal Government Spending

	1960[a] Spending ($ billions)	Proportion	2010[a] Spending ($ billions)	Proportion
National Defense	42.9	_____	668.0	_____
Health	2.5	_____	884.4	_____
Income Security	21.7	_____	1,168.6	_____
Interest	8.4	_____	254.0	_____
All Other	11.3	_____	482.5	_____
Total	86.8		3,457.5	

[a] Fiscal Year

20

© 2012 Cengage Learning. All Rights Reserved. May not be scanned, copied or duplicated, or posted to a publicly accessible website, in whole or in part.

3. Who is going to work outside the home now? The labor force participation rate is an important measure of labor markets. It is computed by looking at the number of people working or looking for work as a proportion of total population. This measure excludes those who are retired and those who are not looking for paid work. **Figure 2-1** shows labor force participation by men and women of various ages in 1950. Complete the missing column in **Table 2-3** to compute labor force participation rates for 2010 and then plot your results in Figure 2-1 to see how labor force participation has changed since 1950. Are you surprised by the differences for men and women? Do the changes over time surprise you? What do you think explains these differences?

Figure 2-1

Labor Force Participation Rate: 1950 and 2007

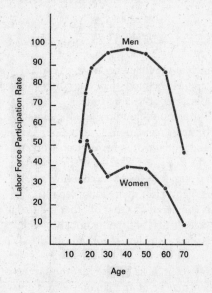

Table 2-3

Labor Force Participation: 2010

| | Men | | | Women | | |
| | Labor Force[a] | Population | Participation | Labor Force[a] | Population | Participation |
Age	(Numbers in thousands)		Rate[b]	(Numbers in thousands)		Rate[b]
16-17	4,990	4,540	_____	1,011	4,403	_____
18–19	2,002	4,038	_____	1,904	3,919	_____
20–24	7,864	10,550	_____	7,164	10,497	_____
25–34	18,352	20,465	_____	15,263	20,438	_____
35–44	18,199	19,807	_____	15,247	20,283	_____
45–54	18,856	21,713	_____	17,104	22,284	_____
55–64	12,103	17,291	_____	11,194	18,594	_____
65 & over	3,701	16,769	_____	3,017	21,937	_____

[a]Labor Force = people working plus those looking for work
[b]Labor Force Participation Rate = Labor Force/Population

Source: Bureau of Labor Statistics, *Current Population Survey*, April 2011, http://www.bls.gov/data

SELF-TESTS FOR UNDERSTANDING

TEST A

Circle the most appropriate answer.

1. Which of the following helps to explain why the output of the American economy is as high as it is? (There may be more than one correct answer to this question.)
   a. The size of the labor force
   b. The amount of money provided by the government
   c. Business regulation
   d. The productivity of American workers

2. Total output of the U.S. economy
   a. is slightly less than that of Japan.
   b. is comparable to that of other industrialized countries.
   c. exceeds that of other national economies.
   d. is among the lowest for industrialized countries.

3. Many economists believe that the success of the American economy reflects, in part, our reliance on (There may be more than one correct answer.)
   a. regulation.
   b. private enterprise.
   c. free markets.
   d. nationalization.

4. Gross domestic product measures
   a. consumer spending.
   b. the vulgarity of many consumer goods.
   c. unpaid economic activity that takes place inside households.
   d. the money value of all the goods and services produced in an economy in a year.

5. American reliance on foreign trade—exports and imports—is _____ most other industrialized countries.
   a. less than
   b. about the same as
   c. greater than

6. Since 1950, the proportion of women employed in the market place has
   a. declined.
   b. shown little change.
   c. increased considerably.

7. Since the mid-1970s, the proportion of the labor force accounted for by teenagers has
   a. declined.
   b. stayed about the same.
   c. increased.

8. Compared to high school graduates, college graduates earn about
   a. the same.
   b. 25 percent more.
   c. 50 percent more.
   d. 67 percent more.

9. The term *recession* refers to
   a. a period of inflation.
   b. a period of above-average economic growth.
   c. reductions in government spending designed to reduce the deficit.
   d. a period when real GDP declines.

10. When referring to inputs, the term *capital* refers to
    a. money business firms need to borrow.
    b. the importance of a firm's head office.
    c. machines and buildings used to produce output.
    d. all of a firm's factors of production.

11. Which of the following would not be classified as an input?
    a. A farmer's time to grow wheat
    b. The farmer's tractor
    c. The farmer's land
    d. The bread that is made from the wheat

12. The majority of American workers work for
    a. manufacturing companies.
    b. the federal government.
    c. state and local governments.
    d. firms that produce a variety of services, including retail and wholesale trade.

13. When businesses pay for factors of production, which of the following gets the largest share of income?
    a. Profits
    b. Labor
    c. Interest
    d. The government (taxes)

14. In the United States there are about
    a. 250,000 business firms or one for every 1,200 people.
    b. 1.5 million business firms or one for every 200 people.
    c. 5 million business firms or one for every 60 people.
    d. 27.5 million business firms or one for every 11 people.

15. When Americans buy goods produced abroad, _____ increase.
    a. exports
    b. taxes
    c. transfer payments
    d. imports

16. When Americans are able to sell goods to foreigners, this adds to
    a. exports.
    b. taxes.
    c. transfer payments.
    d. imports.

17. Consumer spending accounts for _____ of American GDP.
    a. about 33 percent
    b. about 50 percent
    c. about 70 percent
    d. about 90 percent

18. The largest share of federal government spending is for
    a. national defense.
    b. interest.
    c. health.
    d. income security.

19. For the most part, the United States has chosen to let markets determine distribution of before-tax incomes, and then use taxes and _____ to reduce income inequalities.
    a. tariffs
    b. inflation
    c. transfer payments
    d. government production

20. Compared to other industrialized countries, taxes as a percent of GDP in the United States are
    a. among the lowest.
    b. about the same as most other industrialized countries.
    c. among the highest.

TEST B

Circle T or F for true or false.

T F 1. An economic system is a social mechanism that organizes inputs to produce outputs.

T F 2. Since World War II, American real GDP has increased every year without interruption.

T F 3. The American economy is a more open economy than other industrialized economies.

T F 4. The American economy relies on free markets and private enterprise to a greater extent than most other industrialized economies.

T F 5. During a recession, unemployment usually increases.

T F 6. Government production accounts for more than one-half of American GDP.

T F 7. Interest on the national debt is now the largest category of federal government spending.

T F 8. Women hold more than one-half of the jobs outside the home.

T F 9. Most American workers still produce goods rather than services.

T F 10. Labor gets most of the income generated in the United States.

ECONOMICS IN ACTION

THE PROPER ROLE FOR GOVERNMENT

How far should the government go when regulating business? If the government is to provide some goods and services, what principles determine which goods and services? How far should the government go in redistributing income?

Noted economist Milton Friedman consistently argued for a limited role for government. In a widely publicized Public Broadcasting Service series, Friedman and his wife Rose advocated four principles as tests of the appropriate business of government. National defense, domestic police and justice, the provision of goods and services in the limited cases where markets do not work well, and protection for citizens who cannot protect themselves (e.g., children) define the Friedmans' four principles. These principles, especially the third, could be seen as justifying a wide range of government action. The Friedmans are as concerned with government failures as with market failures. They note that once started, government initiatives are rarely stopped. In their view, the burden of proof should be on the proponents of government action.

The Friedmans argued that government should be organized to maximize individual "freedom to choose as individuals, as families, as members of voluntary groups." They endorsed the view of Adam Smith that as long as individuals do not violate the laws of justice, they should be free to pursue their own interests and that competitive markets rather than government regulation are usually the most effective forms of social organization. "We can shape our institutions. Physical and human characteristics limit the alternatives available to us. But none prevents us, if we will, from building a society that relies primarily on voluntary cooperation to organize both economic and other activity, a society that preserves and expands human freedom, that keeps government in its place, keeping it our servant and not letting it become our master."[1]

The equally renowned John Kenneth Galbraith, on the other hand, argued that increasing affluence led to an imbalance between private and public goods. Goods and services that are marketable to individuals allow private producers to accumulate the financial resources that give them control of labor, capital, and raw materials. Sophisticated advertising creates and sustains demand for private goods, generating more income and profits. This affluence of the private sector is in marked contrast to the poverty of the public sector. Galbraith argues that society needs a balance between private and public goods but that the pernicious effects of advertising that creates the demand that sustains the production of private goods gives rise to a serious imbalance. One result is an increasing demand for private goods and services to protect individuals from the poverty of public goods and services, such as elaborate alarm systems and private guards to counteract the lack of police.

How much increase in public spending is necessary to redress the balance? Galbraith will only say that the distance is considerable. "When we arrive, the opulence of our private consumption will no longer be in contrast with the poverty of our schools, the unloveliness and congestion of our cities, our inability to get to work without a struggle, and the social disorder that is associated with imbalance . . . the precise point of balance will

---

[1]Milton and Rose Friedman, *Free to Choose: A Personal Statement,* Harcourt Brace Jovanovich, 1980.

25

never be defined. This will be of comfort only to those who believe that any failure of definition can be made to score decisively against the larger idea."[2]

1. How would you define the proper role of government? Where would you draw the line between those activities best left to individual initiative and markets and those that are the appropriate business of government?

STUDY QUESTIONS

1. What is the difference between inputs and outputs? Is steel an input or an output? What about the steel used to build factories compared to the steel used in home appliances?

2. How can output of the American economy be greater than that of countries like China and India with larger populations?

3. What does the historical record show regarding the growth in real GDP and real GDP per capita in the United States?

4. What is meant by a closed or an open economy? How would you characterize the United States?

5. In the United States, who works outside the home for wages and salary and what types of jobs do they hold?

6. How is income in the United States distributed among factors of production?

7. How does the role of government in the American economy compare with that of other industrialized countries?

8. What is meant by the term "mixed economy"?

ECONOMICS ONLINE

The *Statistical Abstract of the United States* is a good place to begin a statistical profile of the United States.
    http://www.census.gov/compendia/statab/.
It is often useful to compare the United States to other countries. Information about the major industrialized countries can be found from the homepage for the Organization for Economic Cooperation and Development (OECD).
    http://www.oecd.org
The *CIA World Factbook* is a useful summary of information about many countries. It is available online.
    http://www.odci.gov/cia/publications/factbook

---

[2]John Kenneth Galbraith, *The Affluent Society*, Houghton Mifflin, 1958.

The Fundamental Economic Problem: Scarcity and Choice

3

Important Terms and Concepts

Resources	Outputs	Principle of increasing costs	Division of labor
Opportunity cost	Inputs	Efficiency	Comparative advantage
Optimal decision	Production possibilities frontier	Allocation of resources	Market system

Learning Objectives

After completing this chapter, you should be able to:

- explain why the true cost of any decision is its opportunity cost.

- explain the link between market prices and opportunity costs.

- explain why the scarcity of goods and services (outputs) must be attributed to a scarcity of resources (inputs) used in production processes.

- draw a production possibilities frontier for a firm or for the economy.

- explain how the production possibilities frontier contains information about the opportunity cost of changing output combinations.

- explain why specialized resources mean that a firm's or an economy's production possibilities frontier is likely to bow outward.

- explain how the shape of the production possibilities frontier illustrates the principle of increasing costs.

- explain why production efficiency requires that an economy produce on, rather than inside, its production possibilities frontier.

- describe the three coordination tasks that every economy must confront.

- explain why specialization and division of labor are likely to require the use of markets.

- describe how the allocation of tasks by the principle of comparative advantage increases the total output of all parties.

- explain how both parties gain from voluntary exchange even if no new goods are produced.

- describe how a market economy solves the three coordination tasks.

CHAPTER REVIEW

"YOU CAN'T ALWAYS GET WHAT YOU WANT"—MICK JAGGER

Even rock stars whose income and wealth are beyond comprehension understand that scarcity and the resulting necessity to make choices are fundamental concerns of economics.[1] This chapter is an introduction to these issues.

(1)   The importance of *choice* starts with the fact that virtually all resources are _____. Most people's desires exceed their incomes, and, thus, everyone makes buying choices all the time. Similarly, firms, educational institutions, and government agencies make choices between what kinds of outputs to produce and what combination of inputs to use.

What is a good way to make choices? The obvious answer is to consider the alternatives. Economists call

(2)   these forgone alternatives the _____ _____ of a decision. Imagine it is the night before the first midterm in Introductory Economics, which will cover Chapters 1–6, and here you are only on Chapter 3. A friend suggests a night at the movies and even offers to buy your ticket so "it won't cost you anything." Do you agree? What will you be giving up?

At first, the idea of choices for the economy may sound strange. It may be easiest to imagine such choices being made by bureaucrats in a centrally planned economy. Even though there is no central planning bureau for the U.S. economy, it is useful to think of opportunities available to the American economy. The opportunities selected result from the combined spending and production decisions of all citizens, firms, and governmental units, decisions coordinated by our reliance on markets.

The *production possibilities frontier* is a useful diagram for representing the choices available to a firm or an

(3)   economy. The frontier will tend to slope downward to the right because resources are [scarce/specialized]. The frontier will tend to bow out because most resources are _____. Opportunity cost is the best measure of the true cost of any decision. For a single firm or an economy as a whole, with choices represented by a production possibilities frontier, the opportunity cost of changing the composition of output can be measured by the _____ of the production possibilities frontier.

As an economy produces more and more of one good, say automobiles, the opportunity cost of fur-

(4)   ther increases is likely to [increase/decrease]. This change in opportunity cost illustrates the principle of _____ cost and is a result of the fact that most resources are [scarce/specialized].

For given amounts of all but one good, the production possibilities frontier for an economy measures the maximum amount of the remaining good that can be produced. Thus, the production possibilities frontier defines maximum outputs or efficient production. Note that all points on the production possibilities frontier represent efficiency in production. There is, of course, no guarantee that the economy will operate on its frontier.

(5)   If there is unemployment, then the economy is operating [on/inside] the frontier. If a firm or economy operates inside its production possibilities frontier, it is said to be _____; that is, with the same

---

[1] Before he was a rock star, Mick Jagger studied economics at the London School of Economics.

resources the firm or the economy could have produced more of some commodities. Assigning inputs to the wrong or inappropriate tasks because market prices are sending the wrong signals or discrimination that limits opportunities for individuals will also result in production inefficiency. Assigning tasks according to the principle of comparative advantage helps to achieve economic efficiency.

All economies must answer three questions:
1. How can we use resources efficiently to operate on the production possibilities frontier?
2. What combinations of output shall we produce: that is, where on the frontier shall we produce?
3. To whom shall we distribute what is produced?

The American economy answers these questions through the use of markets and prices. If markets are functioning well, then money prices [will/will not] be a reliable guide to opportunity costs. Problems arise when markets do not function well and when items do not have explicit price tags.   (6)

IMPORTANT TERMS AND CONCEPTS QUIZ

Choose the best definition for each of the following terms.

1. _____ Resources
2. _____ Opportunity cost
3. _____ Optimal decision
4. _____ Outputs
5. _____ Inputs
6. _____ Production possibilities frontier
7. _____ Principle of increasing costs
8. _____ Efficiency
9. _____ Allocation of resources
10. _____ Division of labor
11. _____ Comparative advantage
12. _____ Market system

a. Resources used to produce goods and services
b. System in which allocation decisions are made in accordance with centralized direction
c. Breaking tasks into smaller jobs
d. Ability to produce goods less inefficiently than other producers
e. Decision on how to divide scarce resources among different uses
f. Instruments used to create the goods and services people desire
g. Graph of combinations of goods that can be produced with available inputs and existing technology
h. Goods and services that firms produce
i. System in which decisions on resource allocation come from independent decisions of consumers and producers
j. Absence of waste
k. Forgone value of the next best alternative
l. Tendency for the opportunity cost of an additional unit of output to rise as production increases
m. A decision that best serves the decision maker's objectives

BASIC EXERCISES

Figure 3-1 shows the production possibilities frontier (PPF) for the economy of Adirondack, which produces bread and computers.

Figure 3-1

Production Possibilities Frontier

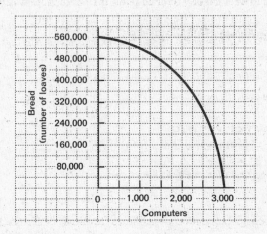

1. If all resources are devoted to the production of bread, Adirondack can produce _____ loaves of bread. In order to produce 1,000 computers, the opportunity cost in terms of bread is _____ loaves. To produce another 1,000 computers, the opportunity cost [rises/falls] to _____ loaves. As long as the PPF continues to curve downward, the opportunity costs of increased computer output will [continue to rise/start to fall]. These changes are the result, not of scarce resources per se, but of _____ resources. (You might try drawing a PPF on the assumption that all resources are equally productive in the production of both outputs. Can you convince yourself that it should be a straight line?)

2. Find the output combination of 2,500 computers and 320,000 loaves on **Figure 3-1.** Label this point A. Is it an attainable combination for Adirondack? Label the output combination 1,500 computers and 400,000 loaves as point B. Is this combination attainable? Finally, label the output combination 1,000 computers and 520,000 loaves as point C. Is this combination attainable? We can conclude that the attainable output combinations for Adirondack are [on/inside/outside] the production possibilities frontier. Among the obtainable output combinations, efficient points of production are located [on/inside/outside] the production possibilities frontier.

3. An output combination is inefficient if it is possible to produce more of one or both goods. Which, if any, of the output combinations identified in question 2 is an inefficient combination? _____ Show that this point is inefficient by shading in all attainable points indicating more of one or both goods.

4. Consider point C in question 2, 1,000 computers and 520,000 loaves of bread, and point D, 2,000 computers and 400,000 loaves of bread. Which point is best for Adirondack and why?

SELF-TESTS FOR UNDERSTANDING

TEST A
Circle the most appropriate answer.

1. Economists define opportunity cost as the
   a. dollar price of goods and services.
   b. hidden cost imposed by inflation.
   c. value of the next best alternative use that is not chosen.
   d. time spent shopping.

2. The position of an economy's production possibilities frontier is determined by all but which one of the following?
   a. the size of the labor force
   b. labor skills and training
   c. the amount of consumption goods the economy can produce
   d. current technology

3. A firm's production possibilities frontier shows
   a. the best combination of output for a firm to produce.
   b. its plans for increasing production over time.
   c. the architectural drawings of its most productive plant.
   d. the different combinations of goods it can produce with available resources and technology.

4. An efficient economy utilizes all available resources and produces the _____ output its technology permits.
   a. minimum amount of
   b. best combination of
   c. one combination of
   d. maximum amount of

5. The fact that resources are scarce implies that the production possibilities frontier will
   a. have a negative slope.
   b. be a straight line.
   c. shift out over time.
   d. bow out from the origin.

6. Which of the following statements implies that production possibilities frontiers are likely to be curved rather than straight lines?
   a. Ultimately all resources are scarce.
   b. Most resources are more productive in certain uses than in others.
   c. Unemployment is a more serious problem for some social groups than for others.
   d. Economists are notoriously poor at drawing straight lines.

7. The set of attainable points for a firm that produces two goods is given by
   a. all points on the production possibilities frontier.
   b. all points inside the production possibilities frontier.
   c. all points on or inside the production possibilities frontier.
   d. none of the above.

8. If an economy is operating efficiently, it will be producing
   a. inside its production possibilities frontier.
   b. on its production possibilities frontier.
   c. outside its production possibilities frontier.
   d. the maximum amount of necessities and the minimum amount of luxuries.

9. The principle of increasing cost is consistent with a _____ production possibilities frontier.
   a. straight-line
   b. bowed-in
   c. shifting
   d. bowed-out

10. The inability of the economy to produce as much as everyone would like is ultimately a reflection of
    a. a lack of money in the economy.
    b. congressional gridlock.
    c. the inability of a market economy to perform the necessary coordination tasks.
    d. a limited amount of productive resources.

11. When, in Figure 3-1, the production of bread is increased from 280,000 loaves to 400,000 loaves, the opportunity cost in terms of reduced output of computers is
    a. 0.
    b. 500.
    c. 2,000.
    d. 2,500.

12. When the output of bread increases by another 120,000 loaves to 520,000, the opportunity cost in terms of reduced output of computers is
    a. 0.
    b. 500.
    c. 1,000.
    d. 2,000.

13. Comparing answers to questions 11 and 12, we can conclude that the production possibilities frontier for Adirondack
    a. is a straight line.
    b. shows a decline in the opportunity cost of more bread.
    c. illustrates the principle of increasing cost.
    d. has a positive slope.

14. Consider a production possibilities frontier showing alternative combinations of corn and computers that can be produced in Cimonoce, a small island in the South Pacific. The opportunity cost of more computers can be measured by the
    a. slope of the production possibilities frontier.
    b. *X*-intercept of the production possibilities frontier.
    c. *Y*-intercept of the production possibilities frontier.
    d. area under the production possibilities frontier.

15. Which of the following implies a shift in the production possiblities frontier for a shoe firm?
    a. raising prices by 10 percent
    b. borrowing money to hire more workers and buying more machines
    c. changing the composition output toward more women's shoes and fewer men's shoes
    d. expanding the advertising budget

16. Which of the following would not shift an economy's production possibilities frontier?
    a. a doubling of the labor force
    b. a doubling of the number of machines
    c. a doubling of the money supply
    d. more advanced technology

17. An optimal decision is one that
    a. will win a majority if put to a vote.
    b. is supported unanimously.
    c. best serves the objectives of the decision maker.
    d. is supported by *The New York Times*.

18. If exchange is voluntary,
    a. there can be mutual gain even if no new goods are produced.
    b. one party will always get the better of the other.
    c. there can be mutual gain only if new goods are produced as a result of the trade.
    d. there can be mutual gain only if the government regulates retail trade.

19. All but which one of the following are examples of waste and inefficiency?
    a. Employment discrimination against women and people of color
    b. Operating on an economy's production possibilities frontier
    c. High levels of unemployment
    d. Quotas that limit the educational opportunities of particular ethnic groups

20. The three coordination tasks that all economies must perform can
    a. only be done by a central planning bureau.
    b. only be done by markets.
    c. only be done inefficiently.
    d. be done by planning bureaus or markets.

TEST B

Circle T or F for true or false.

T F 1. There can never be any real scarcity of manufactured goods because we can always produce more.

T F 2. Market prices are always the best measure of opportunity cost.

T F 3. The principle of increasing costs is a reflection of the fact that most productive resources tend to be best at producing a limited number of things.

T F 4. Markets are incapable of solving the three coordination tasks that all economies must address.

T F 5. Because they have the power to tax, governments do not need to make choices.

T F 6. The existence of specialized resources means that a firm's production possibilities frontier will be a straight line.

T F 7. The existence of widespread unemployment means that an economy is operating inside its production possibilities frontier.

T F 8. An economy using its resources efficiently is operating on its production possibilities frontier.

T F 9. Because they are nonprofit organizations, colleges and universities do not have to make choices.

T F 10. A sudden increase in the number of dollar bills will shift the economy's production possibilities frontier.

SUPPLEMENTARY EXERCISES

1. THE COST OF COLLEGE

Those of you paying your way through college may not need to be reminded that the opportunity cost of lost wages is an important part of the cost of education. You can estimate the cost of your education as follows: Estimate what you could earn if instead of attending classes and studying, you used those hours to work. Add in the direct outlays on tuition, books, and any differential living expenses incurred because you go to school. (Why only differential and not your total living expenses?)

2. PRODUCTION POSSIBILITIES FRONTIER

Consider an economy with a production possibilities frontier between cars (C) and tanks (T) given by

$$C = 6L^5K^5 - 0.3T^2$$

where L is the size of the labor force (50,000 people) and K is the number of machines, also 50,000.
a. What is the maximum number of cars that can be produced? Call this number of cars C^*. The maximum number of tanks? Call this number of tanks T^*.
b. Draw the PPF graph for this economy.
c. Is this frontier consistent with the principle of increasing costs?

d. Is the output combination $(1/2C^*, 1/2T^*)$ attainable? Is the output combination $(1/2C^*, 1/2T^*)$ efficient? Why or why not?

e. What is the opportunity cost of more tanks when 10 tanks are produced? 50 tanks? 200 tanks?

f. Find a mathematical expression for the opportunity cost of tanks in terms of cars. Is this mathematical expression consistent with the principle of increasing cost?

ECONOMICS IN ACTION

FREE THEATER?

In the summer of 2001, New York City's Public Theater presented Chekhov's *Seagull* at the Delacorte Theater in Central Park. The director was Mike Nichols, and the production starred Meryl Streep, Kevin Kline, and Marcia Gay Harden. The tickets were free, or were they?

Tickets were given away each day at 1 p.m. on a first-come, first-served basis. As Joyce Purnick reported, arriving at 6 a.m. and waiting seven hours would not necessarily get you a ticket. The day she reported on, the first person in line arrived at 12:30 a.m., more than twelve hours before the tickets were distributed. Ms. Purnick concluded that "[t]he scene . . . strongly suggested that free tickets were for the retired, the unemployed, and the vacationing only."

If you were not up for spending the night in Central Park, you could call Peter London. Mr. London would hire students and underemployed actors to stand in line for you. He charged up to $200 for this service.

When there were objections, Mr. London responded that he was not doing anything illegal. "Only unemployed people should see this? I don't see this as being fair," he said.

Were the tickets free? How do you value your time? Would you pay $200 for someone to stand in line for you? Would you be willing to stand in line for someone else for $200? Who was likely to use Mr. London's service: those who felt the opportunity cost of their time was high or low? Who was likely to be interested in working for Mr. London? What is fair?

Source: Joyce Purnick, "Free Theater, but the Lines Unspeakable," *The New York Times,* July 30, 2001.

STUDY QUESTIONS

1. How do markets help an economy address the three coordination tasks of deciding "how," "what," and "to whom"?

2. What do economists mean by opportunity cost and why do they say it is the true measure of the cost of any decision?

3. Explain when market prices are likely to be a good measure of opportunity cost and when they are not.

4. What are the factors that determine the location of a country's production possibilities frontier?

5. What is the difference between resources being scarce and resources being specialized? What are the implications of scarcity and specialization for the production possibilities frontier?

35

6. How do specialization and the division of labor enhance economic efficiency? Why do they require a system of exchange?

7. What is the difference between attainable points of production and efficient points of production? (It may be easiest to illustrate your answer using a diagram of a production possibilities frontier. Be sure that you can define and identify those points that are attainable and those points that are efficient.)

8. What is meant by the principle of comparative advantage? What does it imply for individuals and economies?

Supply and Demand: An Initial Look

4

Important Terms and Concepts

Invisible hand	Shift in a demand curve	Supply-demand diagram	Law of supply and demand
Quantity demanded	Quantity supplied	Shortage	Price ceiling
Demand schedule	Supply schedule	Surplus	Price floor
Demand curve	Supply curve	Equilibrium	

Learning Objectives

After completing this chapter, you should be able to:

- explain why the quantity demanded and the quantity supplied are not fixed numbers but rather depend upon a number of factors including price.

- draw a demand curve, given appropriate information from a demand schedule of possible prices and the associated quantity demanded.

- draw a supply curve, given appropriate information from a supply schedule of possible prices and the associated quantity supplied.

- explain why demand curves usually slope downward and supply curves usually slope upward.

- determine the equilibrium price and quantity, given a demand curve and a supply curve.

- explain what forces tend to move market prices and quantities toward their equilibrium values.

- list major factors that will affect the quantity demanded by shifting the demand curve.

- list major factors that will affect the quantity supplied by shifting the supply curve.

- distinguish between a shift in and a movement along either the demand or supply curve.

- analyze the impact on prices and quantities of shifts in the demand curve, supply curve, or both.

- explain why sellers are unlikely to be able to pass on the full increase in excise or sales taxes.

- distinguish between price ceilings and price floors.

- explain the likely consequences of government interference with market-determined prices.

CHAPTER REVIEW

Along with scarcity and the need for choice, demand and supply analysis is a fundamental idea that pervades all of economics. After studying this chapter, look back at the Ideas for Beyond the Final Exam in Chapter 1 and see how many concern the "law" of supply and demand.

Economists use a demand curve as a summary of the factors influencing people's demand for different commodities. A demand curve shows how, during a specified period, the quantity demanded of some good changes

(1) as the _____ of that good changes, holding all other determinants of demand constant. A demand curve usually has a (<u>negative/positive</u>) slope, indicating that as the price of a good declines, people will demand (<u>more/less</u>) of it. A particular quantity demanded is represented by a point on the demand curve. The change in the quantity demanded as price changes is a (<u>shift in/movement along</u>) the demand curve. Quantity demanded is also influenced by other factors, such as consumer incomes and tastes, population, and the prices of related goods. Changes in any of these factors will result in a (<u>shift in/movement along</u>) the demand curve.

Economists use a supply curve to summarize the factors influencing producers' decisions. Like the demand

(2) curve, the supply curve is a relationship between quantity and _____. Supply curves usually have a (<u>negative/positive</u>) slope, indicating that at higher prices producers will be willing to supply (<u>more/less</u>) of the good in question. Like quantity demanded, quantity supplied is also influenced by factors other than price. The size of the industry, the state of technology, the prices of inputs, and the price of related outputs are important determinants. Changes in any of these factors will change the quantity supplied and can be represented by a (<u>shift in/movement along</u>) the supply curve.

Demand and supply curves are hypothetical constructs that answer what-if questions. For example, the supply curve answers the question, "What quantity of milk would be supplied if its price were $10 a gallon?" At this point it is not fair to ask whether anyone would buy milk at that price. Information about the quantity

(3) demanded is given by the _____ curve, which answers the question, "What quantity would be demanded if its price were $10 a gallon?" The viability of a price of $10 will be determined when we consider both curves simultaneously.

Figure 4-1 shows a demand and supply curve for stereo sets. The market outcome will be a price of

(4) $_____ and a quantity of _____. If the price is $400, then the quantity demanded will be (<u>less/more</u>) than the quantity supplied. In particular, from Figure 4-1 we can see that at a price of $400, producers would supply _____ sets while consumers would demand _____ sets. This imbalance is a (<u>shortage/surplus</u>) and will lead to a(n) (<u>increase/reduction</u>) in price as inventories start piling up and suppliers compete for sales. If, instead, the price of stereo sets is only $200, there will be a (<u>shortage/surplus</u>) as the quantity (<u>demanded/supplied</u>) exceeds the quantity _____. Price is apt to (<u>decrease/increase</u>) as consumers scramble for a limited number of stereos at what appear to be bargain prices.

These forces working to raise or lower prices will continue until price and quantity settle down at values

(5) given by the _____ of the demand and supply curves. At this point, barring outside

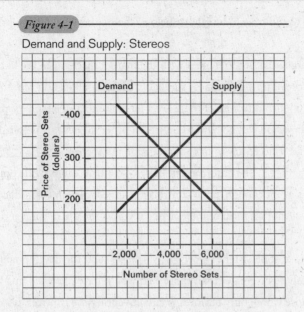

Figure 4-1

Demand and Supply: Stereos

changes that would shift either curve, there will be no further tendency for change. Market-determined price

and quantity are then said to be in _____. This price and quantity combination is the

only one in which consumers demand exactly what producers supply. There are no frustrated consumers or pro-

ducers. However, equilibrium price and quantity will change if anything happens to shift either the demand or

supply curves. The Basic Exercise in this chapter asks you to examine a number of shifts in demand and supply

curves.

Often factors affect demand but not supply, and vice versa. For example, changes in consumer incomes

and tastes will shift the (demand/supply) curve but not the _____ curve. Following a   (6)

shift in the demand curve, price must change to reestablish equilibrium. The change in price will lead to a

(shift in/movement along) the supply curve until equilibrium is reestablished at the intersection of the new

demand curve and the original supply curve.[1] Similarly, a change in technology or the price of inputs will shift

the _____ curve but not the _____ curve. Equilibrium will be reestablished as the

price change induced by the shift in the supply curve leads to a movement along the _____

curve to the new intersection.

In many cases governments intervene in the market mechanism in an attempt to control prices. Some

price controls dictate a particular price; other controls set maximum or minimum prices. A price ceiling is a

(maximum/minimum) legal price, typically below the market-determined equilibrium price. Examples of price   (7)

ceilings include rent controls and usury laws. A price floor sets a(n) _____ legal price. To

---

[1]If following an increase in consumer income the increase in price were sufficiently large to induce an increase in the size of the industry, the supply curve
would shift. However, such a change would take some time. The analysis here focuses on immediate or short-run impacts. Questions of long-run industry
equilibrium are addressed in Chapters 8, 9, and 10.

39

be effective, the price floor would have to be (above/below) the market equilibrium price. Price floors are often used in agricultural programs.

In general, economists argue that interferences with the market mechanism are likely to have a number of undesirable features. Price controls will almost surely lead to a misallocation of resources, as it is unlikely legislated prices will equal opportunity cost. If there are a large number of suppliers, price controls will be
(8) (hard/easy) to monitor and evasion will be hard to police. In order to prevent the breakdown of price controls, governments quite likely find it necessary to introduce a large number of _____
_____. The enforcement of price controls can provide opportunities for favoritism and corruption. If all of this is not enough, price controls are almost certain to produce groups with a monetary stake in preserving controls. Another form of inefficiency involves the use of time and resources to evade effective controls.

(9)   Price ceilings have a history of persistent (shortages/surpluses) and the development of black markets. Prices in the illegal market are likely to be greater than those that would have prevailed in a free market, with substantial income going to those whose only business is circumventing the controls. Over a longer period of time, new investment is likely to (decrease/increase) as controlled prices reduce the profitability of investment in the industry.

Firms try to get around effective price floors by offering nonprice inducements for consumers to buy from them rather than from someone else. (Remember that effective price floors result in excess supply.) These nonprice inducements are apt to be less preferred by consumers than would a general reduction in prices. Price
(10) floors will also result in inefficiencies as high-cost firms are protected from failing by artificially (high/low) prices.

IMPORTANT TERMS AND CONCEPTS QUIZ

Choose the best definition for each of the following terms.

1. _____ Invisible hand

2. _____ Quantity demanded

3. _____ Demand schedule

4. _____ Demand curve

5. _____ Shift in a demand curve

6. _____ Quantity supplied

7. _____ Supply schedule

8. _____ Supply curve

9. _____ Supply-demand diagram

10. _____ Shortage

11. _____ Surplus

12. _____ Equilibrium

13. _____ Law of supply and demand

14. _____ Price ceiling

15. _____ Price floor

a. Observation that in a free market, price tends to a level where quantity supplied equals quantity demanded

b. Legal minimum price that may be charged

c. Graph depicting how quantity demanded changes as price changes

d. Change in price causing a change in quantity supplied or demanded

e. Number of units consumers want to buy at a given price

f. Individual actions to pursue self-interest in a market system promote societal well-being

g. Table depicting how the quantity demanded changes as price changes

h. Situation in which there are no inherent forces producing change

i. Table depicting how quantity supplied changes as price changes

j. Legal maximum price that may be charged

k. Number of units producers want to sell at a given price

l. Table depicting the changes in both quantity demanded and quantity supplied as price changes

m. Change in a variable other than price that affects quantity demanded

n. Excess of quantity supplied over quantity demanded

o. Graph depicting the changes in both quantity supplied and quantity demanded as price changes

p. Excess of quantity demanded over quantity supplied

q. Graph depicting how quantity supplied changes as price changes

BASIC EXERCISES

These exercises ask you to analyze the impact of changes in factors that affect demand and supply.

1. a. Table 4-1 has data on the quantity of candy bars that would be demanded and supplied at various prices. Use the data to draw the demand curve and the supply curve for candy bars in Figure 4-2.

   b. From the information given in Table 4-1 and represented in Figure 4-2, the equilibrium price is _____ cents and the equilibrium quantity is _____ million candy bars.

Table 4-1

Demand and Supply Schedules for Candy Bars

Quantity Demanded	Price per Bar	Quantity Supplied
1,200	55	1,050
1,100	60	1,100
900	70	1,200
800	75	1,250
700	80	1,300

Figure 4-2

Demand and Supply: Candy Bars

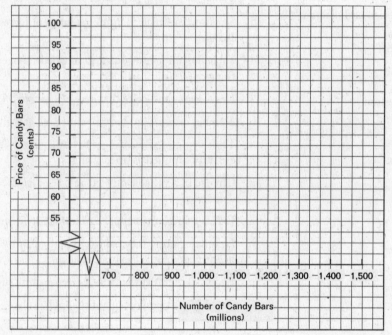

   c. Now assume that increases in income and population mean the demand curve has shifted. Assume the shift is such that, at each price, the quantity demanded has increased by 300 candy bars. Draw the new demand curve. At the new equilibrium, price has (increased/decreased) to _____ cents, and quantity has (increased/decreased) to _____ million candy bars. Note that the change in the equilibrium quantity is (less/more) than the shift in the demand curve. Can you explain why?

   d. Next assume that Congress imposes a tax of 15 cents on every candy bar sold. As sellers must now pay the government 15 cents for each candy bar sold, the tax can be modeled as a 15 cent upward shift in the supply curve. This tax-induced shift in the supply curve will (<u>increase/decrease</u>) the equilibrium price and _____ the equilibrium quantity. Draw this new supply curve in Figure 4-2. Using the demand curve you drew in part c, the new equilibrium price following the imposition of the candy tax will be _____ cents and the equilibrium quantity will be _____ million candy bars. Compared to the equilibrium price you identified in part c, the increase in the market price of candy bars is (<u>less than/equal to/more than</u>) the new tax.

2. Figure 4-3 shows the demand and supply of chicken. Use Figure 4-3 while you fill in Table 4-2 to trace the effects of various events on the equilibrium price and quantity.

Figure 4-3

Demand and Supply: Chicken

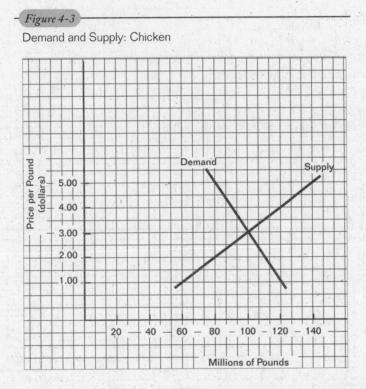

Table 4-2

Event	Which curve shifts?	Is the direction left or right?	Does the equilibrium price rise or fall?	Does the equilibrium quantity rise or fall?
a. A sharp increase in the price of beef leads many consumers to switch from beef to chicken.				
b. A bumper grain crop cuts the cost of chicken feed in half.				
c. Extraordinarily cold weather destroys a significant number of chickens.				
d. A sudden interest in Eastern religions converts many chicken eaters to vegetarians.				

43

3. Figure 4-4 shows the demand and supply of DVDs. Complete Table 4-3 to examine the impact of alternative price ceilings and price floors on the quantity demanded and the quantity supplied. What conclusion can you draw about when ceilings and floors will affect market outcomes?

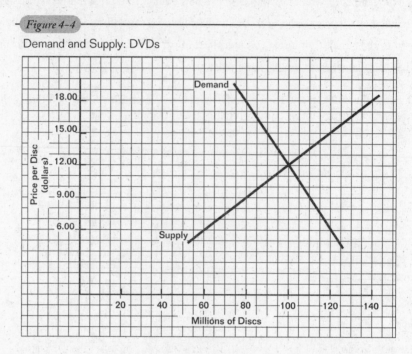

Figure 4-4

Demand and Supply: DVDs

Table 4-3

	Quantity Demanded	Quantity Supplied	Shortage or Surplus
a. Price ceiling = $18			
b. Price ceiling = $9			
c. Price floor = $15			
d. Price floor = $6			

SELF-TESTS FOR UNDERSTANDING

TEST A

Circle the most appropriate answer.

1. A demand curve is a graph showing how the quantity demanded changes when _____ changes.
   a. consumer income
   b. population
   c. price
   d. the price of closely related goods

44

2. The slope of a demand curve is usually _____, indicating that as price declines the quantity demanded increases.
   a. negative
   b. positive
   c. infinite
   d. zero

3. Quantity demanded is likely to depend upon all but which one of the following?
   a. consumer tastes
   b. consumer income
   c. price
   d. the size of the industry producing the good in question

4. A supply curve is a graphical representation of information in a(n)
   a. demand schedule.
   b. equilibrium.
   c. supply schedule.
   d. balance sheet.

5. If price decreases, the quantity supplied usually
   a. increases.
   b. is unchanged.
   c. decreases.
   d. goes to zero.

6. The entire supply curve is likely to shift when all but which one of the following change?
   a. the size of the industry
   b. price
   c. the price of important inputs
   d. technology that reduces production costs

7. There will likely be a movement along a fixed supply curve if which one of the following changes?
   a. price
   b. technology that reduces production costs
   c. the price of important inputs
   d. the size of the industry

8. There will be a movement along a fixed demand curve when which one of the following changes?
   a. price
   b. population
   c. consumer incomes
   d. consumer preferences

9. Graphically, the equilibrium price and quantity in a free market will be given by the
   a. *Y*-axis intercept of the demand curve.
   b. *X*-axis intercept of the supply curve.
   c. point of maximum vertical difference between the demand and supply curves.
   d. intersection of the demand and supply curves.

10. When the demand curve shifts to the right, which of the following is likely to occur?
    a. Equilibrium price rises and equilibrium quantity declines.
    b. Both equilibrium price and quantity rise.
    c. Equilibrium price declines and equilibrium quantity rises.
    d. Both equilibrium price and quantity decline.

11. If equilibrium price and quantity both decrease, it is likely that the
    a. supply curve has shifted to the right.
    b. demand curve has shifted to the right.
    c. demand curve has shifted to the left.
    d. supply curve has shifted to the left.

12. A shift in the demand curve for sailboats resulting from a general increase in incomes will lead to
    a. higher prices.
    b. lower prices.
    c. a shift in the supply curve.
    d. lower output.

13. Which of the following is likely to result in a shift in the supply curve for dresses? (There may be more than one correct answer.)
    a. an increase in consumer incomes
    b. an increase in tariffs that forces manufacturers to import cotton cloth at higher prices
    c. an increase in dress prices
    d. higher prices for skirts, pants, and blouses

14. From an initial equilibrium, which of the following changes will lead to a shift in the supply curve for Chevrolets?
    a. import restrictions on Japanese cars
    b. new environmental protection measures that raise the cost of producing steel
    c. a decrease in the price of Fords
    d. increases in the price of gasoline

15. If the price of oil (a close substitute for coal) increases, then the
    a. supply curve for coal will shift to the right.
    b. demand curve for coal will shift to the right.
    c. equilibrium price and quantity of coal will not change.
    d. quantity of coal demanded will decline.

16. If the price of shoes is initially above the equilibrium value, which of the following is likely to occur?
    a. Stores' inventories will decrease as consumers buy more shoes than shoe companies produce.
    b. The demand curve for shoes will shift in response to higher prices.
    c. Shoe stores and companies will reduce prices in order to increase sales, leading to a lower equilibrium price.
    d. Equilibrium will be reestablished at the original price as the supply curve shifts to the left.

17. A new tax on backpacks that shifts the supply curve should increase the market price of backpacks
    a. not at all.
    b. by less than the increase in the tax.
    c. by an amount equal to the increase in the tax.
    d. by more than the increase in the tax.

18. Binding price floors are likely to
    a. lead to a reduction in the volume of transactions, as we move along the demand curve, above the equilibrium price to the higher price floor.
    b. result in increased sales as suppliers react to higher prices.
    c. lead to shortages.
    d. be effective only if they are set at levels below the market equilibrium level.

19. Effective price ceilings are likely to
    a. result in surpluses.
    b. increase the volume of transactions as we move along the demand curve.
    c. increase production as producers respond to higher consumer demand at the low ceiling price.
    d. result in the development of black markets.

20. A surplus results when
    a. the quantity demanded exceeds the quantity supplied.
    b. the quantity supplied exceeds the quantity demanded.
    c. the demand curve shifts to the right.
    d. effective price ceilings are imposed.

TEST B

Circle T or F for true or false.

T F 1. The Law of Supply and Demand was passed by Congress in 1776.

T F 2. The demand curve for hamburgers is a graph showing the quantity of hamburgers that would be demanded during a specified period at each possible price.

T F 3. The slope of the supply curve indicates the increase in price necessary to get producers to increase output.

T F 4. An increase in consumer income will shift both the supply and demand curves.

T F 5. Both demand and supply curves usually have positive slopes.

T F 6. If at a particular price the quantity supplied exceeds the quantity demanded, then price is likely to fall as suppliers compete for sales.

T F 7. Equilibrium price and quantity are determined by the intersection of the demand and supply curves.

T F 8. Because equilibrium is defined as a situation with no inherent forces producing change, the equilibrium price and quantity will not change following an increase in consumer income.

T F 9. A change in the price of important inputs will change the quantity supplied but will not shift the supply curve.

T F 10. Increases in commodity specific taxes typically lead to equal increases in market prices.

T F 11. When binding, price ceilings are likely to result in the development of black markets.

T F 12. Price controls, whether floors or ceilings, likely will increase the volume of transactions from what it would be without controls.

T F 13. An effective price ceiling is normally accompanied by shortages.

T F 14. An effective price floor is also normally accompanied by shortages.

T F 15. An increase in both the market price and quantity of beef following an increase in consumer incomes proves that demand curves do not always have a negative slope.

SUPPLEMENTARY EXERCISE

Imagine that the demand curve for tomatoes can be represented as:

$$Q = 1,000 - 250P.$$

The supply curve is a bit trickier. Farmers must make planting decisions on what they anticipate prices to be. Once they have made these decisions, there is little room for increases or decreases in the quantity supplied. Except for disastrously low prices, it will almost certainly pay for a farmer to harvest and market his tomatoes. Assuming that farmers forecast price on the basis of the price last period, we can represent the supply curve for tomatoes as:

$$Q = 200 + 150P_{-1},$$

where P_{-1}, refers to price in the previous period. Initial equilibrium price and quantity of tomatoes are $2 and 500, respectively. Verify that at this price the quantity supplied is equal to the quantity demanded. (Equilibrium implies the same price in each period.)

Now assume that an increase in income has shifted the demand curve to:

$$Q = 1,400 - 250P.$$

Starting with the initial equilibrium price, trace the evolution of price and quantity over time. Do prices and quantities seem to be approaching some sort of equilibrium? If so, what? You might try programming this example on a computer or simulating it with a spreadsheet program. What happens if the slope of the demand and/or supply curve changes?

Ask your instructor about cobweb models. Do you think looking at last period's price is a good way to forecast prices?

ECONOMICS IN ACTION

HEY, BUDDY . . .

Scalping tickets—selling tickets at whatever the market will bear rather than at face value—is illegal in a number of states, including New York City. In 1992 the high demand for tickets to a retrospective exhibition of Henri Matisse at the Museum of Modern Art prompted renewed interest in the economic effects of scalping. Admission to the exhibition was by special ticket. By the time the exhibit opened, all advance sale tickets had been sold. A limited number of tickets were available each day. Art lovers had to wait in line for up to two hours early in the morning to purchase these tickets at $12.50 each. Tickets also were available without the wait at $20 to $50 from scalpers who evaded the police.

The Monet retrospective exhibit at the Art Institute in Chicago in 1995 attracted such interest that scalpers were reported to be getting $100 for tickets with a face value of $10. Scalpers also do a lively business at the Super Bowl, the Final Four of the NCAA basketball playoffs, and other major sporting and entertainment events.

Why don't museums, the National Football League, and the NCAA simply raise the price of tickets? Some argue that these organizations, along with other businesses, are concerned with "goodwill." Even if higher profits could be earned from higher ticket prices, it might come by sacrificing profits over the long run as goodwill is replaced by ill will and a growing lack of consumer interest.

Some economists view scalpers as providing a service to those who have not planned ahead or do not wish to stand in line. They point out that other businesses, such as airlines, charge a hefty price for last-minute purchases.

It is often argued that scalping should be illegal, as it makes events unaffordable for the average person. Others wonder whether the average person ever gets tickets to such events and, if she does, whether she might not prefer the option of selling her tickets at a handsome profit.

The following two-tier price system has been proposed by some economists. First, a limited number of tickets would be sold at lower prices to those willing to stand in line or enter a lottery. Then the remaining tickets would be sold at whatever price the market will bear.

In fall 2001, the producers of the hit Broadway show "The Producers" announced just such a plan. Their top ticket price had been $100, and it was rumored that scalpers were getting up to $1,000 a ticket. The producers announced a plan under which 50 seats for each performance would be available at $480 a piece.

1. Who is harmed when scalping is illegal? Who would be harmed if scalping were legal?

2. Would you expect legalizing scalping to affect the price of tickets from scalpers? Why?

3. Evaluate the pros and cons of the two-tier price system.

Source: "Tickets: Supply Meets Demand on Sidewalk," *The New York Times*, December 26, 1992; "For the Asking, a $480 Seat," *The New York Times*, October 26, 2001.

STUDY QUESTIONS

1. Why do economists argue that neither quantity demanded nor quantity supplied is likely to be a fixed number?

2. What adjustment mechanisms are likely to ensure that free-market prices move toward their equilibrium values given by the intersection of the demand and supply curves?

3. What important factors help to determine the quantity demanded? The quantity supplied?

4. Why are changes in all of the supply determinants, except price, said to shift the entire supply curve while changes in price are said to give rise to a movement along a fixed supply curve?

5. How do factors that shift the supply curve give rise to movements along a given demand curve?

6. Why do economists expect that an increase in a tax on a specific commodity will not lead to an equal increase in market prices?

7. If price cannot adjust, say due to an effective price ceiling, what factors will likely allocate the quantity supplied among consumers?

8. Consider the demand for a necessity (for example, food), and the demand for a luxury (for example, home hot tubs). For which good would you expect the quantity demanded to show a greater response to changes in price? Why? For which good would you expect the demand curve to be steeper? Why? For which good would you expect the demand curve to show a greater shift in response to changes in consumer income? Why?

Consumer Choice: Individual and Market Demand

5

Important Terms and Concepts

Total monetary utility

Marginal utility

The "law" of diminishing marginal utility

Marginal analysis

Consumer's surplus

Inferior good

Market demand curve

The "law" of demand

Learning Objectives

After completing this chapter, you should be able to:

- distinguish between total and marginal utility.

- explain how the law of diminishing marginal utility can be used to derive an optimal purchase rule.

- explain how the optimal purchase rule can be used to derive a demand curve.

- understand the true cost of any purchase—the opportunity cost.

- explain the role of marginal utility as a guide to maximizing consumer surplus.

- explain the difference between inferior and normal goods.

- derive a market demand curve given information on individual demand curves.

- explain why a market demand curve can have a negative slope even if individual demand curves do not.

- describe the "law" of demand and exceptions to this law.

- understand the limits of rational decision making.

CHAPTER REVIEW

This chapter discusses economic models of consumer choice. These models are what lie behind the negatively sloped demand curves we encountered in Chapter 4. The appendix to the chapter discusses indifference curve analysis, which is a more sophisticated treatment of the same material. This chapter is also an introduction to *marginal analysis,* an extremely powerful tool of economic analysis.

Economists derive implications for individual demand curves by starting with assumptions about individual behavior. One relatively innocent assumption should be sufficient. It concerns consumer preferences and is called the "law" of diminishing marginal utility. Perhaps we should first start with utility.

The term utility refers to the benefits people derive from consuming goods and services. Actual utility is unique to each one of us and thus is unmeasurable. To get around the measurement problem, we will use the term total utility to refer to the maximum amount a consumer will pay for a given quantity of the commodity. (It should be obvious that this amount will differ from person to person. For an individual consumer, total utility will be influenced by her income and preferences.) Rather than focusing on total utility, however, economists have found it useful to pay attention to the additional amount of money that a consumer would pay for

(1) one more unit of the commodity, or _____ utility, measured in money terms. (Marginal utility (will/will not) also be influenced by a person's income and preferences.) The law of diminishing marginal utility is a hypothesis about consumer preferences. It says that additional units of any commodity normally provide less and less satisfaction. As a result, the additional amount a consumer would pay for an additional unit of some commodity will (increase/decrease) the more units he is already consuming. Note that total utility will (decrease/increase) as long as marginal utility is positive, even if marginal utility itself is decreasing.

The law of diminishing marginal utility can be used as a guide to optimal commodity purchases. Optimal purchases are those that maximize the difference between total utility and total expenditures on a commodity.

(2) This difference is called _____ surplus.[1] Our optimal purchase rule says that an individual consumer should buy additional units of a commodity as long as the marginal utility of the additional units exceeds the _____ of the commodity. If marginal utility exceeds price, the addition to total utility from consuming one more unit will be (greater/less) than the addition to total spending, and consumer's surplus will (increase/decrease).

This notion of optimal purchases and purchasing more as long as marginal utility is greater than price is all well and good for a single commodity, but couldn't a consumer run out of income before she has considered optimal purchases of all goods and services? When one looks at demand curves commodity by commodity, this seems a real possibility. But remember, income and preferences influence utility and demand. Total utility measures what people are willing to pay, given their preferences, their income, and the prices of other goods, not

---

[1]There is a geometric interpretation of consumer's surplus. As the demand curve is the curve of marginal utility, the area under the demand curve equals total utility. If a consumer can buy as much as he wants at market prices, total expenditures are price times the quantity purchased. The difference between total utility and total expenditure is consumer surplus and can be represented as the area under the demand curve and above the horizontal line drawn at the market price. For a straight-line demand curve, consumer surplus is a triangle. This triangle is analogous to the shaded bars of Figure 5-3 in the text.

what they desire. As Mick Jagger and the Rolling Stones said, "You can't always get what you want." The appendix to this chapter shows geometrically how total income constrains the demand for individual commodities.

With our optimal purchase rule, it is easy to derive an individual demand curve. A demand curve shows the quantity demanded at different prices, holding all other things constant. (Look back at Chapter 4 if necessary.) To derive an individual demand curve, we confront our consumer with different prices and see how the quantity demanded changes. Our optimal purchase rule tells us that he will purchase more units as long as the marginal utility is (greater/less) than the price of the unit. He will stop when the two are equal. If we now lower the price, (3) we know that he will again try to equate price and (marginal/total) utility, which he does by considering buying (more/less). Thus, as price goes down the quantity demanded tends to go (down/up), and this individual demand curve has a (positive/negative) slope. In fact, an individual's demand curve will be the same as her curve of (marginal/total) utility.

Income also affects an individual's demand for various commodities. We saw in Chapter 4 that a change in income will mean a (shift in/movement along) the demand curve. In terms of the concepts of this chapter, a (4) change in income will influence how much a person would spend to buy various commodities; that is, a change in income will influence total and marginal _____. Following a change in income, we could again conduct our demand curve experiment, and it would not be surprising if the resulting demand curve had shifted. An increase in income will typically mean an increase in the demand for most commodities, but occasionally the demand for some commodity decreases following an increase in income. Commodities whose demand decreases when income increases are called _____ goods. For example, if potatoes were an inferior good, then increased income would lead our consumer to demand (fewer/more) potatoes.

Individual demand curves are a critical building block to market demand curves. If people determine their own demands without regard to others' purchases, then we can derive the market demand curve by the (horizontal/vertical) summation of individual demand curves. For each price we simply add up the individual (5) quantities demanded. If individual demand curves each have a negative slope, the market demand curve must have a(n) _____ slope. Even if individual demand curves are vertical, that is, individuals purchase only a fixed quantity, the market demand curve is still likely to have a negative slope as long as lower prices attract new consumers and higher prices drive some consumers away.

IMPORTANT TERMS AND CONCEPTS QUIZ

Choose the best definition for each of the following terms.

1. _____ Total utility
2. _____ Marginal utility
3. _____ The "law" of diminishing marginal utility
4. _____ Marginal analysis
5. _____ Consumer's surplus
6. _____ Inferior good
7. _____ Market demand curve
8. _____ The "law" of demand

a. Horizontal summation of individual demand curves
b. Difference between total utility and total expenditures for a given quantity of some commodity
c. Observation that additional units of a given commodity generally have decreasing value for a consumer
d. Maximum amount of money a consumer will give in exchange for a quantity of some commodity
e. Maximum amount of money a consumer will pay for an additional unit of some commodity
f. Quantity demanded increases when consumer real income rises
g. Quantity demanded declines when consumer real income rises
h. Method for calculating choices that best promote the decision maker's objective
i. Observation that a lower price generally increases the amount of a commodity that people in a market are willing to buy

BASIC EXERCISES

These exercises review how we use the law of diminishing marginal utility to derive a negatively sloped demand curve.

1. **Table 5-1** presents data on Dolores' evaluation of different quantities of dresses.

Table 5-1

Dresses	Total Utility	Marginal Utility
1	$110	$ _____
2	$210	$ _____
3	$290	$ _____
4	$360	$ _____
5	$410	$ _____
6	$440	$ _____
7	$460	$ _____

a. Use these data to compute the marginal utility of each dress.
b. The optimal purchase rule says to buy more dresses as long as the marginal utility of the next dress exceeds the price of the dress. According to this rule, how many dresses should Dolores buy if they cost

$90 each? _____ $60 each? _____ $40 each? _____

c. The text defines total utility as the maximum amount Dolores would pay for various quantities of dresses. The difference between what she would be willing to pay and what she has to pay is called _____ surplus.

Table 5-2

Dresses	Price = $90 Total Expenditure	Difference* (Consumer's Surplus)	Price = $60 Total Expenditure	Difference* (Consumer's Surplus)	Price = $40 Total Expenditure	Difference* (Consumer's Surplus)
1	$90	——	$60	——	$40	——
2	180	——	120	——	80	——
3	270	——	180	——	120	——
4	360	——	240	——	160	——
5	450	——	300	——	200	——
6	540	——	360	——	240	——
7	630	——	420	——	280	——

*Differences between total utility and total expenditures

d. Now, fill in columns 3, 5, and 7 of **Table 5-2** to compute Dolores' consumer's surplus at each price. What quantity maximizes consumer's surplus when price equals

$90? _____ $60? _____ $40? _____

How do these quantities compare to your answers to (b)?

e. Use the information in Table 5-1 to plot Dolores' demand curve for dresses in **Figure 5-1**. Is your demand curve consistent with your answers to questions b and c? (It should be.)

Figure 5-1

Demand for Dresses

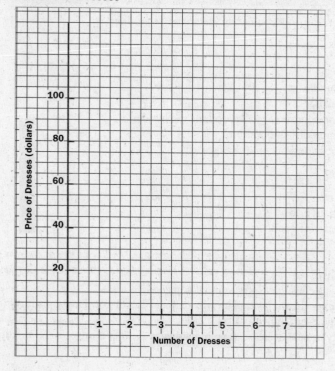

55

2. Consider the following information about Joel's total utility for sweaters:

Number of Sweaters	Total Utility
1	$100
2	$190
3	$27
4	$330
5	$380
6	$410
7	$435
8	$455

a. What marginal utility is associated with the purchase of the third sweater? _____

b. What is Joel's consumer's surplus if he purchases three sweaters at $45 apiece? _____

c. What would happen to Joel's consumer's surplus if he purchased a fourth sweater at $45?

_____

d. How many sweaters should Joel buy when they cost $45 apiece? _____

e. What is Joel's consumer's surplus at the optimal number of sweater purchases? _____

f. If sweaters go on sale and their price drops to $27.50, how many sweaters do you expect Joel to buy?

Why? _____

SELF-TESTS FOR UNDERSTANDING

TEST A

Circle the most appropriate answer.

1. The total utility of any commodity bundle
   a. should be the same for all individuals.
   b. is defined as the maximum amount a consumer will spend for the bundle.
   c. will equal expenditures on the commodity in question.
   d. is not likely to change even if a consumer's income changes.

2. Total utility will increase
   a. as long as marginal utility is positive.
   b. only if marginal utility is greater than price.
   c. if the good in question is not an inferior good.
   d. if consumer surplus is positive.

3. The law of diminishing marginal utility
   a. implies that total utility declines as a consumer buys more of any good.
   b. is an important psychological premise that helps explain why demand curves may have a positive slope.
   c. must hold for every commodity and every individual.
   d. says that increments to total utility usually decrease as an individual consumes more of a commodity.

4. Rick is willing to spend up to $400 for one ski trip this winter and up to $500 for two trips. The marginal utility of the second trip to Rick is
    a. $100.
    b. $200.
    c. $300.
    d. $500.

5. The optimal purchase rule says that consumers should maximize
    a. total utility.
    b. the difference between total utility and consumer surplus.
    c. marginal utility.
    d. the difference between total utility and total expenditures on the good in question.

6. The optimal purchase rule says that to maximize the difference between total utility, measured in money terms, and total expenditures, a consumer should purchase additional units
    a. as long as total utility is increasing.
    b. until marginal utility equals zero.
    c. as long as marginal utility exceeds price.
    d. until marginal utility equals total utility.

7. Consumer surplus refers to the
    a. money a consumer has left over at the end of the month.
    b. accumulation of garbage that could be, but is not, recycled.
    c. difference between total expenditures and what a consumer would have been willing to pay for the same purchases.
    d. the pleasure a consumer takes when he finds an especially good deal.

8. Consumer surplus will increase as long as the marginal utility of each additional purchase is
    a. positive.
    b. increasing.
    c. greater than total utility.
    d. greater than the price of the commodity.

9. If consumers act to maximize consumer surplus, price will be closely related to
    a. total utility.
    b. average utility.
    c. marginal utility.
    d. consumer surplus.

10. On a demand curve diagram, consumer surplus is equal to the
    a. *Y*-axis intercept of the demand curve.
    b. the market price.
    c. the areas between the demand curve and the horizontal line indicating the market price.
    d. the slope of the demand curve.

11. The law of diminishing marginal utility implies that individual demand curves will typically
    a. have a negative slope.
    b. show no response to a change in price.
    c. slope up and to the right.
    d. have a positive slope.

12. A downward-sloping demand curve means that the quantity demanded will
    a. not change when price changes.
    b. increase when price falls.
    c. increase when price rises.
    d. increase when income increases.

13. Scarcity raises _____ utility but lowers _____.
    a. total; price
    b. marginal; price
    c. marginal; total utility
    d. total; marginal utility

14. The diamond–water paradox indicates that
    a. contrary to economists' assumptions, consumers are really irrational.
    b. price is more closely related to marginal utility than to total utility.
    c. water is an inferior good.
    d. the demand for diamonds is very elastic.

15. The effect of an increase in income on quantity demanded
    a. is always positive.
    b. may be positive or negative.
    c. is positive for necessities and negative for luxuries.
    d. depends on the price elasticity of demand.

16. When economists say that some commodity is an inferior good, they are referring to the impact of a(n)
    a. change in price on the quantity demanded.
    b. increase in the quantity consumed on total utility.
    c. increase in the quantity consumed on marginal utility.
    d. change in income on the quantity demanded.

17. The term *inferior good* refers to goods
    a. made with substandard materials.
    b. that economists dislike.
    c. for which the quantity demanded declines when real income increases.
    d. advertised in the *National Enquirer*.

18. The opportunity cost of a purchase _____ its money cost.
    a. is always less than
    b. is always equal to
    c. is always greater than
    d. may be greater or less than

19. Market demand curves can be constructed by
    a. the vertical summation of individual demand curves.
    b. varying the number of people in the market.
    c. charging different people different prices and observing their behavior.
    d. the horizontal summation of individual demand curves.

20. A market demand curve will have a negative slope (there may be more than one correct answer)
    a. if all individual demand curves are downward sloping.
    b. only if the good in question is an inferior good.
    c. even if individual demands are not affected by price, but a lower price attracts new buyers.
    d. if a higher price increases the quantity demanded.

TEST B

Circle T or F for true or false.

T F 1. The term *marginal utility* refers to the amount of dollars that consumers will pay for a particular commodity bundle.

T F 2. If the law of diminishing marginal utility holds for pizza, then the demand curve for pizza should have a negative slope.

T F 3. If a consumer is interested in maximizing the difference between total utility and expenditures, it is optimal to consume more of a commodity as long as the marginal utility of additional units exceeds the market price.

T F 4. Consumer surplus is defined as the difference between price and marginal utility.

T F 5. Maximizing the difference between total utility and total expenditures is the same as maximizing consumer surplus.

T F 6. The term *inferior good* refers to those commodities that economists do not like.

T F 7. If the quantity of ramen demanded decreases when income increases, we can conclude that ramen is an inferior good.

T F 8. If a consumer is rational, he will never buy an inferior good.

T F 9. The opportunity cost of making a purchase is always equal to the money cost of the good being bought.

T F 10. A market demand curve can have a negative slope only if all individual demand curves have a negative slope.

| APPENDIX | *Indifference Curve Analysis*

Important Terms and Concepts

Budget line

Indifference curve

Marginal rate of substitution

Slope of an indifference curve (marginal rate of substitution)

Slope of a budget line

Learning Objectives

After completing this appendix, you should be able to:

- draw a budget line, given data on prices and money income.

- explain the logic behind the four properties of indifference curves:

    (1) higher is better,

    (2) they never intersect,

    (3) they have a negative slope, and

    (4) they are bowed in toward the origin.

- determine optimal commodity bundle(s) for a consumer, given a budget line and a set of indifference curves.

- explain why, if indifference curves are smooth and bowed in to the origin, the optimal commodity bundle is the one for which the marginal rate of substitution equals the ratio of commodity prices.

- use indifference curve analysis to derive a demand curve, that is, show the change in the quantity demanded of a good as its price changes.

- use indifference curve analysis to analyze the impact on commodity demands of a change in income.

APPENDIX REVIEW

Indifference curve analysis is a more rigorous treatment of the material covered in Chapter 5. As the appendix shows, we can study consumer choices by confronting a consumer's desires or preferences, indicated by indifference curves, and with a consumer's opportunities, indicated by a budget line. This approach clearly shows how total purchases are constrained by income.

The budget line represents all possible combinations of commodities that a consumer can buy, given his
(1) income. The arithmetic of a budget line for two commodities shows that it is a (straight/curved) line with a (positive/negative) slope. An increase in money income will change the (intercept/slope) of the budget line. A change in the price of either commodity will mean a change in the _____ of the budget line. The

slope of the budget line is equal to the ratio of the prices of the two commodities. (The price of the commodity measured along the horizontal axis goes on top.)[2]

The budget line indicates all the different ways a consumer could spend her income. In order to figure out what consumption bundle is best for her, we must examine her own personal preferences. Economists use the concept of _____ curves to summarize an individual's preferences. These curves are de-   (2)
rived from a person's ranking of alternative commodity bundles. For two commodities, a single indifference curve is a line connecting all possible combinations (bundles) of the two commodities between which our con-
sumer is _____. From the assumption that more is better, we can deduce (1) that higher indifference curves (are/are not) preferred to lower indifference curves, (2) that indifference curves (never/often) intersect, and (3) that indifference curves will have a (positive/negative) slope.

Indifference curves are usually assumed to be curved lines that are bowed (in/out). The slope of an indiffer-   (3)
ence curve indicates the terms of trade between commodities about which our consumer is indifferent. For a given reduction in one commodity the slope tells us how much (more/less) of the other commodity is necessary to keep our consumer as well-off as before. The slope of the indifference curve is also known as the mar-
ginal rate of _____. If indifference curves are bowed in, or convex to the origin, the marginal rate of substitution (increases/decreases) as we move from left to right along a given indifference curve. This change in the marginal rate of substitution is a psychological premise similar to our earlier assumption about declining marginal utility, and it is what makes the indifference curves convex to the origin.[3]

We can now determine optimal consumer choices. The optimal choice is the commodity bundle that makes our consumer as satisfied as possible, given his opportunities. In this case, opportunities are represented by the _____ line, and the evaluation of alternative commodity bundles is given by the   (4)
_____ curves. The best choice is the commodity bundle that puts our consumer on his (highest/lowest) possible indifference curve. This consumption bundle is indicated by the indifference curve that is just tangent to the _____ _____.

From the definition of the slope of a curved line (Appendix to Chapter 1) we know that at the point of tan-
gency the slope of the associated indifference curve will equal the slope of the budget line. Because the slope of the budget line is given by the ratio of the prices of the two goods, we know that at the optimal decision the slope of the indifference curve, or the marginal rate of substitution, will equal the ratio of prices.

The marginal rate of substitution tells how our consumer *is willing* to trade goods, and the price ratio tells us how she *can* trade goods in the market by buying more of one good and less of the other. If these two trading

---

[2]The equation for the budget line is Income $= P_V Q_V + P_H Q_H$, where V refers to the commodity measured on the vertical axis and H refers to the commodity measured on the horizontal axis. Solve this equation for Q_V and you should get $Q_V = \text{Income}/P_V - (P_H/P_V)Q_H$. Income$/P_V$ is the Y-axis intercept and P_H/P_V is the slope of the budget line. You can use this equation to examine the impact of changes in income and prices on the budget line.
[3]Moving to the left along an indifference curve we see that our consumer is willing to trade fewer and fewer units of the horizontal good for each additional unit of the good measured on the vertical axis. That is, each additional unit of the vertical good is worth less and less to our consumer.

ratios are different, our consumer can make herself better off by changing her purchases. It is only when the two trading ratios are equal that her opportunities for gain have been eliminated.

Once you master the logic and mechanics of indifference curve analysis, you can use it to investigate the impact on demand of changes in price or incomes. A change in either income or prices will shift the (5) _____ _____. It is the resulting change in the optimal commodity bundle that helps trace out a movement along the demand curve in the case of a change in the price of the commodity, or the shift in the demand curve in the case of a change in income or a change in the price of the other commodity.

IMPORTANT TERMS AND CONCEPTS QUIZ

Choose the best definition for each of the following terms.

1. _____ Budget line
2. _____ Indifference curve
3. _____ Slope of an indifference curve
   (Marginal rate of substitution)
4. _____ Slope of a budget line

a. Maximum amount of one commodity a consumer will give up for an extra unit of another commodity
b. Lines connecting all combinations of commodities on a consumer's utility function
c. Line showing all possible combinations of two commodities a consumer can purchase given prices and the consumer's income
d. Line connecting all combinations of commodities that a consumer finds equally desirable
e. Ratio of commodity prices

BASIC EXERCISES

These problems are designed to review the logic of the rule for optimal consumer choice using indifference curve analysis, which says that a consumer should choose the commodity bundle associated with the point of tangency between the budget line and the highest indifference curve.

1. **Figure 5-2** shows Gloria's set of indifference curves between books and hamburgers.
   a. Gloria has an income of $240 that she will spend on books and hamburgers. Hamburgers cost $3 each and paperback books $12 each. Draw the budget line in Figure 5-2 that constrains Gloria's choices. (You might first compute the maximum number of hamburgers Gloria can buy and then

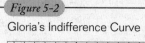

Figure 5-2

Gloria's Indifference Curve

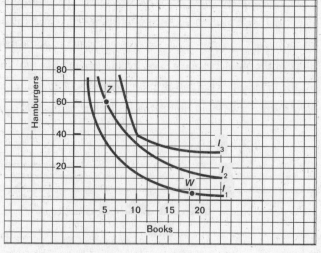

determine the maximum number of books; connect these points on the vertical and horizontal axes with a straight line.)

b. How many hamburgers will Gloria buy? _____ How many books will she buy? _____ In Figure 5-2, label this combination *B* for best choice. (If you drew the budget line correctly, this point should lie on indifference curve I_3.)

c. The combination of 60 hamburgers and 5 books, point *Z*, is obviously not a better choice, as it lies on a lower indifference curve. Assume that Gloria tentatively chooses point *Z* and is considering whether this choice is best. If you put a ruler along indifference curve I_2, you should be able to verify that at point *Z* the marginal rate of substitution of hamburgers for books is 6. This means that Gloria is willing to give up _____ hamburgers in order to be able to buy one more book. However, because books cost only $12 while hamburgers cost $3, Gloria has only to give up _____ hamburgers in order to buy one book. This is clearly a good deal for Gloria, and she should reduce her consumption of hamburgers in order to buy more books; that is, she will move down the budget line away from point *Z*.

d. Consider point *W* on indifference curve I_1. Think about the trade-off Gloria would accept as given by the slope of her indifference curve and the trade-off available in the market as given by the slope of the budget line. Explain why Gloria will be better off moving to the left along the budget line away from point *W*.

e. Arguments similar to those in parts c and d indicate that for smooth indifference curves as in Figure 5-2, the optimal consumer choice cannot involve a commodity bundle for which the marginal rate of substitution differs from the ratio of market prices. The conclusion is that the optimal decision must be the commodity bundle for which the marginal rate of substitution

_____ .

2. **Figure 5-3** assumes that Sharon spends all of her income on pizza and baseball tickets. The budget line P_1B_1 reflects Sharon's initial income and market prices for pizza and baseball tickets. Her preferences are shown by the curved indifference curves. Initially, Sharon chooses to consume at point *X*.

a. Change in income: Where will Sharon consume following a change in income that shifts the budget line to P_2B_2? _____ Is either good an inferior good? How do you know?

b. Change in price: Where will Sharon consume following a reduction in the price of pizzas that shifts the budget line from P_1B_1 to P_3B_1? _____

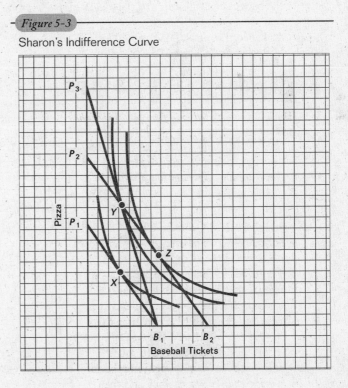

Figure 5-3

Sharon's Indifference Curve

SELF-TESTS FOR UNDERSTANDING

TEST A

Circle the most appropriate answer.

1. The budget line
   a. determines an individual's optimal consumption bundle.
   b. will not shift at all if prices of both commodities increase and income is unchanged.
   c. determines an individual's possible consumption bundles.
   d. is a straight line whose slope is given by the rate of inflation.

2. The slope of the budget line
   a. is equal to the marginal rate of substitution.
   b. depends upon a consumer's income.
   c. is determined by commodity prices.
   d. should be positive.

3. Following a change in income,
   a. a consumer's indifference curves will shift.
   b. the slope of the budget line will increase.
   c. individual commodity demand curves will not shift.
   d. the budget line will shift in a parallel fashion.

4. A change in the price of one good will
   a. lead to a parallel shift of the budget line.
   b. shift the indifference curves in closer to the origin.
   c. change the slope of the budget line.
   d. have no effect on either the budget line or indifference curves.

5. A set of indifference curves is
   a. usually assumed to have a positive slope.
   b. used by economists to represent a person's preferences among different commodity bundles.
   c. the same for everyone.
   d. usually represented by a set of straight lines.

6. The marginal rate of substitution refers to the slope of
   a. an individual's demand curve.
   b. the budget line.
   c. the market demand curve.
   d. indifference curves.

7. The slope of an indifference curve
   a. is constant if the indifference curve is bowed in toward the origin.
   b. always equals the slope of the budget line.
   c. indicates commodity trades about which an individual would be indifferent.
   d. is usually positive.

8. The assumption that more is preferred to less is sufficient to prove all but which one of the following?
   a. Indifference curves never intersect.
   b. Indifference curves bow in toward the origin.
   c. Higher indifference curves are preferred to lower ones.
   d. Indifference curves have a negative slope.

9. If, when choosing between beer and pretzels, a consumer is always willing to trade one beer for one bag of pretzels, the resulting indifference curve will
   a. still bow in toward the origin.
   b. be a straight line.
   c. bow out away from the origin.

10. On an indifference curve diagram, optimal purchases are given by
    a. the point where the budget line intersects the *Y* axis.
    b. the intersection of a ray from the origin and the budget line.
    c. the highest indifference curve that is attainable given the budget line.
    d. any indifference curve that crosses the budget line.

11. The optimal purchases from question 10 occurs where
    a. the quantity of all commodities is equal.
    b. all goods are inferior goods.
    c. demand curves begin to slope up.
    d. the highest indifference curve is tangent to the budget line.

12. If an indifference curve is tangent to the budget line, then the marginal rate of substitution is
    a. less than the ratio of prices.
    b. just equal to the ratio of prices.
    c. greater than the ratio of prices.
    d. zero.

13. On an indifference curve diagram, an increase in the price of one commodity will
    a. cause the resulting budget line to lie inside the original budget line.
    b. lead a consumer to choose a new commodity bundle, but one that is on the same indifference curve.
    c. shift consumer preferences.
    d. have no effect on the demand for either commodity.

TEST B

Circle T or F for true or false.

T F 1. The budget line is a curved line, convex to the origin.

T F 2. A change in the price of one commodity will change the slope of the budget line.

T F 3. A change in income will also change the slope of the budget line.

T F 4. The assumption that consumers prefer more to less is sufficient to establish that indifference curves will be convex to the origin.

T F 5. The slope of indifference curves at any point is given by the ratio of commodity prices.

T F 6. The slope of an indifference curve is also called the marginal rate of substitution.

T F 7. Optimal decision making implies that a consumer should never choose a commodity bundle for which the marginal rate of substitution equals the ratio of market prices.

T F 8. Indifference curve analysis shows that consumers should be indifferent about all the commodity bundles along the budget line, e.g., consumers should be indifferent as between points Y and Z in Figure 5-3.

T F 9. Indifference curve analysis shows us that the demand for all goods is interrelated in the sense that changes in the price of one good can affect the demand for other goods.

T F 10. Indifference curve analysis suggests that a doubling of all prices and a doubling of income will not change optimal consumption bundles.

SUPPLEMENTARY EXERCISE

Consider a consumer whose total utility can be represented as

$$U = (F + 12)(C + 20)$$

where F = quantity of food, C = quantity of clothing, and U = the arbitrary level of utility associated with a particular indifference curve. (A different value for U will imply a different indifference curve.)

1. Draw a typical indifference curve. (Try $U = 7,840$.)

2. Can you derive an expression for the demand for food? For clothing? (Try using the equation for the budget line and what you know about optimal consumer choice to derive an equation that expresses F or C as a function of prices and income. The particular form of these demand curves comes from the mathematical specification of the indifference curves. A different specification of the indifference curves would lead to a different demand function.)

3. If food costs $1.50, clothing $3, and income is $300, what combination of food and clothing will maximize utility?

4. Assume the price of food rises to $2. Now what combination of food and clothing maximizes utility?

5. Assume income increases to $330. What happens to the demand for food and clothing? Is either good an inferior good?

ECONOMICS IN ACTION

DRIP, DRIP, DRIP

In spite of periodic wet winters, drought is a consistent threat to residents of Arizona, California, Nevada, and western Colorado. A year or two of below-average rain and snowfall can seriously deplete water reserves. As the effects of a water shortage become progressively more severe, various schemes for water rationing are discussed, but typically these schemes do not involve using prices to ration water. Most water districts set price to cover cost and do not think very much about price as a variable that might limit demand when drought limits supply.

A typical sequence of events will start with a campaign to encourage voluntary reduction in water usage. As drought persists, many areas establish quotas for water usage, usually based on family size, with stiff increases in price for water consumption in excess of the quota. (The dashed line in Figure 5-4 illustrates such a "quota–high price" scheme. The dashed line indicates the total water bill. The price per gallon is given by the slope of the line.)

The "quota–high price" scheme offers a strong incentive to limit water consumption to the basic quota, but there is little monetary incentive to reduce water consumption below the quota. In 1977, when California was in the midst of a significant drought, economist Milton Friedman suggested that rather than impose quotas with high prices for excess consumption, water districts should charge a high price for all water consumption, offering a rebate to consumers with low water consumption. (See *Newsweek,* March 21, 1977.)

The solid line in **Figure 5-4** illustrates a possible "high price–rebate" scheme. To ensure that a water district has enough money to cover its fixed costs, the position and/or slope of the solid line could be adjusted. Parallel shifts of the solid line would affect the maximum rebate and the no-charge point, but not the price of a gallon of water. Shifts in the slope would change the price. For example, pivoting the solid line on point A would change both the price and the maximum rebate, while leaving the cost of the basic water quota unchanged.

Ross and Judy live in San Francisco. During 1976, in response to the growing concern about water conservation, they voluntarily cut their water consumption significantly below the quotas established by other water districts. The San Francisco rationing scheme, not adopted until early 1977, mandated that all San Francisco residents reduce their consumption below 1976 levels by the same percentage.

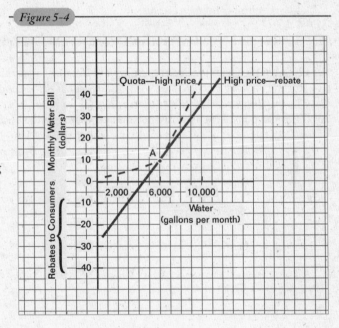

— *Figure 5-4* —————————————————————————

When drought returned to California in the mid-80s, Ross and Judy were heard telling their friends that they were using all the water they could to increase their base use.

1. What advice would you give to a water district facing a drought? How much reliance should be placed on campaigns for voluntary reductions? How much reliance should be placed on prices? If prices, what sort of scheme would you recommend and why? Do you think price affects people's demand for water? What about businesses, government, and farmers?

STUDY QUESTIONS

1. What is the difference between total and marginal utility?

2. How is it that total utility can increase while marginal utility decreases?

3. Why do economists expect a close relationship between price and *marginal utility* rather than *total utility?*

4. How does the difference between total and marginal utility resolve the diamond–water paradox?

5. What is the logic behind the optimal purchase rule?

6. Why does the law of diminishing marginal utility imply that demand curves are likely to have a negative slope?

7. How do we know that purchasing more of a commodity as long as marginal utility exceeds prices will also maximize consumer surplus?

8. How can there be mutual gain from voluntary trade even when no new goods are produced?

9. Economists have a particular definition of inferior goods that does not refer to the quality of product directly but may be correlated with quality. What is the economist's definition of an inferior good?

10. How can one derive a market demand curve from individual demand curves?

Demand and Elasticity

6

Important Terms and Concepts

(Price) elasticity of demand

Elastic, inelastic, and unit-elastic demand curves

Income elasticity of demand

Complements

Substitutes

Cross elasticity of demand

Optimal decision

Learning Objectives

After completing this chapter, you should be able to:

- compute the price elasticity of demand given data from a demand curve.

- explain why the price elasticity of demand is a better measure of the price sensitivity of demand than the slope of the demand curve.

- explain how the impact of a change in price on total revenue and consumer expenditures depends on the price elasticity of demand.

- describe how various factors affect the elasticity of demand.

- use elasticity in measuring how any one economic variable responds to changes in another.

- compute the cross elasticity of demand given information on the change in the price of good X and the associated change in the quantity of good Y demanded.

- explain how the concept of cross elasticity of demand relates to the concepts of substitutes and complements.

- explain how factors other than price can affect the quantity demanded.

- compute the income elasticity of demand given information on how a change in income changes the quantity demanded.

- understand the time period of the demand curve and economic decision making.

CHAPTER REVIEW

The material in this chapter offers an intensive look at demand curves. Demand curves provide important information for analyzing business decisions, market structures, and public policies.

An important property of demand curves is the responsiveness of demand to a change in price. If a firm raises its price, how big a sales drop is likely? If a firm lowers its price, how large an increase in sales will there be?

To avoid problems with changing units, economists find it useful to measure these changes as percentages. If, for a given change in price, we divide the percentage change in the quantity demanded by the percentage change in the price producing the change in quantity and ignore the negative sign, we have just computed the

(1) price _____ of _____. Remember, this calculation ignores minus signs and uses the *average* price and quantity to compute percentage changes.

It is useful to know the elasticity properties of certain, special types of demand curves. If the demand curve is truly a vertical line, then there is no change in the quantity demanded following any change in price, and the

(2) elasticity of demand is _____. (No demand curve is likely to be vertical for all prices, but it may be for some.) The other extreme is a perfectly horizontal demand curve where a small change in price produces a very large change in the quantity demanded. Such a demand curve implies that if price declines, even just a little, the quantity demanded will be infinite, while if the price rises, even a little, the quantity demanded will fall to zero. In this case, a very small percentage change in price produces a very large percentage change in the quantity demanded, and the price elasticity of demand is, in the limit, _____. The price elasticity of demand along a negatively sloped straight-line demand curve (is constant/changes). One of the Basic Exercises illustrates just this point.

A demand curve with a price elasticity of demand greater than 1.0 is commonly called

(3) _____ while a demand curve with a price elasticity of demand less than 1.0 is called _____. If the price elasticity of demand is exactly 1.0, the demand curve is said to be a(n) _____ _____ demand curve.

Some simple arithmetic, not economics, can show the connection between the price elasticity of demand and the change in total consumer expenditure (or, equivalently, the change in sales revenue) following a change in price. We know that total expenditures or revenues are simply price times quantity, or

$$\text{Consumer expenditures} = \text{Sales revenues} = PQ.$$

A decrease in price will increase quantity as we move along a given demand curve. Whether total revenue increases clearly depends on whether the increase in quantity is big enough to outweigh the decline in price. (Remember the old saying: "We lose a little on each sale but make it up on volume.")

It is mathematics, not economics, that tells us the percentage change in total expenditures or revenue is equal to the sum of the percentage change in price and the percentage change in quantity.[1]

---

[1]This result is strictly true only for very small changes in P and Q. Total revenue always equals $P \times Q$, but this simple way of calculating the percentage change in total revenue is only true for small changes.

$$\begin{array}{ccc} \text{Percentage change} \\ \text{in sales revenues} \end{array} = \begin{array}{c} \text{Percentage change} \\ i \text{ price} \end{array} + \begin{array}{c} \text{Percentage change} \\ \text{in quantity} \end{array}$$

Remember that as we move along a given demand curve, a positive change in price will lead to a negative change in quantity, and vice versa.

If the absolute value of the percentage change in quantity is equal to the absolute value of the percentage change in price, then total revenue (will/will not) change following a change in price. In this case, the price elas- (4) ticity of demand is equal to _____.

When the elasticity of demand is greater than 1.0, the absolute value of the percentage change in quantity will be (greater/less) than the percentage change in price. In this case, an increase in price that reduces the (5) quantity demanded will (decrease/increase) total revenue, and a reduction in price that increases the quantity demanded will (decrease/increase) total revenue. Opposite conclusions apply when the price elasticity of demand is less than 1.0. In this case, the percentage change in quantity will be (greater/less) than the percentage change in price. An increase in price that reduces the quantity demanded will (decrease/increase) total revenue, and a reduction in price that increases the quantity demanded will (decrease/increase) total revenue.

The price elasticity of demand refers to the impact on the quantity demanded of a change in a commodity's price. A related elasticity concept compares the change in the quantity demanded of one good with a change in the price of another good. This quotient is called the _____ elasticity of demand. In this case we must (6) keep track of any negative signs.

Some goods, such as knives and forks, cereal and milk, are usually demanded together. Such pairs are called _____ and are likely to have a (positive/negative) cross elasticity of demand. For example a de- (7) cline in the price of milk is likely to (decrease/increase) the demand for cereal. That is, following a decline in the price of milk, the demand curve for cereal will likely shift to the (left/right).

Other goods, such as different brands of toothpaste, are probably close _____ and are likely (8) to have a(n) _____ cross elasticity of demand. What is the likely impact of a change in the price of Crest toothpaste on the demand for Colgate? A decrease in the price of Crest toothpaste would likely (decrease/increase) the demand for Colgate toothpaste. Alternatively, one could say that a decrease in the price of Crest will likely shift the Colgate demand curve to the (left/right).

The price of a commodity is not the only variable influencing demand. Changes in other factors, say, advertising, consumers' income, tastes, and, as we just saw, the price of a close substitute or complement, will mean a (shift in/movement along) a demand curve drawn against price. Finally, remember that a demand curve refers (9) only to a particular period of time.

IMPORTANT TERMS AND CONCEPTS QUIZ

Choose the best definition for each of the following terms.

1. _____ Price elasticity of demand
2. _____ Elastic demand curve
3. _____ Inelastic demand curve
4. _____ Unit-elastic demand curve
5. _____ Income elasticity of demand
6. _____ Complements
7. _____ Substitutes
8. _____ Cross elasticity of demand
9. _____ Optimal decision

a. Ratio of percent change in quantity demanded of one product to the percent change in the price of another
b. A change in price leads to a less than proportionate change in quantity demanded

c. Good for which an increase in price leads to higher demand
d. An increase in price of one good decreases the demand for the other
e. A change in price leads to a more than proportionate change in quantity demanded
f. Ratio of percent change in quantity demanded to percent change in price
g. A change in price accompanied by an equal proportionate change in quantity demanded
h. An increase in the price of one good increases the demand for the other
i. Ratio of percentage change in quantity demanded to percentage change in income
j. Decision that best serves the objectives of the decision maker, whatever those objectives may be

BASIC EXERCISES

These exercises offer practice in calculating and interpreting price elasticities of demand.

1. **The Price Elasticity of Demand**
   a. **Table 6-1** has data on possible prices and the associated demand for schmoos and gizmos. Use these data to plot the demand curves in **Figures 6-1** and **6-2**. Looking at these demand curves, which curve looks more elastic? More inelastic?
   b. Use the data in Table 6-1 to calculate the elasticity of demand for schmoos for a change in price from $60 to $50.[2] It is _____.
   c. Now calculate the elasticity of demand for gizmos for a change in price from $1 to 50 cents. It is _____.
   d. For these changes, which demand curve is more elastic? In fact, if you look closely at the underlying data for both curves—for example, by computing the total revenue—you will see that for both curves the elasticity of demand is _____.

2. **The Price Elasticity of Straight-Line Demand Curves**
   a. Use the data in **Table 6-2** to plot the demand curve for jeans in **Figure 6-3**. It is a (curved/straight) line.

Table 6-1

Demand for Schmoos		Demand for Gizmos	
Price (dollars)	Quantity	Price (dollars)	Quantity
60	200	2.00	2,000
50	240	1.25	3,200
48	250	1.00	4,000
40	300	0.50	8,000

[2]Remember to use the average of the two prices or quantities when computing each percentage change. For example, compute the elasticity of demand when the price changes from $60 to $50 as $\left[\frac{40}{220}\right] \div \left[\frac{10}{55}\right]$.

Figure 6-1

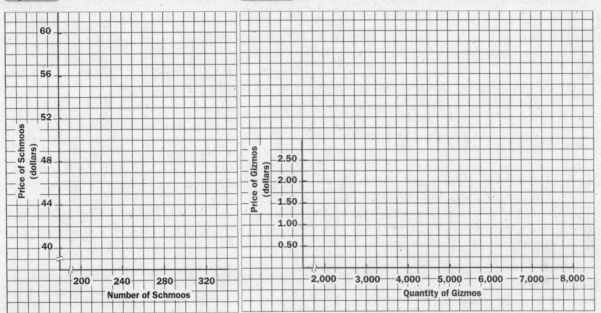

Figure 6-2

Table 6-2

Price (dollars)	Quantity Demanded	Percentage Change Price	Percentage Change Quantity	Elasticity of Demand	Total Revenue
40	15,000				
36	18,000	————	————	————	————
32	21,000	————	————	————	————
28	24,000	————	————	————	————
24	27,000	————	————	————	————

Figure 6-3

b. Using the data in Table 6-2, compute the elasticity of demand for each change in price.[3] What general conclusion can you draw about the elasticity of demand along a straight-line demand curve? The elasticity of demand (increases/decreases) as one moves down and to the right along a straight-line demand curve.

c. Use the same data to compute total revenue for each price-quantity pair in Table 6-2. Compare the change in total revenue to the elasticity of demand. What conclusion can you draw about this relationship?

---

[3]Remember to use the average of the two prices or quantities when computing each percentage change. For a change in price from $40 to $36, compute the elasticity of demand as $\left[\dfrac{3,000}{16,500}\right] \div \left[\dfrac{4}{38}\right]$.

73

SELF-TESTS FOR UNDERSTANDING

TEST A

Circle the most appropriate answer.

1. Looking just at the demand curve, the price responsiveness of demand is given by the
   a. Y-intercept.
   b. slope of the demand curve.
   c. slope of a ray from the origin to a point on the demand curve.
   d. product of price times quantity.

2. If when price increases the quantity demanded declines, we know that
   a. the demand curve has a negative slope.
   b. the price elasticity of demand is less than 1.0.
   c. total sales revenue will increase.
   d. total sales revenue will decrease.

3. The price elasticity of demand is defined as the _____ change in the quantity demanded divided by the _____ change in price.
   a. percentage; absolute
   b. absolute; absolute
   c. percentage; percentage
   d. absolute; percentage

4. If the price elasticity of demand is less than 1.0, then for a 10 percent change in price the quantity demanded will change by
   a. less than 10 percent.
   b. exactly 10 percent.
   c. more than 10 percent.
   d. There is not enough information.

5. If the units in which the quantity demanded is measured are changed, say from pounds to ounces, then the price elasticity of demand will
   a. decrease.
   b. increase.
   c. be unaffected.
   d. increase by a factor of 16.

6. If a 10 percent price increase leads to a 12 percent decline in the quantity demanded, the price elasticity of demand is
   a. (10/12) = .83.
   b. (12/10) = 1.2.
   c. (12 − 10) = 2.
   d. (12 + 10) = 22.

7. If the elasticity of demand is equal to 1.0, then a change in price leads to
    a. no change in the quantity demanded.
    b. a reduction in total revenue.
    c. a shift in the demand curve.
    d. (ignoring any negative signs) an equal, proportionate change in the quantity demanded.

8. If the elasticity of demand is greater than 1.0, a reduction in price will
    a. decrease total sales revenue.
    b. leave total sales revenue unchanged.
    c. increase total sales revenue.
    d. lead to a reduction in the quantity demanded.

9. Sales revenue will not change following an increase in price if the
    a. price elasticity of demand is equal to 1.0.
    b. demand curve is a straight line.
    c. cross elasticity of demand is positive.
    d. quantity demanded doesn't change.

10. If the demand for apples is inelastic, apple producers could increase total revenue by
    a. decreasing price.
    b. increasing price.
    c. Changing price will not affect total revenue.

11. If a 20 percent decrease in the price of long-distance phone calls leads to a 35 percent increase in the quantity of calls demanded, we can conclude that the demand for phone calls is
    a. elastic.
    b. inelastic.
    c. unit elastic.

12. From the data given above, what would happen to total revenue following a 20 percent decrease in the price of long-distance phone calls? It would
    a. decrease.
    b. increase.
    c. remain the same.

13. Angelita manufactures artificial valves used in open-heart surgery. She is contemplating increasing prices. Total revenue will decrease unless the demand for valves is
    a. elastic.
    b. inelastic.
    c. unit elastic.

14. Goods that are usually used together are said to be
    a. complements.
    b. inelastic.
    c. spin-offs.
    d. substitutes.

15. If goods are substitutes, then the cross elasticity of demand is likely to be
    a. equal to 1.0.
    b. negative.
    c. positive.
    d. zero.

16. The cross elasticity of demand between frozen pizza and home-delivered pizza would be computed as the percentage change in the quantity of frozen pizza demanded divided by the
    a. percentage change in the price of frozen pizza.
    b. percentage change in the quantity of home-delivery pizza demanded.
    c. percentage change in the price of home-delivery pizza.
    d. change in the price of mozzarella cheese.

17. If following an increase in the price of schmoos the quantity demanded of gizmos declined, we would conclude that
    a. the demand for gizmos is inelastic.
    b. gizmos and schmoos are substitutes.
    c. gizmos and schmoos are complements.
    d. schmoos are likely to be a luxury good.

18. If the cross elasticity of demand between two goods is negative, we would conclude that the two goods are
    a. substitutes.
    b. complements.
    c. necessities.
    d. both likely to have inelastic demand curves.

19. If skis and boots are complements, then which one of the following statements is false?
    a. A reduction in the price of skis is likely to increase the sales of boots.
    b. Revenue from ski sales will increase following a reduction in the price of ski boots.
    c. An increase in the price of boots will likely reduce the sales of skis.
    d. The cross elasticity of demand between skis and boots will likely be positive.

20. The income elasticity of demand is measured as the percentage change in
    a. price divided by the percentage change in income.
    b. the quantity demanded divided by the percentage change in income that changes demand.
    c. income divided by the change in demand.
    d. income divided by the percentage change in price.

TEST B

Circle T or F for true or false.

T F 1. The price elasticity of demand is defined as the change in quantity divided by the change in price.

T F 2. The elasticity of demand will be the same at all points along a straight-line demand curve.

T F 3. A vertical demand curve would have a price elasticity of zero.

T F 4. A demand curve is elastic if, following a decrease in price, the quantity demanded increases.

T F 5. If demand is inelastic, an increase in price will actually increase the quantity demanded.

T F 6. If the demand for airplane travel is elastic, then a reduction in the price of airline tickets will increase total expenditures on airplane trips.

T F 7. If two goods are substitutes, then an increase in the price of one good is likely to reduce the demand for the other good.

T F 8. The cross elasticity of demand between complements is normally negative.

T F 9. If sales of Whoppers at Burger King increase following an increase in the price of Big Macs at McDonald's, we can conclude that Whoppers and Big Macs are complements.

T F 10. The price elasticity of demand for Chevrolets is likely to be greater than that for cars as a whole.

T F 11. A demand curve will shift to the left following an increase in price of a close complement.

T F 12. An increase in consumer income will shift the demand curve for most goods to the left.

T F 13. The income elasticity of demand is defined as the percentage change in income divided by the percentage change in price.

T F 14. Plotting price and quantity for a period of months or years is a good way to estimate a demand curve.

| APPENDIX | *Statistical Analysis of Demand Relationships*

BASIC EXERCISES

Completing these exercises should help underscore the necessity and difficulty of distinguishing between a demand curve and observations on price and quantity that are determined by the intersection of demand and supply curves.

1. Consider the data on the consumption and prices of fresh apples for the period 1994 to 2006 in **Table 6-3.** Plot these data on a piece of graph paper. What does this graph say about the demand for apples? Why?

— *Table 6-3* —

Year	Quantity (millions of pounds)	Price (dollars per pound)
1990	4,926.7	$0.72
1991	4,618.0	$0.89
1992	4,944.2	$0.89
1993	4,972.2	$0.83
1994	5,126.4	$0.80
1995	5,006.4	$0.83
1996	5,061.9	$0.93
1997	4,961.9	$0.91
1998	5,268.9	$0.94
1999	5,197.2	$0.90
2000	4,958.6	$0.92
2001	4,478.1	$0.87
2002	4,633.7	$0.95

2. Assume that the demand for handheld calculators depends on aggregate consumer income and price as follows:

$$Q_D = -110 + 0.2Y - 5P$$

where

Q_D = quantity demanded (thousands),

Y = consumer income (millions), and

P = price (dollars).

Supply is assumed to be determined as follows:

$$Q_S = 50 + 15P$$

where Q_S = quantity supplied (thousands).

a. Compute the equilibrium price and quantity for 2005, 2006, and 2007, given that consumer income was as follows:

Year	Consumer Income
2005	$3,000
2006	3,100
2007	3,200

Plot these price–quantity pairs for each year on a two-variable diagram. Are these points a good estimate of the demand curve? Why or why not?

b. Assume now that the supply curve for calculators shifts each year in response to technical advances in the production process. To capture these technical advances, we need a new supply curve for each year as follows:

2005 $Q_S = 50 + 15P$

2006 $Q_S = 100 + 15P$

2007 $Q_S = 300 + 15P$

Compute and plot equilibrium price and quantity for each year. (Remember to include the effect of the change in consumer income in the demand curve.) Are these points a good estimate of the demand curve? Why or why not?

ECONOMICS IN ACTION

1. Howard Grant operates a movie theater in New Jersey, just across the Hudson River from New York. He used to show the most recently released movies at a ticket price of $6.50. He was especially discouraged when attendance dropped to 212 people over a full weekend. He then changed the format of his theater to show still current but previously released movies, and he reduced his ticket price to $1. Weekend attendance jumped to 3,782 people. (*The New York Times*, March 20, 1992.)
   a. Using the numbers above, what is the elasticity of demand for movies at Mr. Grant's theater?
   b. What is likely to happen to Mr. Grant's attendance if other theaters adopt his format and lower their prices?

2. In the late spring of 1992, Northwest Airlines offered a promotional fare advertised as parents fly free with children. The program cut fares in half for family travel. American Airlines responded by halving all fares purchased seven days in advance, a move matched by most other airlines. To avoid the anger of passengers who had bought tickets earlier, the airlines agreed that these passengers could reticket at the new, lower fares. Not surprisingly, airlines and travel agents were swamped with calls. At one point, new

bookings were so heavy that some airline executives were reported saying that total sales revenue might not drop "because of the extraordinary high response." (*The New York Times,* June 2, 1992.)

    a. What would the price elasticity of demand for air travel have to be if these airline executives were correct?

    b. How would we know whether the reduction in ticket prices did double the demand for air travel? Consider the following. In the summer of 1991, June through September, travel on domestic airlines totaled 120 billion passenger miles. In 1992, summer travel totaled 134.5 billion passenger miles. Discuss the relevance of this information for an evaluation of the impact of the reduction in airfares.

3. In December 2001, Leonard Riggio, Chairman of Barnes and Noble, argued that publishers should rethink book pricing. Mr. Riggio was quoted as saying "publishers and retailers would both make more money if books cost less." (*New York Times*, December 16, 2001.) Paul Ingram, a bookstore owner in Iowa City, Iowa, agreed. He was quoted as saying, ". . . they would sell more books and make more money if they lowered the prices."

    a. What must be true about the elasticity of demand for books if Mr. Riggio and Mr. Ingram are correct?

STUDY QUESTIONS

1. Why is elasticity measured as the ratio of percentage changes and not just as the ratio of the change in quantity demanded to the change in price?

2. What is the logic behind the statement that the demand for narrowly defined commodities, for example a particular brand of clothing, is more elastic than the demand for broadly defined commodities, that is, all clothing?

3. Which is likely to be larger and why—the price elasticity of demand for luxuries or the price elasticity of demand for necessities?

4. What is meant by the terms "perfectly elastic" and "perfectly inelastic"? What do these demand curves look like and why?

5. How does the elasticity of demand help determine whether a change in price will raise or lower total sales revenue?

6. If a government is interested in increasing revenue, will it want to impose or raise sales taxes on goods with a high or low price elasticity of demand? Why?

7. What is the cross elasticity of demand and how does its numerical value help to determine whether goods are complements or substitutes?

8. Consider the demand for pretzels. Why does the change in the price of a complement, say, beer, or the change in the price of a close substitute, say, potato chips, lead to shifts in the demand curve for pretzels rather than a movement along the curve? What exactly is the nature of the shifts?

Production, Inputs, and Cost: Building Blocks for Supply Analysis

7

Important Terms and Concepts

Short run	Variable cost	Average physical product (APP)	Marginal revenue product (MRP)	Economies of scale (increasing returns to scale)
Long run	Total physical product (TPP)	Marginal physical product (MPP)		
Fixed cost				

Learning Objectives

After completing this chapter, you should be able to:

- describe the difference between the short run and long run.

- compute the average and marginal physical product for a single input given data on total output at different input levels.

- explain the "law" of diminishing marginal returns.

- compute the marginal revenue product for additional units of some input given information on the marginal physical product of the input and the price of the output.

- explain why a profit-maximizing firm will expand the use of each input until its marginal revenue product equals the price of the input.

- distinguish between diminishing returns following an increase of a single productive input.

- explain the importance of opportunity cost when distinguishing between total cost and total expenditure.

- explain the difference between fixed and variable costs.

- explain why fixed costs, administrative problems of large organizations, and the law of diminishing returns imply that the short-run average cost curve is usually U-shaped.

- explain how to determine the long-run average cost curve from a set of short-run average cost curves.

- explain how and why the ratio of input prices and the ratio of marginal physical products is relevant to the optimal choice of input combinations.

- explain how total cost—and hence average cost as well as marginal cost—can be computed.

- determine whether a firm's operations show increasing, decreasing, or constant returns to scale, given data on output and on various input combinations.

- explain the relationship between returns to scale and the long-run average cost curve.

- distinguish between diminishing returns to increases of a single productive input and economies of scale when all inputs change.

- explain the difference between analytical and historical cost curves.

CHAPTER REVIEW

In this chapter we will make extensive use of the concept of marginal analysis as a guide to optimal decision making. We will see how marginal analysis can help a firm make optimal decisions about the use of production inputs and how these decisions can be used to derive cost curves. In Chapter 5, we saw how marginal analysis helps to understand optimal consumer decisions. We use it here in an analogous way to understand optimal firm decisions about the use of inputs.

This chapter introduces a potentially bewildering array of curves and concepts—marginal physical product, marginal revenue product, fixed costs, variable costs, long run, and short run. All of these curves and concepts relate to each other and underlie optimal firm decisions. Spending time now to get these relationships clear will save you time in later chapters and the night before the exam.

In deciding whether to use an additional unit of some input, say, hiring more workers, a firm should look at the contribution of the additional workers to both total revenue and total cost. If the increase in revenue

(1) exceeds the increase in cost, then profits will (increase/decrease). The increase in revenue comes from producing and selling additional units of output. Economists call the amount of additional output from the use of one more unit of input the marginal (physical/revenue) product of the input. For a firm selling its output at a constant price, the increase in revenue comes from multiplying the additional output by the price at which it can be sold. Economists call this the marginal _____ product.

Consider a small firm that faces fixed market prices for its production inputs. Common sense tells us that a profit-maximizing firm should use additional units of any input if the addition to total revenue exceeds the addition to total cost. Another way of saying the same thing is that the firm should consider using more of an

(2) input as long as the marginal (physical/revenue) product exceeds the price of the input. A firm has clearly gone too far if additions to revenue are less than additions to cost. Thus a profit-maximizing firm should expand the use of any factor until the marginal revenue product equals the _____ of the input.

If the price of an input is constant, firms will use more and more units of this input until the marginal revenue product falls to a point where it equals the input price. As a result, firms will usually expand the use of any input past any region of increasing marginal returns and into the region of decreasing returns to the one input.

So far we have talked about the optimal use of only one input. What if production involves trade-offs between more than one input? Our rule holds true for more than one input. The idea is to adjust the use of all inputs until the marginal revenue of each is equal to the price of the input. In symbols, assuming the use of two inputs A and B, we have $MRP_A=P_A$ and $MRP_B=P_B$. A little multiplication and division should show that when the prices of inputs and output are constant, our condition for optimal input use can be rewritten as MPP_A/P_A and MPP_B/P_B.[1]

---

[1]For input A, we can write our condition for optimal input use as $MPP_A \times P_{OUTPUT}=P_A$. Dividing both sides of this equality by MPP_A we see that $P_{OUTPUT}=P_A/MPP_A$. Similar results hold for input B. That is, setting MRP_B equal to the price of input B also sets $P_{OUTPUT}=P_B/MPP_B$. Since both fractions are equal to the price of output, they are equal to each other and their reciprocals are also equal, that is if $P_A/MPP_A=P_B/MPP_B$ then $MPP_A/P_A=MPP_B/P_B$, our condition for the optimal input combination.

Either fraction shows how output will change per dollar spent on that input. When the fraction is high, one gets a lot of output per dollar spent. A low fraction means less output per dollar spent. If this ratio were initially high for input B and low for input A, a firm would want to use (<u>less/more</u>) of input B and _____ of input (3) A. Making these adjustments should (<u>increase/reduce</u>) the MPP of input B and _____ the MPP of input A, moving the fractions toward the equality necessary for the optimal input combination.

If the price of an input changes, it is natural to expect the firm's optimal input combination to change. Specifically, it is natural to expect that a profit-maximizing firm will (<u>reduce/increase</u>) the use of any factor (4) whose price has risen. Changing the quantity of one input will typically affect the marginal physical product of other inputs. As a result, a firm will want to rethink its use of all inputs following a change in price of any one input. It is quite likely that following an increase in the price of one input, a profit-maximizing firm will decide to use relatively (<u>less/more</u>) of the more expensive input and relatively _____ of the inputs with unchanged prices.

If all inputs are increased by the same percentage amount, then the percentage increase in output is used to indicate the degree of economies of scale. If output increases by more than the common percentage increase in all inputs, the production function exhibits _____ returns to scale. If output increases by less, (5) there are _____ returns to scale, and if output increases by the same percentage, we would say that returns to scale are _____.

Information about inputs and outputs can be used to construct cost curves for a firm. Over a very short time horizon, previous commitments may limit a firm's ability to adjust all inputs. These commitments often imply that at least one input is predetermined and cannot be adjusted immediately. Imagine a farmer with a five-year lease on a parcel of land and unable to rent additional land. The interval of time over which a firm's fixed commitments cannot be adjusted is called the (<u>long/short</u>) run. (6)

When computing the total cost of producing each level of output in the short run we will be interested only in minimum total costs for every level of output. We first use what we know about optimal factor use to determine the most efficient combination of variable inputs. We can then compute minimum total cost. As an example, assume that production requires two inputs, one of which is fixed in the short run. To compute total cost, the firm must identify what amount of the variable input is necessary to produce different levels of output. Then it can compute total cost for each level of output by multiplying the quantity of the fixed input and the optimal quantity of the variable input by their prices, remembering relevant opportunity costs, and adding the results. After computing total cost, the firm can compute average cost by dividing total cost by the associated level of _____. To compute marginal cost the firm must examine how (<u>average/total</u>) cost changes (7) when output changes.

The period of time over which a firm can adjust all its fixed commitments is called the _____ _____. Long-run cost curves can be derived by either of two equivalent methods. (8) One procedure would first derive short-run cost curves for each possible amount of the fixed input. The long-run cost curve is then determined by joining the _____ segments of the short-run cost curves.

An alternative and equivalent method would treat both factors as variable. One would first use information on the marginal physical product for each input along with input prices to determine the optimal level of both inputs to produce every level of output. Total cost for each output level can then be computed by multiplying optimal input levels by their respective prices and adding the results. Average and marginal cost are then easily computed.

Since in the long run all factors can be changed, the shape of the long-run average cost curve is related to economies of scale. Constant returns to scale imply that a doubling of output requires twice as much of all (9) inputs. In this case, total costs also double and average cost (falls/is unchanged/rises). Increasing returns to scale mean that twice the output can be produced with (more/less) than twice the inputs and average cost will (fall/rise). With decreasing returns to scale, twice the output requires _____ than twice the inputs and average cost _____.

We've covered a lot of ground and a lot of curves. You may want to take a deep breath before a quick review. One starts with the basic technical information about inputs and output. From this information we can derive total physical product and marginal physical product for a single input. By itself the technical information is not sufficient to determine the minimum cost combination of inputs. Knowing the price of output will let us compute marginal revenue product for each input. Comparing marginal revenue product with input prices will then determine the optimal input quantities. Optimal input quantities, in turn, determine (minimum) total cost for alternative levels of output. Once we know total cost, we can easily compute average and marginal cost. In the short run, there may be fixed costs. In the long run, all inputs, and hence all costs, are variable. In either run, the same optimizing principles apply.

IMPORTANT TERMS AND CONCEPTS QUIZ

Choose the best definition for each of the following terms.

1. _____ Short run
2. _____ Long run
3. _____ Fixed costs
4. _____ Variable costs
5. _____ Total physical product (TPP)
6. _____ Average physical product (APP)
7. _____ Marginal physical product (MPP)
8. _____ Marginal revenue product (MRP)
9. _____ Economies of scale (increasing returns to scale)

a. A graph showing how average cost has changed over time

b. Costs which do not change when output rises or falls

c. Increase in output greater than the proportionate increase in all inputs

d. Period of time long enough for all of a firm's commitments to end

e. Dollar value of output produced by an extra unit of input

f. Graph of output generated by various quantities of one input, holding other inputs fixed

g. Total output divided by total quantity of input

h. Costs that change as the level of production changes

i. Increase in output that results from an additional unit of a given input, holding all other inputs constant

j. Period of time during which none of a firm's commitments will have ended

BASIC EXERCISES

These questions review the concept of optimal input decisions.

Megan and Jamie have invested in Greenacre Farms to grow cornbeans. Since they both work in the city, they will need to hire workers for the farm. **Table 7-1** has data on various input combinations and the resulting output of cornbeans.

1. **Figure 7.1** shows the relationship between total output and labor input for 100 acres of land.

    What is the region of increasing marginal returns? _____

    What is the region of decreasing marginal returns? _____

    What is the region of negative marginal returns? _____

2. Use Figure 7-1 to draw the relationship between total output and labor input, assuming the use of 200 acres of land. Identify the regions of increasing, decreasing, and negative returns.

    Do the same assuming 300 acres of land. How does the output–labor curve, i.e., the curve of total physical product, shift when more land is used?

3. Fill in the middle part of Table 7-1 by computing the marginal physical product of each worker. Check to see that the regions of increasing, diminishing, and negative returns that you identified above correspond to information about the marginal physical product of labor. (The marginal physical product of labor is equal to the slope of the total physical product curve. Check to see that your entries for each row in the middle of Table 7-1 equal the slope of the relevant total product curve in Figure 7-1.)

Table 7-1

Total Output of Cornbeans (thousands of tons)

Number of Workers		1	2	3	4	5	6
Acres	100	1	4	6	7	6	4
of	200	2	6	9.5	12	13	12
Land	300	3	7.5	11	14	16	17

Marginal Physical Product of Labor		1	2	3	4	5	6
Acres	100	___	___	___	___	___	___
of	200	___	___	___	___	___	___
Land	300	___	___	___	___	___	___

Marginal Revenue Product of Labor		1	2	3	4	5	6
200 Acres of Land		___	___	___	___	___	___

Figure 7-1

Output of Cornbeans

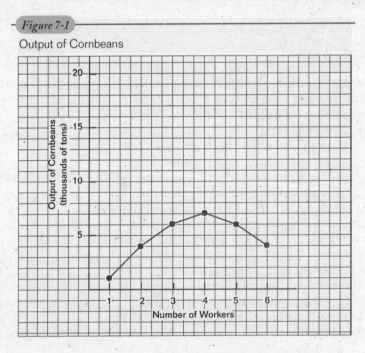

4. Your answers to questions 1, 2, and 3 should confirm that the production of cornbeans eventually shows decreasing returns to labor for all three potential farm sizes. (What about returns to the increased use of land for a fixed amount of labor?)

5. Now consider the following pairs of inputs (acres, workers) and indicate for each whether economies of scale are increasing, decreasing, or constant.

Economies of Scale

(100, 1) to (200, 2) _____
(100, 2) to (200, 4) _____
(100, 3) to (200, 6) _____
(200, 2) to (300, 3) _____
(200, 4) to (300, 6) _____

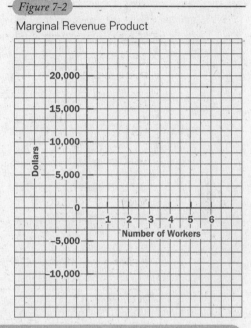

Figure 7-2

Marginal Revenue Product

6. Assume that cornbeans can be sold for $5 a ton and that Greenacre Farms has 200 acres of land. Calculate the marginal revenue product of labor for 200 acres of land in the bottom part of Table 7-1. Plot the marginal revenue product in **Figure 7-2**. Hired help costs $8,000 for a growing season. Draw a horizontal line in Figure 7-2 at $8,000 to indicate the price of labor. How many workers should Megan and Jamie hire? _____. At the level of labor input you just determined, what is the difference between the proceeds from selling cornbeans (output) and labor costs? _____ (Check to see that your labor input choice maximizes this difference by considering the use of one more or one fewer worker.)

SELF-TESTS FOR UNDERSTANDING

TEST A

Circle the most appropriate answer.

1. A graph of total physical product shows how output changes as
   a. all inputs are increased simultaneously.
   b. the firm adopts new technologies.
   c. the scale of production varies.
   d. one input is increased, holding all others constant.

2. For a production process that uses just one input, average physical product is found by
   a. graphing total output against the number of units of input.
   b. computing the change in output for a unit change in input.
   c. dividing total output by the number of units of input.
   d. multiplying the number of units of input by their cost.

3. The "law" of diminishing marginal returns
   a. says that eventually the marginal physical product of any input must become negative.
   b. applies to only a simultaneous increase in all inputs.
   c. can only be true when there are decreasing returns to scale.
   d. refers to what happens to output as only one factor is increased, all other inputs being held constant.

87

4. Marginal physical product refers to
   a. the increased revenue from employing an additional worker.
   b. the change in total output from a one-unit increase in a variable input.
   c. total output divided by total input.
   d. total output divided by total cost.

5. When looking at the curve for total physical product, the region of diminishing marginal returns is given by the region where marginal physical product is
   a. negative.
   b. positive.
   c. positive and increasing.
   d. positive and decreasing.

6. Consider the following data on workers and output.

Workers	1	2	3	4	5
Output	10	25	35	42	40

   Where do diminishing marginal returns to workers begin to set in?
   a. after the first worker
   b. after the second worker
   c. after the third worker
   d. after the fourth worker

7. For a production process that uses just one input, a firm should expand output as long as marginal
   a. revenue is positive.
   b. physical product is positive.
   c. revenue product is greater than the price of the input.
   d. physical product is greater than average physical product.

8. The rule for optimal input use implies that a firm should use additional units of an input until
   a. average cost equals the price of the input.
   b. marginal physical product is maximized.
   c. marginal revenue product equals the price of the input.
   d. increasing returns to scale are exhausted.

9. A change in fixed costs affects
   a. marginal physical product of the variable input.
   b. average physical product of the variable input.
   c. marginal cost associated with changes in the variable input.
   d. average cost associated with changes in total output.

10. In the short run, decisions to vary the amount of output will affect all but which one of the following?
    a. fixed costs
    b. variable costs
    c. marginal physical product
    d. average costs

11. As output increases, average fixed costs
    a. first decline and then increase.
    b. decrease continuously.
    c. are constant.
    d. increase more or less continuously.

12. As output increases, average total costs typically
    a. first decline and then increase.
    b. decrease continuously.
    c. are constant.
    d. increase more or less continuously.

13. A change in which of the following will not shift the short-run average cost curve?
    a. the price of output
    b. the price of inputs
    c. the quantity of fixed factors
    d. the marginal physical product of variable inputs

14. The term economies of scale refers to
    a. the change over time in average cost as firms grow larger.
    b. the percentage change in the marginal revenue product divided by the percentage change of the associated input.
    c. the increase in output when only one input is increased.
    d. what happens to total output following a simultaneous and equal percentage increase in all inputs.

15. If all inputs are doubled and output more than doubles, one would say that the production relationship
    a. shows decreasing returns to scale.
    b. shows constant returns to scale.
    c. shows increasing returns to scale.
    d. violates the "law" of diminishing returns.

16. In the long run,
    a. inputs are likely to be less substitutable than in the short run.
    b. all firms will exhibit constant returns to scale.
    c. a firm is assumed to be able to make adjustments in all its fixed commitments.
    d. average cost must decline.

17. The optimal choice of input combinations
    a. is a purely technological decision, unaffected by input prices, and better left to engineers than economists.
    b. can be determined by looking at information on the marginal revenue product and price of various inputs.
    c. will always be the same in both the short and long run.
    d. is likely to include more of an input if its price rises and if other input prices are unchanged.

89

18. Assume that on a small farm with ten workers, the hiring of an eleventh worker actually lowers total output. Which of the following statements is not necessarily true?
    a. The marginal physical product of the last worker is negative.
    b. The marginal revenue product of the last worker is negative.
    c. A profit-maximizing firm would never hire the eleventh worker.
    d. The operations of the farm show decreasing returns to scale.

19. Marginal revenue product (MRP) is equal to
    a. MPP/P_{OUTPUT}
    b. $MPP \times P_{OUTPUT}$
    c. P_{OUTPUT}/MPP.
    d. $MPP \times P_{INPUT}$

20. The ratio of a productive input's marginal physical product (MPP) to its price is a measure of the
    a. marginal cost of expanding output.
    b. average cost of expanding output.
    c. efficiency of production.
    d. increase in output from spending an extra dollar on this input.

TEST B

Circle T or F for true or false.

T   F   1. The "law" of diminishing returns says that economies of scale can never be increasing.

T   F   2. The marginal physical product of an input refers to the increase in output associated with an additional unit of that input when all other inputs are held constant.

T   F   3. The marginal revenue product measures the total revenue that a firm will have at different use levels of a particular input.

T   F   4. If a firm's operations show increasing returns to scale from the additional use of all inputs, it violates the "law" of diminishing returns.

T   F   5. If a firm's operations show decreasing returns to scale, it is likely that long-run average costs will be increasing.

T   F   6. The short run is defined as any time less than six months.

T   F   7. The curve of average fixed cost is usually U-shaped.

T   F   8. Long-run cost curves will always lie above short-run cost curves.

T   F   9. Inputs are likely to be more substitutable in the long run than in the short run.

T   F   10. Historical data on costs and output is a good guide to the relevant cost curves for a firm's current decisions.

| APPENDIX | *Production Indifference Curves*

Learning Objectives

After completing this appendix, you should be able to:

- describe how diminishing returns to a single factor help determine the shape of a typical production indifference curve.

- determine what input combination will minimize costs for a given level of output, given information about production indifference curves and input prices.

- explain how a firm's expansion path helps determine (minimum) total cost for every possible output level.

- use a production indifference curve to explain how a change in the price of one productive factor can affect the least cost combination of inputs.

Important Terms and Concepts

Production indifference curve

Budget line

Expansion path

APPENDIX REVIEW

A set of production indifference curves (or isoquants) is a geometrical device that can be used to represent a production function involving two inputs and one output. The horizontal and vertical axes are used to measure quantities of each input. A line connecting all input combinations capable of producing the same amount of output is called the _____ _____ curve. Each separate curve represents a   (1) particular output level. Higher curves will mean (more/less) output.

Production indifference curves will have a (negative/positive) slope as a reduction in the use of one in-   (2) put must be compensated for by an increase in the use of the other input. Production indifference curves (will/will not) bow in toward the origin. This last property follows from the "law" of _____ _____ returns. Production indifference curves (do/do not) cross.

Production indifference curves tell a firm what alternative combinations of inputs it could use to produce the same amount of output. An optimizing firm should not be indifferent to these alternatives. To determine the least costly combination of inputs, the firm will need to know the price of each input. From this information, the firm can construct a budget line showing combinations of inputs that can be purchased for the same total cost. The budget line is a (curved/straight) line. The slope of the budget line is given by the ratio of input prices.   (3) The price of the input measured on the horizontal axis goes on the top of the ratio. The intercept on each axis comes from dividing the total budget by the price of input measured on that axis.

To minimize cost for a given level of output, the firm chooses that combination of inputs lying on the

(4) (highest/lowest) budget line consistent with the given level of output. For smooth and convex production indifference curves, the least costly input combination is given by the point of tangency between the budget line and the relevant production indifference curve. A change in the price of either input will change the slope of the budget line and result in a new optimal input combination. It is now easy to see that an increase in the price of one input will typically lead firms to use (less/more) of that input and _____ of the input whose price has not changed.

The procedure described in the previous paragraph will determine the optimal input combination to minimize cost for a given output target. Using the same procedure to find the lowest cost input combination for dif-

(5) ferent levels of output defines the firm's _____ path. It also allows us to compute total cost for any level of output. At this point, division and subtraction will allow us to compute average and marginal cost. What level of output maximizes profits is considered in the next chapter.

Is the solution to the question of optimal input combinations in this appendix consistent with the earlier discussion that determined optimal inputs by comparing input prices and marginal revenue products? Yes. Although it may not be immediately obvious, the slope of the production indifference curve equals the ratio of marginal physical products. When we choose the optimal input combination from the point of tangency where the slope of the production indifference curve equals the slope of the budget line, we set the ratio of marginal products equal to the ratio of input prices. In symbols, assuming that our two inputs are A and B, choosing the point of tangency between the production indifference curve and the budget line means that

$$MPP_A/MPP_B = P_A/P_B.$$

Some multiplication and division[2] allows us to rewrite this expression as

$$MPP_A/P_A = MPP_B/P_B,$$

which we have seen is equivalent to our earlier condition for the optimal use of inputs.

IMPORTANT TERMS AND CONCEPTS QUIZ

Choose the best definition for each of the following terms.

1. _____ Production indifference curve
2. _____ Budget line
3. _____ Expansion path

a. Locus of firm's cost-minimizing input levels for different output levels
b. Graph showing how total output varies as one input is increased
c. Graph depicting all combinations of input quantities that yield a given level of output
d. Representation of equally costly input combinations

[2]Multiply both sides of the expression by MPP_B and divide each side by P_A.

BASIC EXERCISES

Figure 7-3 shows a production indifference curve for producing 6,000 tons of cornbeans. This curve is derived from data given in Table 7-1.

1. (Read all of this question before answering.) If land can be rented at $65 an acre a year and if labor costs are $8,000 a worker per year, what is the least cost combination for producing 6,000 tons of cornbeans? Restrict your answer to the dots in Figure 7-3 that correspond to data in Table 7-1.

   _____ acres and _____ workers

   If land rents for $125 a year and labor costs $8,000 a worker, what is the least cost input combination for producing 6,000 tons of cornbeans?

   _____ acres and _____ workers

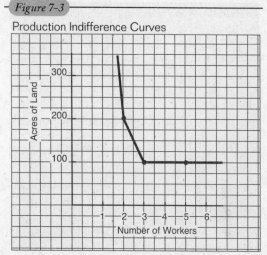

Figure 7-3

Production Indifference Curves

Remember that the ratio of input prices determines the slope of the budget line. For a given set of input prices draw the budget lines that pass through each of the possible input combinations. Remember that for a given set of input prices, these lines should be parallel and the least cost combination is given by the lowest budget line. Can you explain why?

2. From your answer to the previous question, you know that if the cost of using land is relatively low, the least cost input combination will use more land with a smaller number of workers. You also know that if the cost of using land rises enough, an optimizing farmer would be induced to use less land and more workers. What is the rental price of land that just tips the balance away from the input combination of 200 acres and two workers to the combination of 100 acres and three workers?

   $ _____ .

The answer to this question comes from "rotating" a budget line around the outside of the production indifference curve. For given input prices, find the lowest budget line that just touches the production indifference curve. This point will show the lowest cost input combination. As one input price changes, the slope of the budget line will change and the lowest cost budget line rotates around the outside of the production indifference curve. If the price of land is low, the input combination of 200 acres and two workers will be on the lowest budget line. As the price of land rises, the slope of the budget line becomes flatter, and there will come a point where suddenly the input combination of 100 acres and three workers is on the lowest budget line.

SELF-TESTS FOR UNDERSTANDING

TEST A

Circle the most appropriate answer.

1. A production indifference curve shows
   a. different levels of output that can be produced with a given amount of inputs.
   b. levels of output about which producers should be indifferent.
   c. what changes in one input are necessary to keep the marginal physical product of a second input constant.
   d. what input combinations can be used to produce a given level of output.

2. Which of the following properties is not true of production indifference curves?
   a. They have a negative slope.
   b. Their slope is always equal to the ratio of input prices.
   c. They bow in toward the origin because of the "law" of diminishing returns.
   d. The amount of output is the same for all points on the production indifference curve.

3. A single budget line shows
   a. how total cost varies when the level of output changes.
   b. how production costs vary when the price of inputs changes.
   c. what different combinations of inputs can be purchased with a fixed budget.
   d. how production costs have changed over time.

4. The budget line
   a. has a positive slope.
   b. will shift in a parallel fashion in response to an increase in the price of one input.
   c. is a straight line with a negative slope reflecting relative input prices.
   d. will have a different slope following an equal percentage change in the price of all inputs.

5. The optimal input combination for a given level of output is determined by
   a. the Y-axis intercept of the budget line.
   b. the point where marginal utility is equal to price.
   c. the point of tangency between the lowest budget line and the relevant production indifference curve.
   d. where the relevant production indifference curve intersects the budget line.

6. Using budget lines to determine the optimal input combination for every possible level of output traces out
   a. the total physical product curve.
   b. a firm's expansion path.
   c. marginal revenue product.
   d. a firm's average cost curve.

7. When the price of one input increases, the
   a. budget line will shift out in parallel fashion.
   b. budget line will shift in toward the origin in parallel fashion.
   c. slope of the budget line will change.
   d. production indifference curves will shift.

8. If production requires two inputs, labor and capital, and the price of both doubles,
   a. the slope of the budget line will double.
   b. production indifference curves will become steeper.
   c. the marginal physical product of the more expensive input will decline.
   d. the slope of the budget line and the least costly input combination do not change.

9. Which one of the following will not occur after a reduction in the price of one input?
   a. The budget line will shift in such a way that a fixed production budget can now buy more of the cheaper input.
   b. The optimal input combination for a given level of output is likely to involve the use of more of the cheaper input.
   c. The minimum total cost for producing a given level of output will fall.
   d. Each production indifference curve will show a parallel shift.

TEST B

Circle T or F for true or false.

T F 1. Production indifference curves have a positive slope because higher output usually requires more of both inputs.

T F 2. Typically, a production indifference curve will bow in at the middle because of the "law" of diminishing returns.

T F 3. A firm minimizes cost for any level of output by choosing the input combination given by the tangency of the budget line to the production indifference curve.

T F 4. An increase in the price of either input will make the budget line steeper.

T F 5. If production requires the use of two inputs, x_1 and x_2, a change in the price of x_1 will never affect the optimal use of x_2.

T F 6. A change in the price of output will change the cost-minimizing input combination for a given level of output.

T F 7. For given input prices, the tangencies of production indifference curves with alternative budget lines trace out a firm's expansion path.

SUPPLEMENTARY EXERCISES

Assume that the production of widgets (W) requires labor (L) and machines (M) and can be represented by the following expression[3]

$$W = L^{1/2} M^{1/2}.$$

1. Measuring machines on the vertical axis and labor on the horizontal axis, draw a production indifference curve for the production of 500,000 widgets.

---

[3]This particular mathematical representation of a production function is called the Cobb-Douglas production function. Charles Cobb was a mathematician. Paul Douglas was an economist at The University of Chicago, president of the American Economic Association, and United States senator from Illinois from 1948 to 1966. You might enjoy reading the comments by Albert Rees and Paul Samuelson about Douglas and his work in the *Journal of Political Economy*, October 1979, Part 1.

2. *L* measures labor hours and *M* measures machine hours. In the long run, both machine and labor hours are variable. If machine hours cost $48 and labor hours cost $12, what is the cost-minimizing number of labor and machine hours to produce 500,000 widgets? (Whether it is profitable to produce 500,000 widgets depends on the price of widgets.)

3. Assume that the firm has 125 machines capable of supplying 250,000 machine hours and that labor hours are the only variable input.
   a. Draw a picture of total output as a function of the number of labor hours.
   b. Use the production function to derive an expression for the marginal physical product of labor conditional on the 250,000 machine hours. Draw a picture of this function. What, if any, is the connection between your pictures of total output and marginal physical product?
   c. Divide your picture of the marginal physical product into regions of increasing, decreasing, and negative marginal returns to labor. (Note: Not all areas need exist.)
   d. If the price of widgets is $50 and the price of labor is $12 per hour, what is the optimal number of labor hours that the firm should use? How many widgets will the firm produce?

4. Graph the expansion path for this production function on the assumption that labor hours cost $12 and machine hours cost $48.

5. Are returns to scale in the production of widgets constant, increasing, or decreasing?

STUDY QUESTIONS

1. What is the difference between diminishing marginal returns and negative marginal returns?

2. Why does the discussion of optimal input use focus on marginal revenue product and not average revenue product?

3. What is the relation between marginal physical product and marginal revenue product?

4. Why is it optimal for a firm to use more of an input as long as marginal revenue product is greater than the price of the input?

5. What is the difference between fixed and variable cost?

6. Why do economists typically use a U-shaped curve to represent an average cost curve?

7. What is the difference between the short run and the long run?

8. If a firm's production function shows increasing returns to scale, what will its long-run average cost curve look like and why?

9. Why isn't a firm's long-run average cost curve found by connecting the minimum points of its short-run average cost curves?

10. Consider a production function that involves the input of two factors. For each factor individually, increases in inputs lead to diminishing returns. However, when both inputs are increased simultaneously, there are increasing returns to scale. Can this be possible? Explain how.

11. If output can be produced with varying quantities of different inputs, how can a firm figure out the cost-minimizing input combination?

12. Is data on how average cost has evolved over time appropriate to analyze the cost implications of different output levels today? Why or why not?

Output, Price, and Profit: The Importance of Marginal Analysis

8

Important Terms and Concepts

Optimal decision	Total revenue (TR)	Marginal profit
Total profit	Average revenue (AR)	
Economic profit	Marginal revenue (MR)	

Learning Objectives

After completing this chapter, you should be able to:

- explain why a firm can make a decision about output or price, but not usually about both.

- explain how and why an economist's definition of profit differs from that of an accountant.

- explain why the demand curve is the curve of average revenue.

- calculate total and marginal revenue from data on the demand curve.

- calculate average and marginal cost from data on total cost.

- use data on costs and revenues to compute the level of output that maximizes profits.

- explain why the point of maximum profit should be associated with a point of zero marginal profit.

- explain why comparing marginal revenue and marginal cost is equivalent to looking at marginal profit.

- explain why profit is maximized only when marginal revenue is (approximately) equal to marginal cost.

- explain how selling at a price below average cost can increase profits if price is above marginal cost.

CHAPTER REVIEW

This is the last of four building block chapters that explore what lies behind the demand and supply curves introduced in Chapter 4. As with Chapters 5 and 7, this chapter makes extensive use of marginal analysis, one of the most important tools an economist has. In this chapter, marginal analysis is used to help decide how much output a firm should produce to maximize its profits.

While marginal analysis is a powerful tool for business decision making, it is applicable in many nonbusiness situations as well. For example, how much should the government spend to clean up the environment? Or a related question: To clean up our lakes and rivers, should the government require all industries and towns to reduce their discharges by an equal percentage, or is there a more efficient alternative? As discussed in Chapter 17, marginal analysis can help answer these questions.

You may already have had more experience with marginal analysis than you realize. Have you ever had to pay federal income taxes? If so, you might dig out your records and make two calculations. Your total taxes divided
(1) by your total income would be your (average/marginal) tax rate. Now assume that you had $100 more income. Figure out how much more taxes you would have owed. This increase in taxes divided by the $100 additional income would be your (average/marginal) tax rate.

Your grade point average is another example of the distinction between marginal and average. If you want to raise your overall GPA, what sorts of grades do you need? The grades you earn this semester are the marginal contribution to your overall grade average. Similarly, a baseball player's batting record for a single game is a marginal measure when compared with his season's batting average.[1]

In whatever context, marginal analysis focuses on the effect of changes. For business output decisions, marginal analysis looks at the effect on costs, revenues, and profits as output changes. The change in total
(2) cost from changing output by one unit is called _____ cost. The change in total revenue from producing and selling one more unit is _____ revenue. Marginal profit is the change in total _____ as output expands by one unit. Because profits equal revenue minus costs, marginal profit equals marginal _____ minus marginal _____.

(3)   Economists usually assume that business firms are interested in maximizing (average/marginal/total) profit. This assumption need not be true for all firms, but economists have found that models based on this assumption provide useful insights into actual events. (Remember the discussion in Chapter 1 about the role of abstraction in theory.) Economists are interested in marginal profit, not as an end in itself, but because marginal profit is an extremely useful guide to maximizing total profit.

---

[1]One could take the position that each time at bat, rather than a whole game, is the real marginal measure. On this view, the marginal measure is either 1.000 (a hit) or 0.000 (no hit). Consistent with Rule 4 in the Appendix to this chapter, every hit increases a player's overall batting average and every at-bat without a hit lowers one's overall batting average.

It should be common sense that any firm interested in maximizing profit will want to expand output as long as the increase in total revenue exceeds the increase in total costs. If the increase in revenue is less than the increase in cost, the firm has gone too far. Rather than looking at total revenue and total cost, we could just as easily look at the changes in revenue and cost as output changes. An increase in output will add to profits if the increase in revenue is greater than the increase in costs. An economist might make the same point by saying that an increase in output will add to profits if (<u>marginal/average</u>) revenue exceeds (<u>marginal/average</u>) cost. We (1) could also say that an increase in output will add to total profits as long as marginal profits are (<u>positive/zero/negative</u>). Total profits will stop rising when marginal profits fall to _____; that is, when marginal revenue _____ marginal cost.

IMPORTANT TERMS AND CONCEPTS QUIZ

Choose the best definition for each of the following terms.

1. _____ Optimal decision

2. _____ Total profit

3. _____ Economic profit

4. _____ Total revenue

5. _____ Average revenue

6. _____ Marginal revenue

7. _____ Marginal profit

a. Net earnings minus a firm's opportunity cost of capital

b. Total revenue divided by quantity of output

c. Addition to profit from producing an additional unit of output

d. Amount firm must spend to produce a given quantity of output

e. Difference between total revenue and total costs

f. Best outcome for the decision maker

g. Price of output times quantity sold

h. Addition to total revenue when producing one more unit of output

BASIC EXERCISES

1. **Wanda's Widget Company**
   This exercise is designed to review the use of marginal revenue and marginal cost as a guide to maximizing profits.
   a. **Table 8-1** has data on demand for widgets from Wanda's Widget Company as well as data on production costs. Total revenue and total cost are plotted in the top panel of Figure 8-1. Fill in the column on total profits by subtracting total cost from total revenue. Plot the data on total profit in the second panel of **Figure 8-1.** Looking just at your graph of total profit, what output level maximizes total profits?

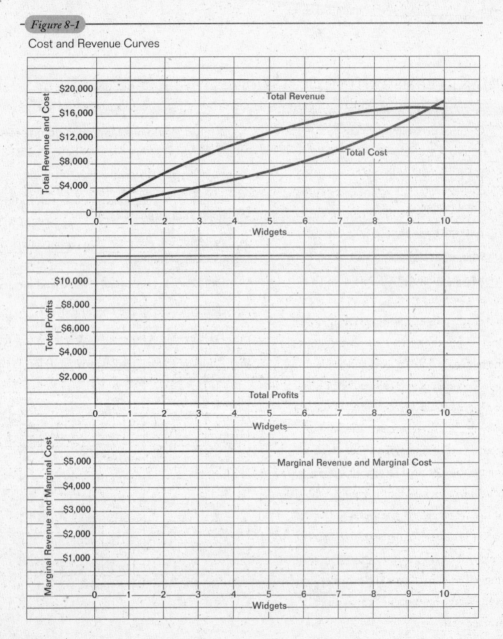

Figure 8-1

Cost and Revenue Curves

Table 8-1

Wanda's Widget Company

| Marginal Revenue | Total Revenue | Demand Curve | | Total Cost (dollars) | Marginal Cost | Total Profits |
		Price (dollars)	Output			
_____	3,500	3,500	1	2,000	_____	_____
_____	6,600	3,300	2	3,000	_____	_____
_____	9,300	3,100	3	4,100	_____	_____
_____	11,600	2,900	4	5,300	_____	_____
_____	13,500	2,700	5	6,900	_____	_____
_____	15,000	2,500	6	8,900	_____	_____
_____	16,100	2,300	7	11,100	_____	_____
_____	16,800	2,100	8	13,400	_____	_____
_____	17,100	1,900	9	15,800	_____	_____
_____	17,000	1,700	10	18,300	_____	_____

b. Complete Table 8-1 by computing marginal cost and marginal revenue. Plot each series in the bottom panel of Figure 8-1. Marginal revenue exceeds marginal cost up to what level of output? _____ Looking just at your graph of marginal cost and marginal revenue, what output level maximizes total profits? Is this the same answer as above?

c. **Figure 8-2** plots the average cost of producing widgets. Use the data on the demand curve from Table 8-1 to plot the curve of average revenue in Figure 8-2. Using the profit-maximizing level of output determined above, find the profit-maximizing price on the demand curve: Draw the rectangle for total revenue and shade it lightly with positively sloped lines. Using the average cost curve, draw the rectangle for total cost and shade it lightly with negatively sloped lines. This rectangle should overlap a part of the rectangle for total revenue. The nonoverlapped part of the total revenue rectangle is a measure of total (cost/profit/revenue). Maximizing total profit maximizes the size of this rectangle. It (does/does not) maximize the difference between average revenue and average cost. It (does/does not) imply that output should increase whenever average revenue, i.e., price, exceeds average cost.

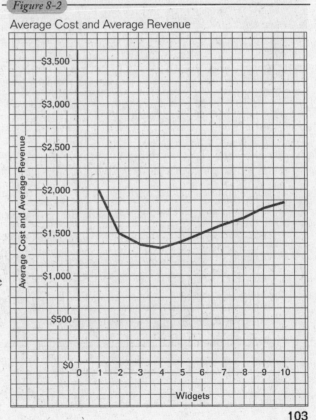

Figure 8-2

Average Cost and Average Revenue

103

d. (Optional) Assume now that there is an increase in the fixed costs Wanda must pay. Specifically assume that all of the entries in the column for total cost in Table 8-1 are now $3,000 higher. Write out a new version of Table 8-1 to determine the profit-maximizing level of output following the increase in fixed costs. What happens to total profits? Consider Figures 8-1 and 8-2. Explain which curves shift and why.

2. **The Geometry of Marginal Revenue**

   a. **Figure 8-3** shows the demand curve for Medalist bicycles. Draw a rectangle for total revenue on the assumption that 55,000 bicycles are sold. Lightly shade this rectangle with horizontal lines.
   Assume now that 70,000 bicycles are sold rather than 55,000. Draw a rectangle for total revenue at this higher level of sales. Lightly shade this rectangle with vertical lines.

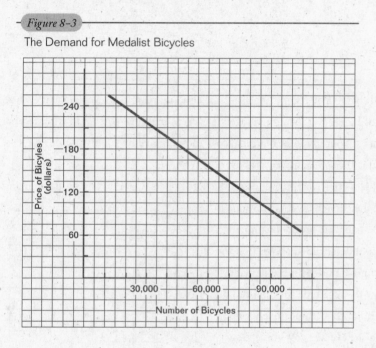

Figure 8-3

The Demand for Medalist Bicycles

If you have drawn and shaded the rectangles correctly, you should have a large, cross-hatched rectangle and two smaller rectangles: a horizontal rectangle on the top of the cross-hatched rectangle and a vertical rectangle on the right side. The vertical rectangle represents revenue from additional sales at the new lower price. This rectangle (is/is not) a complete measure of marginal revenue. It measures the receipts of additional sales but neglects the drop in revenue from the reduction in price that was necessary to expand sales in the first place. The reduction in revenue on previous units is represented by the _____ rectangle. The geometric representation of marginal revenue is the (vertical/horizontal) rectangle minus the _____ rectangle.

   b. What is the marginal revenue associated with increasing output from 55,000 to 70,000 bicycles?

SELF-TESTS FOR UNDERSTANDING

TEST A

Circle the most appropriate answer.

1. The logic of the demand curve says that business firms can choose
   a. both the level of output and the level of prices.
   b. the level of output or the level of prices but not both.
   c. to sell whatever quantity they want at whatever price.
   d. only those levels of output where marginal cost equals marginal revenue.

2. The assumption of profit maximization is
   a. likely to be true for all firms.
   b. the same as the assumption of satisficing.
   c. a useful abstraction that gives sharp insights.
   d. the best description of what firms actually do.

3. Total profit is equal to
   a. average revenue minus average cost.
   b. marginal revenue minus marginal cost.
   c. total revenue minus total cost.
   d. zero when marginal cost equals marginal revenue.

4. Marginal profit is
   a. the difference between total revenue and total cost.
   b. only positive at the profit-maximizing output level.
   c. another term for the return on an owner's own time and resources.
   d. the change in profit when output increases by one unit.

5. Marginal cost equals
   a. total cost divided by total output.
   b. the change in total cost associated with an additional unit of output.
   c. the change in average cost.
   d. the slope of the average cost curve.

6. Average cost is found by
   a. dividing total cost by output.
   b. multiplying marginal cost by output.
   c. looking at how total cost changes when output changes.
   d. considering how price changes with quantity along the demand curve.

7. If total costs are increasing then
   a. marginal cost must also be increasing.
   b. marginal cost must be positive.
   c. average cost must be greater than marginal costs.
   d. average cost must be increasing.

105

8. The demand curve is the curve of
   a. total revenue.
   b. marginal revenue.
   c. variable revenue.
   d. average revenue.

9. Marginal revenue to a firm is
   a. the same as the demand curve for the firm's output.
   b. found by dividing price by output.
   c. found by dividing output by price.
   d. the change in revenue associated with an additional unit of output.

10. When output increases by one unit, marginal revenue will typically be
    a. less than the new lower price.
    b. equal to the new lower price.
    c. greater than the new lower price.

11. Marginal profit equals the difference between
    a. total revenue and total cost.
    b. average revenue and average cost.
    c. marginal revenue and marginal cost.
    d. the demand curve and the marginal cost curve.

12. As long as total revenue is greater than total cost,
    a. marginal profit must be positive.
    b. total profit must be increasing.
    c. total profit will be positive.
    d. marginal revenue will be greater than marginal cost.

13. If marginal revenue is greater than marginal cost, then a firm interested in maximizing profits should probably
    a. reduce output.
    b. expand output.
    c. leave output unchanged.

14. To maximize profits, a firm should produce where
    a. marginal cost is minimized.
    b. average cost is minimized.
    c. marginal revenue equals marginal cost.
    d. marginal revenue is maximized.

15. If a firm has chosen an output level that maximizes profits, then at this level
    a. marginal profits are also maximized.
    b. average cost is minimized.
    c. further increases in output will involve negative marginal profits.
    d. the difference between average revenue and average cost is maximized.

16. Once a firm has determined the output level that maximizes profits, it can determine the profit-maximizing price from
    a. the demand curve.
    b. setting its usual markup on average cost.
    c. adding marginal cost to marginal revenue.
    d. adding marginal cost to average cost.

17. Producing where marginal revenue equals marginal cost is the same as producing where
    a. average cost is minimized.
    b. total profit is maximized.
    c. average cost equals average revenue.
    d. marginal profit is maximized.

18. An economist's definition of profit differs from that of an accountant because
    a. the economist is only interested in marginal cost and marginal revenue.
    b. the economist includes the opportunity cost of owner-supplied inputs in total cost.
    c. accountants cannot maximize.
    d. economists cannot add or subtract correctly.

19. If accounting profits are zero, it is likely that economic profits are
    a. negative.
    b. also zero.
    c. positive.

20. If marginal revenue is less than average cost, a firm
    a. should reduce output; it loses the additional revenue but saves more in cost.
    b. must be losing money.
    c. should consider a temporary shutdown.
    d. can still increase profits if marginal revenue exceeds marginal cost.

TEST B

Circle T or F for true or false.

T F 1. Business firms can decide both the price and quantity of their output.

T F 2. Firms always make optimal decisions.

T F 3. The demand curve for a firm's product is also the firm's marginal revenue curve.

T F 4. Marginal revenue is simply the price of the last unit sold.

T F 5. An output decision will generally not maximize profits unless it corresponds to a zero marginal profit.

T F 6. Marginal profit will be zero when marginal revenue equals marginal cost.

T F 7. An economist's measure of profit would typically be smaller than an accountant's.

T F 8. A reduction in fixed costs should lead a firm to increase output.

T F 9. As long as average revenue exceeds average cost, a firm is making profits and should increase output.

T F 10. It never pays to sell below average cost.

| APPENDIX | *The Relationships Among Total, Average, and Marginal Data*

BASIC EXERCISES

These questions are designed to help review the relationships between total, average, and marginal measures described in the appendix to Chapter 8.

1. **Table 8-2** contains information on Heather's first ten games with the college softball team. The table includes her batting performance for each game, a marginal measure, as well as her season average updated to include the results of each game. Answer the following questions to see if the marginal and average data from Heather's batting record are consistent with the rules in the Appendix to Chapter 8. It may be useful to first plot both the marginal and average data in **Figure 8-4**.

   a. According to Rule 3, the marginal and average records should be equal on the first day of the season. Is this the case?

   b. According to Rule 4, if the marginal data are equal to the average, the average should be unchanged. Check to see if this is always the case.

Table 8-2

Heather's Batting

Game	At-bats	Hits	Daily Batting Average	Season Batting Average
1	4	2	.500	.500
2	4	2	.500	.500
3	4	1	.250	.417
4	3	1	.333	.400
5	4	3	.750	.474
6	3	1	.333	.455
7	6	2	.333	.429
8	3	0	.000	.387
9	4	2	.500	.400
10	5	2	.400	.400

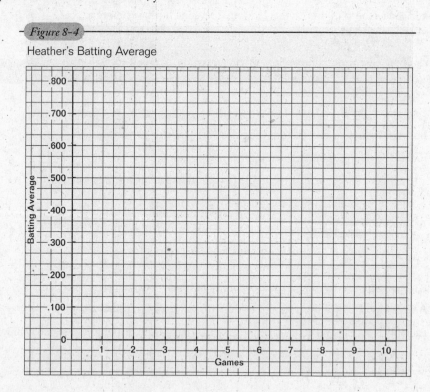

Figure 8-4

Heather's Batting Average

Figure 8-5

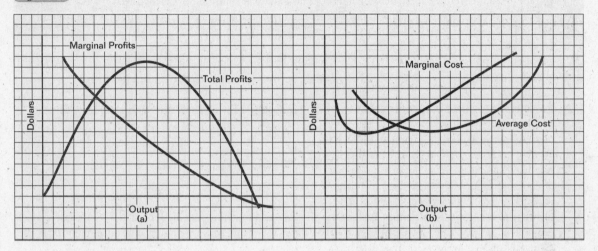

c. According to Rule 4, if the marginal data are less than the average, the average should decline. Check to see if this is always the case.
d. According to Rule 4, if the marginal data are greater than the average, the average should increase. Check to see if this is always the case.

2. Explain what is wrong with both of the illustrations in **Figure 8-5.**
   a. For part (a) of Figure 8-5, assume that the total profit curve is correct and draw an appropriate marginal profit curve.
   b. For part (b) of Figure 8-5, assume that the average cost curve is correct and draw an appropriate marginal cost curve.

SUPPLEMENTARY EXERCISES

MATHEMATICAL EXAMPLES OF PROFIT MAXIMIZATION

1. The demand for Acme stereos is

$$Q = 1,200 - 4P$$

where Q represents output measured in thousands of sets and P represents price. The total cost of producing stereos is given by

$$TC = 16,000 + 120Q - .4Q^2 + .002Q^3.$$

   a. What are Acme's fixed costs?
   b. What mathematical expression describes average costs? Marginal costs?
   c. Plot average cost and marginal cost. Does your marginal cost curve go through the minimum point of your average cost curve?
   d. Use the information from the demand curve to derive a mathematical expression for marginal revenue.
   e. On the same graph as in c draw the demand curve (the average revenue curve) and the marginal revenue curve.

109

f. What does your graph suggest about the profit-maximizing level of output?

g. Does your answer in f coincide with a direct mathematical solution for Q when MR = MC? It should. (To answer this question, you will need to set the expressions you derived for marginal revenue and marginal cost equal and solve the resulting equation for Q.)

h. What is Acme's maximum profit?

i. Shade in the portion of your graph that represents maximum profit.

j. What if fixed cost were $20,000? How, if at all, do your answers to b, c, d, g, and h change?

2. Consider the mathematical representation of the production of widgets in the Supplementary Exercise to Chapter 7.

Assume the demand for widgets is given by

$$W = 2,500,000 - 25,000 P_W$$

where P_W = price of widgets.

a. If a firm can purchase labor services at $12 per hour and machines can be rented at $48 per hour, what is the marginal cost of increases in output? What is the profit-maximizing level of output? What is the market price of widgets?

b. Assume now that the firm owns 100 machines that supply 200,000 machine hours and that the firm can purchase labor at a cost of $12 per hour. Derive an expression for marginal cost and determine the profit-maximizing level of output on the assumption that the number of machines is fixed at 100. What is the market price of widgets?

3. **Profit Maximization and the Elasticity of Demand**

A profit-maximizing firm will not try to produce so much output that it is operating in the inelastic portion of its demand curve. Why not? What about the firm producing stereos and widgets in problems 1 and 2 above? What is the elasticity of demand at the profit-maximizing point of output?

ECONOMICS IN ACTION

FAIR TRADE, FREE TRADE, AND MARGINAL COST

American trade laws, like those of many other countries, include antidumping provisions. Foreign producers are not supposed to have access to American markets if they sell their output at unfairly low prices. The concern is that a foreign producer might drive American competitors out of business and then be in a position to act as a monopolist, raising prices and restricting output. Such actions are sometimes called ruinous competition.

Complaints about dumping by foreign firms are typically initiated by American producers, not consumers, and investigated by an office of the U.S. government. If a complaint is found to have cause, the government can impose antidumping tariffs on specific foreign manufacturers that are intended to establish prices that reflect "fair value," that is, raise prices to a level sufficient to cover fully allocated costs plus a normal profit. Recent examples involve imports of computer chips and steel.

Fully allocated cost is another term for the average cost of purchased inputs, including labor. Normal profit refers to the opportunity cost of the investment by a firm's owners. (As we have seen, economists include both measures when they talk of average cost.)

1. Are there conditions under which domestic producers would willingly sell output for less than "fair value," that is, less than average cost? (For example, from an initial position of equilibrium, how might a domestic producer respond to a temporary shift of the demand curve to the left during a recession?)

2. How does one distinguish possible ruinous competition from normal market fluctuations and the natural tendency of all producers to exploit opportunities to limit competition? Should foreign producers be prohibited from behavior that domestic producers are likely to engage in on a regular basis?

SOURCE: "Cement Shoes for Venezuela," Peter Passell, *New York Times,* September 25, 1991. "Thriving Steel Industry Needs No Import Curb, Experts Say; Trade: House vote illustrates lure of protectionism. Production last year was second highest in history"; Donald W. Nauss, *Los Angeles Times,* March 22, 1999.

STUDY QUESTIONS

1. Why can't firms sell as much output as they want at whatever price they want?

2. How can it be that expanding output when average revenue is greater than average cost is not guaranteed to increase profits?

3. The condition for profit maximization is stated in terms of marginal revenue and marginal cost. What would happen to total profits if instead a firm produced where average revenue equaled average cost?

4. Why isn't marginal revenue equal to the price of the last unit sold?

5. Why is the demand curve also the curve of average revenue?

6. Why is it better to produce where marginal profit is zero rather than at some point where marginal profit is greater than zero?

7. What are the differences between profits as measured by an economist and profits as measured by an accountant? Which is likely to be larger? Why?

8. Should a firm raise or lower its price following a decrease in fixed costs? Why?

9. How can it be rational for a firm to continue producing if the price it receives is less than the (average) cost of production?

Securities, Business Finance, and the Economy: The Tail that Wags the Dog?

9

Important Terms and Concepts

Corporation	Plowback (retained earnings)	Leverage
Limited liability	Takeover	Mortgage
Common stock	Speculation	Mortgage-backed security
Bond	Random walk	Securities
Inflation	Credit Default Swap	Subprime mortgage
Interest rate	Derivative	

Learning Objectives

After completing this chapter, you should be able to:

- describe the unique characteristics of corporations.

- explain how limited liability limits the risks faced by investors in corporate stock.

- explain why bond prices fall when interest rates go up and vice versa.

- explain the similarities between stocks and bonds.

- explain how the use of stocks or bonds shifts risk between a corporation and financial investors.

- explain the advantages of plowback as a source of funds to a corporation.

- explain why the stock market is of critical importance to the financing of corporations even if new stock issues account for only a small proportion of new funds raised by corporations.

- discuss the importance of regulation of the stock market.

- discuss the advantages and disadvantages of corporate takeovers.

- discuss the role of speculation both in the economy and in the securities markets.

- understand the nature of risk inherent in the stock market.

- explain how leverage contributed to the 2007–2009 financial crisis.

CHAPTER REVIEW

This chapter explores the advantages and disadvantages of corporations as a way of organizing businesses. Special attention is given to the different ways in which corporations raise funds and to the markets on which corporate securities are traded.

A corporation is a firm with the legal status of a fictional individual, owned by a large number of stock-holders and run by an elected board of directors and officers. A major advantage of forming a corpora-tion is that stockholders, the legal owners of the business, are not liable for the firm's debts. Having (1) _____ liability makes it possible for corporations to raise very large sums of money in the pursuit of profits. Although accounting for only about 20 percent of businesses, corporate revenues total more than 70 percent of gross domestic product.

A corporation that raises funds by selling shares of ownership and offering a stake in profits is issuing (2) (stock/bonds). If a corporation issues securities that promise to pay fixed sums as interest and principal, it is issuing _____. Corporations can also borrow directly from large financial institutions, such as banks or insurance companies. The most common way of raising funds is to directly reinvest part of a corpora-tion's profits. This method of raising funds is called _____. Corporations typically prefer to use plow-back to finance corporate investments as it avoids the cost and scrutiny that accompany new issues of stocks and bonds.

Assuming a firm does not become bankrupt, a bond that is held to maturity offers the bondholder a fixed (3) stream of payments. Investing in stock promises dividend payments and stock prices that (are/are not) known at the time of purchase. The greater uncertainty of dividends and stock prices as compared to bond payments leads many investors to conclude that stocks are (more/less) risky than bonds. From the viewpoint of a firm, (bonds/stocks) are more risky, because a failure to (meet bond payments/pay dividends) can force bankruptcy.

This comparison understates the risk to individual investors of investing in bonds. If a bond must be sold before maturity and interest rates have changed, the market price of the bond will also change. If interest rates have risen, previously issued bonds with low coupon payments will look less attractive unless their price (4) (rises/falls). Holders of these bonds will suffer a (gain/loss). Conversely, if interest rates have fallen, competition for existing bonds with high coupon payments will (increase/decrease) the price of previously issued bonds.

Stocks and bonds are traded in markets that sometimes have a specific location, such as the New York Stock Exchange, but they are also traded by dealers and brokers who keep track, by telephone or computer, of the lat-(5) est price changes. New stock issues (are/are not) usually sold through established exchanges. Two important functions served by established exchanges include reducing the _____ of stock ownership by providing a secondary market in existing shares and determining the current price of a company's stock. In the latter role, established exchanges help allocate the economy's resources to those firms that, in the market's judgment, are expected to make the most profitable use of those resources.

Speculators are not much different from most investors who hope to profit from increases in stock prices. From a general perspective, speculation serves two important functions. First, it can help decrease price fluctuations. Buying at low prices in anticipation of being able to sell next year at high prices will, in fact, make prices today (<u>higher/lower</u>) than they otherwise would be and will also make prices next year _____ (6) than they otherwise would be. The second function of speculation is that it can provide _____ for those who want to avoid taking risks. Commodity speculators will agree now on a price to be paid for buying crops next year, thus insuring a farmer against the adverse effects of a decrease in price. Other speculators may agree now on a price at which to sell crops next year to a milling company, thus insuring the miller against the adverse effects of an increase in price.

The behavior of individual stock prices has long fascinated investors. Much time and effort is spent trying to forecast price movements. Some investors look at things like a firm's earnings and its current stock price; others plot recent stock prices and try to discover laws of motion in their graphs. Economists have also studied the changes in individual stock prices. Much of this research supports the conclusion that changes in stock prices are essentially unpredictable; that is, they look like a(n) _____ _____. Such a (7) result could arise because of essentially random waves of buying and selling as investors try to outguess each other. It could also arise from investors' careful study and analysis of individual companies, study that is so complete that all anticipated events are fully reflected in current stock prices. From this perspective, changes in stock prices can only reflect currently unanticipated events, events that will likely look like random events.

Derivatives are a type of security that have recently become very popular. They can be used to (<u>reduce/eliminate</u>) risk. A particular type of derivative, Credit Default Swaps, played a significant role in the financial crisis of 2007-2009. CDS are bought by investors as _____ to protect their investments. (8) When the housing market crashed and homeowners began to default on their mortgages, returns on these investments that were _____ from homeowner's mortgage payments, (<u>fell/rose</u>) and the value of these mortgage-related products declined rapidly. Insurers, unprepared for such widespread default (<u>could/could not</u>) cover their CDS contracts and a(n) _____ followed.

Another contributor to the 2007–2009 financial crisis was the extensive use of leverage. Leverage refers to the use of (<u>borrowed/laundered</u>) money for the purchase of risky securities. Leverage (<u>magnifies/minimizes</u>) (9) both the possible gains and losses from an investment.

IMPORTANT TERMS AND CONCEPTS QUIZ

Choose the best definition for each of the following terms.

1. _____ Corporation
2. _____ Limited liability
3. _____ Common stock
4. _____ Bond
5. _____ Inflation
6. _____ Interest rate
7. _____ Plowback (retained earnings)
8. _____ Takeover
9. _____ Speculation
10. _____ Random walk
11. _____ Credit Defaults Swap
12. _____ Derivative
13. _____ Leverage
14. _____ Mortgage
15. _____ Mortgage-backed security
16. _____ Securities
17. _____ Subprime mortgage

a. A financial instrument that derives its value from some underlying investment(s)
b. Change in variable is completely unpredictable
c. Legal obligation of owners to repay company debts only with money already invested in the firm
d. The use of borrowed money to purchase assets
e. Purchase of risky assets in anticipation of favorable price changes
f. Stocks and bonds
g. Corporation's promise to pay a fixed sum at maturity plus annual interest
h. Portion of a corporation's profits that management returns to shareholders
i. A group of individuals not currently in control of a firm buys enough stock to gain control
j. A financial instrument that functions like an insurance policy that protects a lender
k. Firm owned by stockholders, with the legal status of a fictitious individual
l. A mortgage made to a borrower who may not be able to repay the loan
m. Piece of paper that gives holder a share of ownership in a company
n. Portion of a corporation's profits that management decides to keep and reinvest
o. Amount borrowers are contracted to pay lenders per dollar borrowed
p. A security whose returns to investors come from a pool of mortgages
q. Increase in average price of goods and services
r. A type of loan used to buy a house

BASIC EXERCISE

1. **Bond Prices and Interest Rates**

   The market price of a $1,000 bond paying interest once a year can be calculated by computing the present value of future payments:

   $$\text{Price} = \sum_{t=1}^{N} \frac{INT}{(1+i)^t} + \frac{1000}{(1+i)^N}$$

   where P = market price, i = market interest rate, N = number of years to maturity, and INT = annual interest payment.

It may be easiest to complete the following exercises if you use a spreadsheet program on a computer or a sophisticated hand calculator.

a. Show that if *INT* = $80 and *i* = .08, the market price of this bond will be $1,000 for *N* = 10.

b. Now vary *i*, holding *INT* constant at $80 and *N* constant at 25 years. Note how the price of a bond issued with a coupon payment of $80 changes as market interest rates change. You should find that price is less than $1,000 when *i* is greater than .08 and price is greater than $1,000 when *i* is less than .08.

c. Choose a particular value for *i*, say .06, and calculate the difference in price from the original $1,000 as *N* varies from one year to 25 years. Remember to keep *INT* = 80. You should find that the difference in price is greater as *N* gets larger; that is, longer term bonds show a greater change in price for a given change in interest rates. Can you explain why?

SELF-TESTS FOR UNDERSTANDING

TEST A

Circle the most appropriate answer.

1. Corporations account for _____ percent of businesses in the United States.
   a. about 10
   b. slightly more than 20
   c. just under 50
   d. more than 70

2. Which of the following actions gives you a share of ownership in a company?
   a. buying a bond
   b. buying a share of stock
   c. extending a loan
   d. selling to a speculator

3. The term *limited liability* refers to
   a. the use of limit orders when buying stocks.
   b. the priority bondholders have on corporate assets in case of liquidation or bankruptcy.
   c. the protection stockholders have against the debts and liabilities of a corporation.
   d. stock market rules that limit trading when there are large declines in stock prices.

4. Bonds are often said to be more risky to _____ while stocks are riskier for _____.
   a. investors; firms
   b. firms; investors

5. The returns to investing in stocks include which of the following? (There may be more than one correct answer.)
   a. dividends
   b. interest
   c. repayment of principal
   d. capital gain or loss when sold

117

6. Corporations can raise money in all but which one of the following ways?
   a. issue shares of stock
   b. borrow money in the form of bonds
   c. reinvestment or plowback profits
   d. pay dividends

7. Which of the following is the most important source of new funds for corporations?
   a. new stock issues
   b. corporate bonds
   c. plowback (i.e., retained earnings)
   d. bank loans

8. If held to maturity and with no risk of bankruptcy, bonds offer investors
   a. the prospect of substantial capital gains if company profits increase.
   b. unknown interest payments that will fluctuate with profits.
   c. the opportunity to sell their bond at its original price at any time.
   d. known interest payments.

9. A decrease in interest rates will tend to _____ the price of existing bonds.
   a. increase
   b. lower
   c. have no effect on

10. Jamal purchased a newly issued General Electric bond several years ago with coupon payments offering an interest rate of 10 percent. Since then, market interest rates on similar bonds have fallen to 6 percent. Which of the following is true?
    a. If Jamal sold his bonds today at their current market price, he would have to sell them for less than he paid.
    b. If held to maturity and General Electric does not default, Jamal will earn 6 percent on his original investment.
    c. Anyone purchasing such bonds today at their current market price and holding them to maturity can expect to earn 10 percent on the investment.
    d. The market value of the bonds that Jamal bought will have increased from the price he paid.

11. Five million shares of stock are outstanding in XYZ Corporation. If the price of XYZ stock rises by $1, then
    a. XYZ Corporation will have $5 million more to invest or use to pay higher dividends.
    b. existing shareholders will benefit by $1 a share.
    c. investors who hold XYZ bonds will have suffered a capital loss.
    d. XYZ Corporation will owe federal tax on the increased stock price.

12. All of the following, except which one, contributed to the financial crisis of 2007–2009?
    a. credit default swaps
    b. leverage
    c. subprime mortgages
    d. diversification

13. Which of the following is an example of leverage?
    a. Samantha buys a risky stock for $100, using $20 of her own money and $80 that she borrows.
    b. Edgar spends $100 on a risky stock rather than for groceries for his family.
    c. Raul buys 100 shares of 10 different stocks.
    d. Jean-Pierre exchanges 1,000 euros for $1,460 for his trip to the United States.

14. A derivative is:
    a. a mortgage made to a customer with questionable credit worthiness.
    b. a type of security whose value is determined by the price movements of some underlying investment(s)
    c. the annual payment made to the owners of corporate stock.
    d. the fixed payment made to the owners of corporate bonds.

15. The important economic functions of organized stock exchanges include all but which one of the following?
    a. Offering investors insurance against the risk of changes in stock prices.
    b. Reducing the risk of purchasing stock by offering investors a place to sell their shares should they need the funds for some other purpose.
    c. Helping allocate the economy's resources, since companies with high current stock prices will find it easier to raise additional funds to pursue investment opportunities.

16. If Maxine is to be a successful speculator, she must buy during a period of excess
    a. supply and sell during a period of excess supply.
    b. supply and sell during a period of excess demand.
    c. demand and sell during a period of excess demand.
    d. demand and sell during a period of excess supply.

17. Which of the following are correct? (There may be more than one correct answer.)
    a. Speculators only make prices higher than they otherwise would be.
    b. Speculators offer a form of insurance to those who want to avoid the risk of price fluctuations.
    c. Speculators tend to smooth out extreme price movements.
    d. Speculators serve no useful social function.

18. Advantages to existing stockholders from takeovers can include all but which one of the following?
    a. the elimination of incompetent management
    b. increasing the price of an undervalued company
    c. a greater chance that low earnings will grow to match their potential
    d. the time and effort of top management in responding to the takeover bid

19. To say that stock prices follow a random walk is to say that
    a. stock prices are easily predicted given information about past prices.
    b. the predictions of stock analysts are uniformly better than those of individual investors.
    c. day-to-day changes in stock prices are essentially unpredictable.
    d. over the long run, individual investors will only lose money by buying stocks.

TEST B

Circle T or F for true or false.

T F 1. Corporations, while constituting a minority of the number of business organizations, are the most important form of organization when measured by total sales revenue.

T F 2. Limited liability means that investors in corporations cannot lose more than what they invested.

T F 3. Assuming no bankruptcy, a corporate bond is a riskless investment even if the bond must be sold before maturity.

T F 4. A diversified portfolio is less risky than investment all of one's money in a single stock.

T F 5. Buying stock only when it reaches a pre-specified price is an example of limited liability.

T F 6. Whenever a share of General Motors' stock is sold on the New York Stock Exchange, General Motors gets the proceeds.

T F 7. A corporation that decides to issue stock will typically offer the shares initially through one of the regional stock exchanges.

T F 8. Established stock exchanges, such as the New York Stock Exchange, are really just a form of legalized gambling and serve no social function.

T F 9. The finding that stock prices follow a random walk implies that investing in stock is essentially a gamble.

T F 10. Profitable speculation involves buying high and selling low.

SUPPLEMENTARY EXERCISES

1. **Portfolio Diversification**

   This exercise is meant to illustrate the principle of diversification. Assume you invested $10,000 on December 31, 2006, and sold your holdings one year later on December 31, 2007. **Tables 9-1 and 9-2** contain data for a number of popular stocks in 2007. Table 9-1 shows the results of dividing your investment among each of the 10 stocks, $1,000 in each. The entries in Table 9-2 assume that your $10,000 was invested in just one company. Column (2) shows the number of shares purchased on December 31, 2006. Column (3) reports stock prices on December 31, 2007.

   a. Column (4) has spaces for the value of your stock holdings on December 31, 2007. Complete this column in both tables by multiplying stock prices on December 31, 2007, by the number of shares bought a year earlier; that is, multiply each entry in column (2) by the corresponding entry in column (3).

   b. Complete column (6) by adding the dividends you received in 2007, column (5), to the value of your stock holdings in column (4). Column (6) shows the total value of your investments, dividends plus the change in stock prices, after one year. Be sure to sum all of the entries in column (6) for Table 9-1.

   c. Each entry in column (6), Table 9-2, shows how you would have done had you invested all of the $10,000 in the stock of just one company. The sum for column (6), Table 9-1, shows the results of a 10-stock portfolio. How do your results illustrate the link between portfolio diversification and risk?

Table 9-1

Portfolio Stock Returns: 2007

Company	Number of Shares if Investing $1,000 12/31/2006	Price per Share on 12/31/2007	Value of Shares on 12/31/2007	Dividends Received During 2007	Value of Stock + Dividend
Apple	46.79	$64.40	_____	$0.00	_____
Best Buy	19.14	$59.42	_____	$8.42	_____
Cisco	41.27	$19.32	_____	$0.00	_____
ExxonMobil	24.39	$51.26	_____	$26.34	_____
FedEx	14.81	$98.49	_____	$4.15	_____
General Electric	32.28	$36.50	_____	$28.41	_____
Home Depot	28.18	$42.74	_____	$9.58	_____
Merck	21.65	$32.14	_____	$32.90	_____
Microsoft	36.54	$26.72	_____	$11.69	_____
Walmart	18.85	$52.82	_____	$9.80	_____
				Total Portfolio:	_____

Table 9-2

Individual Stock Returns: 2007

Company	Number of Shares if Investing $10,000 12/31/2006	Price per Share on 12/31/2007	Value of Shares on 12/31/2007	Dividends Received During 2007	Value of Stock + Dividend
Apple	467.95	$64.40	_____	$0.00	_____
Best Buy	191.42	$59.42	_____	$84.23	_____
Cisco	412.71	$19.32	_____	$0.00	_____
ExxonMobil	243.90	$51.26	_____	$263.41	_____
FedEx	148.15	$98.49	_____	$41.48	_____
General Electric	322.79	$36.50	_____	$284.05	_____
Home Depot	281.77	$42.74	_____	$95.80	_____
Merck	216.45	$32.14	_____	$329.00	_____
Microsoft	365.36	$26.72	_____	$116.92	_____
Walmart	188.50	$52.82	_____	$98.02	_____

ECONOMICS IN ACTION

IF YOU'RE SO SMART, WHY AREN'T YOU RICH?

Can you or your stockbroker consistently beat the market? Many economists would answer no unless you have inside information on which it is illegal to trade. Presumptions about the inability of individuals to beat the market are closely linked to notions of efficient markets and random walks. Formally the hypothesis of efficient markets implies that stock prices reflect all available information about future profitability. For example, should there be new information about increased profits from investing in stock X, the price of stock X should rise immediately as investors and stock managers seek to take advantage of this information. In this way all available information is incorporated into current stock prices.

On this view, stock prices change only as new information becomes available. New information that is easily foreseen would already be incorporated into stock prices. The conclusion is that new information must be unpredictable and changes in the price of individual stocks will tend to look random. Some stocks are riskier than others and need to offer a higher expected return to compensate for the possibility that they may turn out to be a bust. Riskier stocks with above average returns are not a violation of the efficient markets hypothesis, as the risk of such investments is part of currently available information.

Does all this mean that one cannot make money in the stock market? No, one can make money, but once you have decided how much risk you are willing to accept, do not expect that you or your stockbroker can consistently do better than other investors who are willing to accept similar risks. In any given year some investors and investment professionals will do better than others. The efficient markets hypothesis suggests that over a period of years it will be hard for anyone to consistently beat the market.

Some have likened beating the market to guessing whether a fair coin toss will come up heads or tails. Imagine you asked this question of everyone attending a Michigan-Notre Dame football game in Ann Arbor. If half the crowd said heads and half said tails, more than 50,000 people would have predicted the coin toss correctly. After 10 flips about 100 people would still have a perfect record of prediction. Do they know something we don't know? Would you want to bet on their continued ability to predict the flip of a coin?

The discussion of efficient markets has a certain surface plausibility, but how does one test whether markets are in fact efficient? Economists have defined three notions of efficiency—weak, semi-strong, and strong. Weak efficiency requires that information on past prices of stock X is of no use in forecasting future prices. Semi-strong efficiency requires that no publicly available information is helpful, while strong efficiency says that no relevant information, published or not, helps to forecast stock prices. Tests for various forms of efficiency involve elaborate computer estimation and/or simulation of trading rules based on past prices and other information. Remember that any profit from a particular trading rule has to be sufficient to offset the brokerage fees for trading as well as any other costs of implementing the rule.

As computers have become more powerful it has been possible to test for a wider range of trading rules. Situations have been identified where there appear to be small but predictable returns in excess of the market average. One of the best known of these is the so-called "January effect" where portfolios of the shares of small companies have consistently done better in January than the stock market as a whole. What explains such inefficiencies? No one is sure. If the decisions of a sufficient number of investors are determined by mood and feeling rather than hardheaded analysis, it might be possible that inefficiencies could persist with smart traders winning at the expense of others. It may also be that the identification of trading rules that beat the market will work to eliminate their profit potential as they are adopted on a wide-scale basis.

What is an individual investor to do?

Source: Mark Hulbert, "Why Small-Cap Stocks are So Hot in Cold Weather," *The New York Times*, November 18, 2001. You might want to look at the symposium of papers on the stock market and speculative bubbles in the Spring 1990 issue of *The Journal of Economic Perspectives*.

STUDY QUESTIONS

1. The text points out that although only a small percentage of business firms, corporations account for a much larger percentage of business sales and output. This difference arises because the biggest firms are corporations. Why are the biggest firms corporations?

2. Why is most business investment financed by plowback or retained earnings rather than by new stock issues or bonds?

3. What explains the inverse relationship between market interest rates and bond prices?

4. Why is it often said that bonds are riskier than stocks to a corporation but stocks are riskier than bonds for investors?

5. Do derivative securities reduce risk or are they a source of added risk?

6. What is a subprime mortgage and how did they contribute to the financial crisis of 2007–2009?

7. How can an investor use leverage and what risk does the use of leverage create?

8. What is the economic role of the stock market if new stock issues are seldom used to finance business investment?

9. Many people would like to regulate speculators on the belief that they are greedy predators who profit only on the misfortune of others. Why do economists often disagree with this assessment?

10. How can one make money investing in stocks if day-to-day changes in stock prices are unpredictable?

ECONOMICS ONLINE

1. There are now lots of ways to follow stocks, bonds, and mutual funds on the web. Many mutual funds and stock exchanges have their own homepages. Here are some popular sites that contain financial information and give access to these other sites.

    CBS MarketWatch

    http://www.marketwatch.com

    CNN Financial

    http://www.Money.cnn.com

    Bloomberg

    http://www.bloomberg.com

123

USA Today

http://www.usatoday.com/money

Yahoo

http://dir.yahoo.com/business_and_economy/finance_and_investment

2. The Securities and Exchange Commission regulates trading in stocks and bonds. See what they are up to at their homepage. You might want to investigate EDGAR, the SEC's electronic database of corporate reports.

http://www.sec.gov

The Firm and the Industry under Perfect Competition

10

Important Terms and Concepts

Perfect competition

Price taker

Variable cost

Firm's supply curve

Industry supply curve

Economic profit

Learning Objectives

After completing this chapter, you should be able to:

- describe the conditions that distinguish perfect competition from other market structures.

- explain why the study of perfect competition can be profitable even if few industries satisfy the conditions of perfect competition exactly.

- explain why under perfect competition the firm faces a horizontal demand curve while the industry faces a downward-sloping demand curve.

- explain the relation of price, average revenue, and marginal revenue as seen by individual firms under perfect competition.

- find the profit-maximizing output level for a perfectly competitive firm given information on the firm's marginal cost curve and the market price for its output.

- understand the case of short-term losses and the rules governing shut-down decisions.

- explain why a perfectly competitive firm's short-run supply curve is the portion of its marginal cost curve that is above average variable costs.

- derive a perfectly competitive industry's short-run supply curve given information on the supply curves for individual firms.

- understand how the equilibrium of a perfectly competitive industry in the long run may differ from the short-run equilibrium.

- use the concept of opportunity cost to reconcile economic and accounting profits.

- explain how freedom of entry and exit imply that in the long run firms operating under perfect competition will earn zero economic profit.

- explain why the long-run supply curve for a competitive industry is given by the industry's long-run average cost curve.

- explain how perfect competition implies the efficient production of goods and services.

CHAPTER REVIEW

This chapter uses the concepts developed in earlier chapters to study in more detail the supply decisions of firms. The discussion also adds important material about market structures. The decisions of individual firms depend not only upon their production functions and cost curves, but also upon the type of market structure the firm faces. Different market structures have important implications for demand conditions that firms face. This chapter focuses on the abstraction of the market structure of perfect competition. Later chapters will investigate other market structures—monopolistic competition, oligopoly, and pure monopoly.

Perfect competition is distinguished from other market structures by four conditions:

(1)   a.   (Few/Many) buyers and sellers.

       b.   (Differentiated/Identical) product.

       c.   (Easy/Difficult) entry and exit.

       d.   (Perfect/Imperfect) information.

Conditions a, b, and d imply that the actions of individual buyers and sellers (do/do not) affect the market price for the identical product. Condition c implies that the number of firms can easily expand or contract and leads to the condition that long-run equilibrium will be characterized by (positive/zero/negative) economic profits.

An important first step to analyzing the firm's decisions in a particular market structure is to be careful about what the market structure implies for the firm's demand curve and its marginal revenue. Let us first consider the short-run supply decision of an individual firm under perfect competition. Since the actions of this firm will not affect the market price, the firm can sell as much or as little as it wants at the prevailing market price.

(2) Alternatively, we may say that the firm faces a (horizontal/vertical) demand curve. In Chapter 8 we saw that the demand curve is also the curve of average revenue. If the demand curve is horizontal, then besides being the curve of average revenue it is also the curve of _____ revenue. (Remember the picture of marginal revenue in the Basic Exercise of Chapter 8. If the demand curve is horizontal, there is no horizontal rectangle to subtract.) As we saw in Chapter 8, the firm maximizes profits by producing where MC = MR. Under perfect competition, MR = P, thus under perfect competition the firm should produce where MC = MR = P.

We can now derive the short-run supply curve for the firm by imagining that the firm faces a variety of possible prices and considering what output the firm would supply at each price. These price–output pairs will define the firm's short-run supply curve. For many possible prices, short-run supply will be given by the inter-

(3) section of price and the (average/marginal) cost curve. If price drops below the minimum of the average total cost curve, the MC = P rule maximizes profits by minimizing _____. Even if price is less than average total cost, the firm should continue to produce as long as price exceeds average _____ cost. If the firm decides to produce nothing, it still must cover its fixed costs. As long as price exceeds average variable cost, there will be something left over to help cover these costs. Putting all of this together, we

can conclude that under perfect competition, a firm's short-run supply curve is given by the portion of the

_____ _____ curve above average _____ cost.

The industry short-run supply curve is given by the (<u>horizontal/vertical</u>) summation of individual firm's sup- (4)

ply curves. Market price, the variable so crucial to individual firms decisions, will be given by the intersection of

the market _____ and _____ curves. In the short run, the number of firms in the

industry is fixed; the short-run industry supply curve will come from the supply decisions of existing firms.

In the long run, existing firms may expand (or contract) and/or there will be more (fewer) firms if the short-

run equilibrium involves economic profits (losses). For example, if general market returns are around 8 percent

and investments in the firm show a return of 6 percent, an economist would conclude that the firm has an

economic (<u>loss/profit</u>) of _____ percent. In this case, by investing elsewhere and earning 8 percent, the firm's (5)

owners would be (<u>better/worse</u>) off. The 8 percent is the _____ cost of capital to the firm

and it is an important part of costs as counted by the economist. Thus, economists focus on economic profits as

the indicator of entry or exit rather than on accounting profits. The condition of long-run equilibrium that (<u>ac-</u>

<u>counting/economic</u>) profits be zero is consistent with _____ profits equal to general market rates

of return.

As firms expand or contract and enter or leave, the industry short-run supply curve will shift appropri-

ately, price will adjust as we move along the industry demand curve, and industry long-run equilibrium will be

achieved when there are no further incentives for the supply curve to shift from expansion/entry or contraction/

exit of new or existing firms. **Figure 10-1**(a) illustrates a firm in a perfectly competitive industry. Figure 10-1(b)

shows the industry demand and supply. The illustrated firm will be making economic (<u>profits/losses</u>). Shade (6)

in the appropriate rectangle showing economic profits or losses. There will be an incentive for some firms to

(<u>enter/leave</u>) the industry. As the number of firms in the industry changes, the supply curve in Figure 10-1(b)

Figure 10-1

Competitive Market Equilibrium

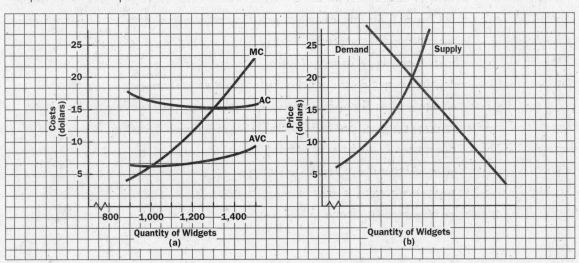

127

will shift to the (right/left) and price will (rise/fall). If the cost curves in Figure 10-1(a) are representative of long-run costs for all current and potential firms in the industry, long-run equilibrium will involve a price of $_____. Note that at all times our representative firm is producing where MC = P. But in the long-run equilibrium, MC = P = minimum _____ _____ _____ cost. It is this last condition that explains the efficiency of perfectly competitive markets.

IMPORTANT TERMS AND CONCEPTS QUIZ

Choose the best definition for each of the following terms.

1. _____ Perfect competition
2. _____ Price taker
3. _____ Variable cost
4. _____ Firms supply curve
5. _____ Industry supply curve
6. _____ Economic profit

a. The portion of the marginal cost curve that exceeds average variable cost
b. Return to an owner's investment in her firm in excess of the return on alternative investments
c. Single buyer in a market
d. Many small firms selling an identical product
e. Costs that depend upon the quantity of output
f. Agent or firm too small to affect the market price
g. Industry's long-run average cost curve

BASIC EXERCISE

*This exercise is designed to explore the short-run supply curve for a firm under perfect competition. Assume that widgets are produced by perfectly competitive firms. The data in **Table 10-1** are consistent with Figure 10-1 and are for a representative widget firm. Although not listed separately in Table 10-1, producing widgets involves fixed costs of $10,140.*

1. If the price of widgets is $19.10, what is the profit-maximizing level of output? _____

   What are economic profits at this level of output? $ _____ Check that this level of output maximizes profits by calculating profits for output levels 100 units higher and lower.

   Economic profits at higher output = $ _____

   Economic profits at lower output = $ _____

2. What is the profit-maximizing level of output if the price of widgets falls

Table 10-1

Costs of Producing Widgets

Quantity	Average Cost (dollars)	Average Variable Cost (dollars)	Marginal Cost (dollars)
900	17.67	6.40	4.60
1,000	16.44	6.30	6.30
1,100	15.62	6.40	8.60
1,200	15.15	6.70	11.50
1,300	15.00	7.20	15.00
1,400	15.14	7.90	19.10
1,500	15.56	8.80	23.80

to $11.50, below all values for average cost? _____ What are economic profits at this level of output? $ _____ Again check that this level of output maximizes profits or minimizes losses by considering output levels 100 units higher, 100 units lower, and no production.

Economic losses at higher output = $ _____

Economic losses at lower output = $ _____

Economic losses at zero output = $ _____

3. If the price of widgets is $6.00, what is the profit-maximizing level of output? Why?

_____

4. What general conclusion can you draw about the short-run supply curve for a firm operating under conditions of perfect competition?

_____

_____

5. Note that in question 1, when the market price was assumed to be $19.10, the profit-maximizing level of output was at a point where price exceeded both average cost and average variable cost. Remembering that under perfect competition a firm can sell as much output as it wants at the given market price, why isn't it profitable for the firm to produce even more when price exceeds average costs?

6. If many firms can produce widgets with the same cost functions, what is the long-run equilibrium price of widgets? $ _____ What is the associated level of production for the representative firm?

_____

SELF-TESTS FOR UNDERSTANDING

TEST A

Circle the most appropriate answer.

1. Which of the following is inconsistent with perfect competition?
   a. perfect information about products
   b. one firm producing the total industry output
   c. freedom of entry
   d. freedom of exit

2. If production is limited to a few large firms, the resulting market structure is called
   a. perfect competition.
   b. monopolistic competition.
   c. oligopoly.
   d. pure monopoly.

3. If a firm can sell any amount of output without affecting price, we say that the demand curve for this firm is
   a. horizontal.
   b. inelastic.
   c. equal to the marginal cost curve.
   d. indeterminate.

4. Which one of the following is not true under perfect competition?
   a. The firm's demand curve is horizontal.
   b. The firm's demand curve is also the curve of average revenue.
   c. The firm's demand curve is also the curve of marginal revenue.
   d. The firm's demand curve is inelastic.

5. If a firm's demand curve is horizontal, marginal revenue equals
   a. average cost.
   b. marginal cost.
   c. average revenue.
   d. minimum long-run average cost.

6. If a firm's demand curve is horizontal, the firm should produce
   a. as much output as it can.
   b. more output as long as price exceeds average variable cost.
   c. at the point where marginal cost equals price.
   d. at the minimum of its long-run average cost curve.

7. Under perfect competition, a profit-maximizing firm should shut down when price falls below
   a. average cost.
   b. average variable cost.
   c. marginal cost.
   d. fixed costs.

8. The short-run supply curve for a firm under perfect competition is the portion of the firm's marginal cost curve that is above the
   a. average total cost curve.
   b. average fixed cost curve.
   c. average variable cost curve.
   d. minimum of the marginal cost curve.

9. Under perfect competition, industry supply in the short run is given by
   a. the intersection of market demand and average cost.
   b. the horizontal sum of firm's short-run supply curves.
   c. the horizontal sum of firm's average cost curves.
   d. a fixed markup over average variable cost.

10. Which of the following is not a characteristic of long-run equilibrium under perfect competition?
    a. production where $P = MC$
    b. zero accounting profits
    c. zero economic profits
    d. production where P = minimum average cost

11. Which of the following explains why economic profits in a perfectly competitive industry will equal zero in the long run?
    a. the assumption of perfect information
    b. the elasticity of market demand
    c. the ease of entry and exit by new and existing firms
    d. the existence of fixed costs that must be covered in the long run

12. When economic profits equal zero, we know that accounting profits will
    a. also be zero.
    b. likely understate economic profits.
    c. be at their minimum.
    d. equal the opportunity cost of an owner's investment in her firm.

13. In long-run equilibrium under perfect competition, all but which one of the following are equal to price?
    a. average cost
    b. marginal cost
    c. marginal revenue
    d. fixed cost

14. Under perfect competition, price will equal average cost
    a. in the short run.
    b. in the long run.
    c. in both the short and long run.
    d. never.

15. Under perfect competition, firms will produce where $MC = P$
    a. in the short run.
    b. in the long run.
    c. in both the short and long run.
    d. never.

16. Under perfect competition, price is determined by the intersection of the industry supply and demand curves
    a. in the short run.
    b. in the long run.
    c. in both the short and long run.
    d. never.

17. Under perfect competition, the industry's long-run supply curve is
    a. horizontal.
    b. its long-run average cost curve.
    c. its long-run average variable cost curve.
    d. its long-run fixed cost curve.

131

18. Economic profits will be positive as long as price
    a. equals marginal cost.
    b. is greater than average variable cost.
    c. is greater than average fixed cost.
    d. is greater than average cost.

19. Imagine that pencils are produced by firms with U-shaped average costs under conditions of perfect competition. Concern about the quality of education has increased government spending on education and disturbed the original long-run equilibrium by shifting the demand curve for pencils to the right. Which one of the following is not a likely response?
    a. Pencil prices rise initially in response to the increase in demand.
    b. Existing firms are likely to earn positive economic profits in the short run.
    c. Existing firms in the industry expand output to the point where average cost equals the new, higher price.
    d. New firms are likely to enter the industry in response to earnings above the opportunity cost of capital.

20. Widgets are produced by perfectly competitive firms. The demand curve for widgets has a negative slope. A technological innovation dramatically reduces average and marginal costs for current and potential widget manufacturers. All but which one of the following will occur?
    a. The quantity supplied increases in the short run.
    b. The price of widgets declines in the short run.
    c. Economic profits increase in the short run.
    d. Economic profits will be positive in the long run.

TEST B

Circle T or F for true or false.

T F   1. Perfect competition is characterized by many firms producing similar but not identical products.

T F   2. Under perfect competition, firms maximize profits by always producing at the minimum of their average cost.

T F   3. Freedom of entry and exit are really unnecessary for the existence of perfect competition.

T F   4. Under perfect competition a firm is always guaranteed to earn positive economic profits if it produces where MC = P.

T F   5. Under perfect competition, the demand curve facing the industry is horizontal.

T F   6. A competitive firm should always expand output as long as price exceeds average cost.

T F   7. The firm's short-run supply curve is given by the portion of its marginal cost curve with a positive slope.

T F   8. In long-run equilibrium, perfectly competitive firms will show positive accounting profits but zero economic profits.

T F   9. If price is less than average cost, a firm is always better off shutting down.

T F 10. Perfect competition is studied because a very large number of markets satisfy the conditions for perfect competition.

SUPPLEMENTARY EXERCISES

Consider a firm with the following total cost curve:

$$TC = 10{,}140 + 0.00001Q_3 - 0.02Q_2 + 16.3Q$$

where Q *is output. (This cost curve is consistent with the Basic Exercise.)*

1. Derive equations for the firm's
   a. average cost.
   b. average variable cost.
   c. marginal cost.

2. Draw a picture showing these various measures of cost as a function of output.

3. Verify that the marginal cost curve goes through the bottom of the average cost curve and the average variable cost curve.

4. Assume this firm operates in a perfectly competitive market. Derive a mathematical expression for the firm's supply curve.

ECONOMICS IN ACTION

MORE COMPETITIVE MARKETS?

The development of the Internet and the web has had an important impact on many consumers. While a number of the early claims about how the web would change the world were clearly overblown, it is appropriate to ask whether the availability of shopping alternatives on the web will make markets more or less competitive. To date it appears that results paint a somewhat mixed but optimistic picture.

One of the conditions for perfectly competitive markets is that buyers need good information about the quality and characteristics of commodities as well as good information about the prices offered by different sellers. Can the Internet help? Some observers point to price comparison sites on the web and the opportunity for customer comments as ways in which the Internet increases consumer information.

A story in the *Los Angeles Times* describes how Internet auction sites have changed the market for collectibles by creating a pricing mechanism that is available to all participants. Buyers, especially novice buyers, are able to see market prices and do not have to negotiate one-on-one with more experienced sellers. Similarly, uninformed sellers can easily check prices. David Welch, an Illinois dealer in collectibles, noted, "The advantage I had was knowledge. If someone had something for $25 and I knew it was worth $300, my knowledge was what gave me the edge." Now eBay gives sellers more information about whether what they have is really as rare as hen's teeth and thus worth a lot or not.

Florain Zettelmeyer, Fiona Morton, and Jorge Silva-Risso concluded that the anonymity of the Internet can help buyers by making it more difficult for salespeople to identify particular buyers who would be willing to pay

133

more. In particular when looking at prices that consumers pay when buying an automobile, the authors conclude that "the Internet is disproportionately beneficial to those who have personal characteristics that put them at a disadvantage in negotiating."

Others are not so sure that the Internet always promotes privacy. Online sites can keep track of buyers and use this information to charge buyers different prices. At one point Amazon.com was forced to issue an apology and refunds when customers complained about differential prices of DVDs. Amazon said it was testing randomly chosen discounts for their effectiveness while cynics argued that Amazon was "discounting heavily to new visitors while repaying old customers for their loyalty by charging them higher prices."

Other economists who have looked at Internet shopping find that firms have found ways to make price comparisons difficult rather than easy. Shipping and restocking charges are not always clear. Differences in model numbers along with custom-made store brands make direct price comparisons difficult.

1. Have you bought over the Internet or used the Internet to gather product information? Did your experience make you a more informed consumer? On balance, do you think the Internet will improve or reduce the efficiency of markets? Why?

SOURCES: Fiona M. Scott Morton, Florian Zettelmeyer, Jorge Silva-Risso, "Consumer Information and Price Discrimination: Does the Internet Affect the Pricing of New Cars to Women and Minorities?" Yale SOM Working Paper No. ES-15; Haas School, UC Berkeley Marketing Working Paper No. 01-2, December 2001; Marcia Pledger, "Finding the best deals online," *The Cleveland Plain Dealer*, December 11, 2001; David Streitfeld, "Dispenser of Instant Treasures," *Los Angeles Times*, November 22, 2001; Tim Jackson, "INSIDE TRACK: Why Amazon looks to Japan," *The Financial Times* (London), November 7, 2000; Mike Meyers, "Economists: Comparison Shipping on the Web a Mixed Bag," *Minneapolis Star Tribune*, January 27, 2002.

STUDY QUESTIONS

1. What conditions are necessary for perfect competition?

2. Which of these conditions helps to ensure that in the long run economic profits are driven to zero? Explain.

3. How can firms in a perfectly competitive industry face a horizontal demand curve when the demand curve for the industry is sloping downward?

4. Explain the difference between average cost, average variable cost, and marginal cost. Which is relevant for the short-run supply decisions of firms in a perfectly competitive industry? Why?

5. How can it be profitable for a firm to stay in business if price is less than average cost?

6. Often firms think that if they raise their price just a bit they might lose a few customers but make enough from those who remain to increase profits. Why wouldn't a firm in a perfectly competitive industry do the same thing? What about reducing price just a bit in an effort to attract more customers?

7. What is meant by the efficient production of commodities and how is it fostered by market forces under perfect competition?

8. The discussion of equilibrium makes a distinction between the short run and the long run. What is it that is different between the short run and the long run for firms and for an industry of perfectly competitive firms?

9. If long-run equilibrium yields zero economic profits, why do any firms stay in a perfectly competitive industry?

Monopoly

11

Important Terms and Concepts

- Pure monopoly
- Barriers to entry
- Patents
- Natural monopoly
- Monopoly profits
- Price discrimination

Learning Objectives

After completing this chapter, you should be able to:

- define a monopoly and explain why unrestrained pure monopolies are rarely found in practice.

- describe what factors allow a particular monopoly to persist.

- explain why a monopolist cannot determine both price and quantity.

- explain why for a monopolist marginal revenue is less than price.

- calculate a monopolist's profit-maximizing price and output, given information on costs and demand.

- explain why, unlike with a competitive firm, there is no supply curve for a monopolist.

- explain why a monopolist will receive positive economic profits in both the short and long runs.

- explain how a monopoly can give rise to an inefficient allocation of resources.

- describe why a monopolist's demand and cost curves may differ from those of a comparable competitive industry.

- identify specific ways in which monopoly can offset some of its undesirable consequences.

- show how price discrimination can increase a monopolist's profit.

CHAPTER REVIEW

In Chapter 10 we studied the decisions of firms operating in markets characterized as perfect competition, that is, markets with lots of firms competing to produce and sell the same commodity. Chapters 7 and 8 considered optimal firm decisions. This chapter will use the tools we developed in Chapter 8 to examine a pure monopoly,

(1) a market with (<u>one/many</u>) firm(s) producing a single good with (<u>no/lots of</u>) close substitutes. Not only is there no competition at the moment, but also the entry and survival of potential competitors is extremely unlikely. The essence of a pure monopoly is one producer without effective competition.

A pure monopoly may arise for one of two broad reasons. If the technology of large-scale production enables one firm to produce enough to satisfy the whole market at lower average costs than a number of smaller firms

(2) can, the result is a(n) _____ monopoly. Legal restrictions such as exclusive licensing or patents; advantages the monopolist acquires for himself, such as control of a vital input or technical superiority; or special risks faced by potential entrants who must spend large amounts on factories or advertising before realizing any revenue can also create a pure monopoly. All of these factors would deter potential competitors and are called _____ to _____.

The study of a pure monopoly often starts by assuming that some enterprising entrepreneur is able to monopolize a previously competitive industry. It is also traditional to assume that the monopolist initially faces the previous industry demand curve and operates with the same cost curves.

Under pure competition, individual firms face demand curves that are horizontal; that is, any firm can sell as much as it wants at the market price. A monopolist will face the industry demand curve with a

(3) (<u>positive/negative/zero</u>) slope. The monopolist who wants to sell more must (<u>raise/lower</u>) his price. A monopolist who raises his price will find that sales (<u>decrease/do not change/increase</u>).

The monopolist maximizes profit just like any other profit-maximizing firm; that is, the monopolist

(4) chooses the output level at which (<u>marginal/average</u>) cost equals (<u>marginal/average</u>) revenue. Now the only trick is to figure out what the relevant cost and revenue curves look like. Marginal cost comes from the monopolist's total costs in exactly the same way that it does for anyone else. The tricky part is marginal revenue. Marginal revenue is the addition to total revenue from producing and selling one more unit. Under perfect competition, the actions of an individual firm have no effect on the market price and marginal revenue equals _____. But with a monopolist, quantity decisions affect price and marginal revenue (<u>is/is not</u>) equal to price.

(5) Remember from Chapter 8 that the demand curve is the curve of (<u>average/marginal</u>) revenue. From Rule 4 in the Appendix to Chapter 8 we know that when average revenue is declining, marginal revenue will be (<u>less/more</u>) than average revenue. In other words, for the monopolist with a downward-sloping demand curve, the curve of marginal revenue will lie (<u>above/below</u>) the curve of average revenue. (Remember the geometry of marginal revenue in the Basic Exercise to Chapter 8 in the Study Guide.) A similar use of Rule 4 indicates that when average cost is rising, the marginal cost curve will lie _____ the average cost curve.

Once we have used the marginal cost and marginal revenue curves to compute the monopolist's profit-maximizing output level, we can use the (demand/supply) curve to figure out what price he should charge. We (6) know that since the curve of marginal revenue lies below the demand curve, the monopolist's market price will be (greater/less) than both marginal revenue and marginal cost. We also know that if average cost is rising, average cost will be (greater/less) than marginal cost and hence also (greater/less) than the market price given by the demand curve. Thus, for a profit-maximizing monopolist, operating at a level where average cost is rising, price will be greater than average cost and the monopolist will receive positive economic profits. Since, by definition, the monopolist is the only supplier, new firms (will/will not) arise to compete away these profits. Compared with results under pure competition, the monopolist's profit-maximizing behavior will result in a (higher/lower) price and a (higher/lower) level of output in both the short and long run. (If average costs are not rising, the long-run viability of the monopolist requires that price exceed average cost.)

In Chapter 14 we will see that pure competition leads to an efficient allocation of resources. Efficient resource allocation requires that the marginal utility (MU) of each commodity equal its marginal cost (MC). In Chapter 5 we learned that optimal consumer decisions lead to the result that MU equals price. In Chapter 10 we saw that under perfect competition, optimal firm decisions imply that MC equals _____. (7) The upshot is clearly that under pure competition MU equals MC. With a pure monopoly as outlined above—that is, with the same demand and cost curves—we know that while consumers will continue to equate MU and P, the monopolist will equate MC to _____ _____, which is (greater/less) than P. The result is that with a pure monopoly, MU is (greater/less) than MC. Increased quantity of the monopolized commodity would yield marginal benefits, measured by MU, that are (less than/the same as/greater than) marginal costs. In this sense, the monopoly leads to an inefficient allocation of resources.

It is important to note that in the discussion above we assumed that the monopolist faces demand and cost curves that are the same as those of the previously competitive industry. However, several factors could shift these curves following a change in market structure. Advertising might shift demand and cost curves. Savings from centralizing various operations and avoiding duplication might shift the cost curves (up/down). (8) Inefficiencies from greater size would have the opposite effect. Particular results will depend upon particular circumstances.

Why do we say there is no supply curve for a monopolist? Remember that the supply curve shows the relationship between each possible market price and the quantity supplied. Under pure competition a firm takes price as given and then decides how much to produce, knowing that its individual quantity decision (will/will not) affect the market price. The firm's supply curve comes from considering its reaction to possible (9) prices. But the monopolist (does/does not) take price as given. The monopolist chooses the one quantity that maximizes profits and receives the price given by the point on the demand curve consistent with the quantity. The monopolist is a price (maker/taker).

IMPORTANT TERMS AND CONCEPTS QUIZ

Choose the best definition for the following terms.

1. _____ Pure monopoly
2. _____ Barriers to entry
3. _____ Patents
4. _____ Natural monopoly
5. _____ Monopoly profits
6. _____ Price discrimination

a. Impediments preventing potential rivals from entering an industry
b. Industry in which advantages of large-scale production enable a single firm to supply the market demand at a lower average cost than a number of smaller firms could
c. Industry with a single buyer for the entire market
d. Charging different prices to different customers when the cost of supplying customers is the same
e. Industry with single supplier of a product for which there are no close substitutes
f. Economic profits that persist in the long run
g. Temporary government grants of exclusive production rights to product's inventors

BASIC EXERCISES

These exercises are designed to offer practice in computing the profit-maximizing quantity and price for a monopolist.

1. Mario has a monopoly in the production of widgets. **Table 11-1** contains data on the demand for widgets and the cost of producing them. Use this data to compute Mario's profit-maximizing quantity and the associated price.
   a. One way is to consider columns 2 and 5 of **Table 11-2**. Choose the output level that maximizes the difference. That level of output is _____ widgets.

Table 11-1

Mario's Cost and Revenue

Quantity	Average Revenue (Price)	Average Cost
12	$9,500	$7,068.00
13	9,300	6,957.00
14	9,100	6,894.00
15	8,900	6,869.40
16	8,700	6,876.00

Table 11-2

Marginal Revenue and Cost

(1) Quantity	(2) Total Revenue	(3) Marginal Revenue	(4) Marginal Cost	(5) Total Cost
12	$114,000			$84,816
13	120,900	_____	_____	90,441
14	127,400	_____	_____	96,516
15	133,500	_____	_____	103,041
16	139,200	_____	_____	110,016

b. The second way is to fill in columns 3 and 4 of Table 11-2 by computing marginal revenue and marginal cost. Mario could maximize profits by increasing production as long as marginal _____ exceeds marginal _____ widgets. In this case, Mario maximizes profits by producing _____ widgets.

c. To maximize profits Mario should charge a price of $ _____.

d. What is Mario's profit? _____

It is sometimes argued that monopolists do not have to worry about what consumers are willing to pay, they can charge what they want. Assume that the production of widgets involves significant pollution, and the government has imposed a pollution charge that costs Mario $1,000 a widget. **Table 11-3** contains the original data on demand along with the new average cost data that reflect the $1,000 a widget pollution charge.

e. Use **Table 11-4** to compute the new profit-maximizing output level. Mario's new profit-maximizing output level is _____ and the associated price is $ _____.

f. Note that while the pollution charge is $1,000 a widget, Mario's profit-maximizing price increases by only $_____. Why doesn't Mario simply raise his price by the full $1,000?

g. What is the new level of profits? $_____.

h. (Optional) What would have happened if, instead of a per-unit tax, the government had simply fined Mario $13,000 for polluting and imposed no further charges? Compared with the initial situation and the situation with the per unit tax, what happens to Mario's profit-maximizing level of output, and actual profits with this lump-sum pollution charge?

Which tax reduces pollution the most? (When answering this question be sure you are working with the correct cost curves. Adjust Table 11-2, remembering that at each output level, total costs will now be $13,000 higher than the entries in column 5.)

Table 11-3

Revenue and Cost after the Pollution Tax

Quantity	Average Revenue (Price)	Average Cost
12	$9,500	$8,068.00
13	9,300	7,957.00
14	9,100	7,894.00
15	8,900	7,869.40
16	8,700	7,876.00

Table 11-4

Marginal Revenue, Total Cost, and Marginal Cost after the Pollution Tax

(1) Quantity	(2) Total Revenue	(3) Marginal Revenue	(4) Marginal Cost	(5) Total Cost
12	114,000			_____
13	120,900	_____	_____	_____
14	127,400	_____	_____	_____
15	133,500	_____	_____	_____
16	139,200	_____	_____	_____

2. This exercise illustrates how a monopolist may be able to increase her profits by engaging in price discrimination. **Table 11-5** contains data on the demand for snow tires in Centerville and Middletown. Centerville does not get much snow, and the demand for snow tires is quite elastic. Middletown is smaller, and gets more snow; it should not be surprising that the demand for snow tires in Middletown is less elastic than in Centerville. Snow tires are supplied to both cities by a monopolist who can produce tires with a fixed cost of $2,500,000 and a constant marginal cost of $10 a tire.

a. Assume that the monopolist charges the same price in both towns. Use the data on total demand to compute the monopolist's profit-maximizing level of output and price. First compute total revenue in order to compute marginal revenue per tire by dividing the change in total revenue by the change in output. Then compare marginal revenue to the monopolist's marginal cost of $10 to determine the profit-maximizing level of output.

Price? $ _____

Output? _____

Profits? $ _____

Table 11-5

Demand for Snow Tires

Price	Quantity Demanded Centerville	Quantity Demanded Middletown	Total Demand	Total Revenue	Marginal Revenue
$48	10,000	40,000	50,000		
45	25,000	43,750	68,750		
42	40,000	47,500	87,500		
39	55,000	51,250	106,250		
36	70,000	55,000	125,000		
33	85,000	58,750	143,750		
30	100,000	62,500	162,500		
27	115,000	66,250	181,250		

b. Assume now that the monopolist is able to charge different prices in the towns; that is, she is a price discriminator. Can the monopolist increase her profits by charging different prices? Complete **Table 11-6** to answer this question.

Profit-maximizing price in Centerville: $ _____

Profit-maximizing price in Middletown: $ _____

Quantity of snow tires in Centerville: _____

Table 11-6

Total and Marginal Revenue

| Price | Centerville | | Middletown | |
	Total Revenue	Marginal Revenue	Total Revenue	Marginal Revenue
$48	_____		_____	
45	_____	_____	_____	_____
42	_____	_____	_____	_____
39	_____	_____	_____	_____
36	_____	_____	_____	_____
33	_____	_____	_____	_____
30	_____	_____	_____	_____
27	_____	_____	_____	_____

Quantity of snow tires in Middletown: _____

Total Profits: $ _____

c. In which town did the monopolist raise the price? In which town did she lower the price? The monopolist should charge a higher price in the town with the lower elasticity of demand. Can you explain why? Is that the case here?

SELF-TESTS FOR UNDERSTANDING

TEST A

Circle the most appropriate answer.

1. Pure monopoly is characterized by
   a. many firms producing slightly different products.
   b. many firms producing slightly different products that are close substitutes.
   c. such a small number of firms that each must figure out how the others will respond to its own actions.
   d. one firm, with no competitors, producing a product with no close substitutes.

2. Which one of the following is not likely to lead to a monopoly?
   a. patents
   b. control of the sole source of an important commodity
   c. a commodity with many close substitutes
   d. significant increasing returns to scale

143

3. A natural monopoly arises when
   a. natural resources are an important input.
   b. there are significant cost advantages to large-scale production.
   c. the government prohibits entry.
   d. patents protect a firm's technology.

4. Which of the following is not an example of a barrier to entry?
   a. patents that give exclusive rights to production
   b. the existence of large fixed costs before one can begin production
   c. a legal charter that grants its holder the right to be the sole supplier
   d. a simple production process with constant average cost and no fixed costs

5. Which of the following is likely to represent a monopoly?
   a. the largest department store in town
   b. the University of Iowa, which is the largest employer in Iowa City
   c. the local gas and electric company, which operates under an exclusive contract from the city
   d. Amtrak

6. If in order to sell more a firm must reduce the price on all units sold, we can conclude that the firm's demand curve
   a. has a positive slope.
   b. is horizontal.
   c. slopes down and to the right.
   d. is vertical.

7. Under the conditions of question 6, we know that marginal revenue will
   a. be less than average revenue.
   b. equal average revenue.
   c. exceed average revenue.

8. If average costs are increasing, marginal cost will be
   a. less than average cost.
   b. equal to average cost.
   c. greater than average cost.
   d. Insufficient information to determine whether marginal cost will be above or below average cost.

9. A monopolist maximizes profit by producing where
   a. marginal cost equals marginal revenue.
   b. marginal cost equals marginal utility.
   c. average cost equals average revenue.
   d. the difference between average cost and average revenue is greatest.

10. Once a monopolist has determined the profit-maximizing level of output, the price she should charge is given by the curve of
    a. marginal revenue.
    b. marginal cost.
    c. average cost.
    d. average revenue.

11. A monopolist's profits are found by multiplying the quantity produced by the difference between
    a. marginal cost and marginal revenue.
    b. marginal cost and average revenue.
    c. average cost and average revenue.
    d. average cost and marginal revenue.

12. A monopolist's economic profits will
    a. be competed away in the long run.
    b. be driven to the opportunity cost of capital.
    c. persist in the long run.
    d. be limited by usury laws.

13. Because a monopolist is a price maker, it is typically said that he has
    a. an inelastic demand curve.
    b. no demand curve.
    c. no supply curve.
    d. an upward-sloping demand curve.

14. An entrepreneur who monopolizes a previously competitive industry and now faces the same demand curve and produces with the same cost function will typically maximize profits by
    a. forcing consumers to buy more at a higher price.
    b. producing less and charging a higher price.
    c. increasing volume.
    d. lowering both output and price.

15. A price-discriminating monopolist producing in one plant and selling in two markets will operate such that
    a. price is equal in both markets.
    b. profits are equal in both markets.
    c. marginal revenue is equal in both markets.
    d. quantities sold are equal in both markets.

16. A monopolist cannot simply pass on any increase in average cost because
    a. marginal cost exceeds average cost.
    b. the average cost curve often has a positive slope.
    c. the monopolist's demand curve is typically downward sloping.
    d. of concerns about excessive profiteering.

17. An increase in a monopolist's average cost will lead to a(n)
    a. increase in price by the same amount, as the monopolist passes on the price increase.
    b. increase in price only if marginal cost increases.
    c. decrease in price as the monopolist needs to sell more in order to cover increased costs.
    d. increase in price only if the elasticity of demand is less than 1.0.

18. Some argue that because they control the whole market and can thus garner all of the benefits, monopolies are more likely to foster innovations. Statistical evidence
    a. confirms this argument.
    b. suggests exactly the reverse.
    c. lacks a firm conclusion.

19. An increase in a monopolist's fixed cost will
    a. reduce the profit-maximizing level of output.
    b. not affect the profit-maximizing level of output.
    c. increase the profit-maximizing level of output as the monopolist needs to sell more to cover costs.

20. If marginal cost is greater than zero, we know that a monopolist will produce where the elasticity of demand is
    a. greater than 1.0.
    b. equal to 1.0.
    c. less than 1.0.

TEST B

Circle T or F for true or false.

T F 1. A pure monopoly results when only a few firms supply a particular commodity for which there are no close substitutes.

T F 2. Significant increasing returns to scale, which reduce average costs as output expands, may result in a natural monopoly.

T F 3. A pure monopolist can earn positive economic profits only in the long run.

T F 4. An entrepreneur who successfully monopolizes a competitive industry will face a horizontal demand curve just like each of the previous competitive firms.

T F 5. A monopolist maximizes profits by producing at the point at which marginal cost equals marginal revenue.

T F 6. If in a monopolistic industry, demand and cost curves are identical to a comparable competitive industry, and the demand curve slopes downward while the average cost curve slopes upward, then the monopolist's price will always exceed the competitive industry's price, but the monopolist's output will be larger.

T F 7. A monopolist has a greater incentive to advertise than does an individual firm under pure competition.

T F 8. When market price is greater than average cost, a monopolist can always increase profits by producing more.

T F 9. A price-discriminating monopolist would increase profits by charging all consumers the same price.

T F 10. Price discrimination always hurts consumers.

SUPPLEMENTARY EXERCISES

1. The demand curve for the first problem in the Basic Exercise is

$$Q = 59.5 - 0.005P.$$

   The total cost curve is

$$TC = 52,416 + 225Q_2.$$

   a. Derive mathematical expressions for total revenue, marginal revenue, average cost, and marginal cost.
   b. Plot the demand, marginal revenue, average cost, and marginal cost curves.
   c. Use your expressions for marginal revenue and marginal cost to solve for the profit-maximizing level of output. Is your answer consistent with your graph in part b and your answer to the Basic Exercise?
   d. What is the impact of the per-unit pollution tax and the fixed-charge pollution tax on your expressions for total, average, and marginal cost? Do differences here help explain the impact of these taxes on the profit-maximizing level of output?

2. Why is (a) the correct answer to question 20 in Test A? (You might want to refer back to Chapter 7.)

ECONOMICS IN ACTION

THE HIGH COST OF NEW DRUGS

In the early 1990s, the debate over health-care reform at the beginning of the Clinton Administration focused attention on the pricing policies of drug companies. This concern has not abated as low-income countries in Africa struggle with the cost of drugs to treat AIDS. The cost of drugs to treat anthrax and the actions of several countries to abridge patent agreements in the face of what looked like national emergencies in the fall of 2001 along with President Bush's successful lobbying of Congress for a prescription drug bill for senior citizens have only intensified concerns about drug prices.

Consider the case of Tacrine, the first drug recommended by an advisory panel of the Food and Drug Administration to treat Alzheimer's disease. Industry observers were expecting Tacrine would cost more than $1,000 a year even though it is not effective for most patients. What explains such high prices for this and other new drugs?

Some point to the high cost of drug research, and the fact that most new ideas are not successful, as justification for the high cost of drugs. Pharmaceutical manufacturers argue that drugs save money, as even expensive drugs are often cheaper than hospitalization or surgery.

Regulating drug prices to allow manufacturers a reasonable rate of return while recognizing the significant research and development costs a company incurs—that is, setting prices on the basis of cost-plus pricing—has been advocated by some. Others are concerned that this approach may only subsidize and encourage wasteful and mediocre research. Sam Peltzman, a professor of economics at the University of Chicago, argues that

147

one should not be surprised by high prices. Patents mean that drug companies enjoy a ten-year monopoly. As Peltzman puts it, "These companies are not charities—they are charging what the market will allow."

Are there other solutions? Peltzman has advocated limiting patent monopolies to five years. Others argue that the concept of managed competition, under which patients are organized into large groups to bargain with drug companies and other health care providers, is necessary for patients to get the best price. Some are less optimistic that patients, even if organized into large groups, will be successful in bargaining with drug companies who hold a monopoly position unless patients are willing to refuse drug treatments that cost too much.

Uwe Reinhardt, a health economist at Princeton University, has advocated a variant on the bargaining approach through the use of a "reference pricing" system, such has been used in Germany. Under this approach, insurers would provide a larger reimbursement for drugs that are truly new, different, and for which its manufacturer agrees to the reference price. Other drugs would be available to consumers, but with a lower reimbursement. Reinhardt has suggested that private insurers and the government set aside 1 percent of their current expenditures on prescription drugs to establish an independent research institute to determine what drugs would qualify for the reference pricing system.

1. How would you determine a fair price for new drugs?

2. What would it take to enforce your concept of fair prices and what side effects are likely to be associated with enforcement?

3. Do you think there should be changes in the terms of patents for new drugs? If so, what and why?

4. What do you think explains the high price of new drugs?

Sources: Elizabeth Rosenthal, "Exploring the Murky World of Drug Prices," *The New York Times*, March 28, 1993; Uwe E. Reinhardt, "How to Lower the Cost of Drugs," *The New York Times*, January 3, 2001; Malcolm Gladwell, "Who's really to blame for the cost of drugs?" *The New Yorker*, October 25, 2004.

STUDY QUESTIONS

1. Why are barriers to entry important for the preservation of a monopolist's monopoly?

2. What is the difference between a price taker and a price maker? Which description is relevant for a monopolist?

3. Why do economists argue that monopoly leads to an inefficient allocation of resources?

4. Who has the greater incentive to advertise and why, a firm in a purely competitive industry or a monopolist?

5. Are there conditions under which society might benefit from a monopoly? Explain.

6. What is meant by the term "price discrimination"?

7. How can a monopolist increase profits by engaging in price discrimination?

8. Will price discrimination always raise prices for customers?

9. Why doesn't a monopolist simply raise her price by the full cost of things like pollution charges?

10. If both monopolists and competitive firms produce where marginal revenue equals marginal cost, why are the results of a competitive industry and a monopolized industry different?

Between Competition and Monopoly

12

Important Terms and Concepts

Monopolistic competition	Price war	Payoff matrix	Zero sum game
Oligopoly	Sales maximization	Dominant strategy	Repeated games
Cartel	Kinked demand curve	Maximin criterion	Credible threat
Price leadership	Sticky price	Nash equilibrium	Perfectly contestable markets

Learning Objectives

After completing this chapter, you should be able to:

- compare the four conditions that define monopolistic competition with those of perfect competition.

- explain why and how the long-run equilibrium of a firm under monopolistic competition differs from that of a firm under pure competition.

- explain why firms under monopolistic competition earn zero profit in the long run even though they face a downward-sloping demand curve.

- explain why monopolistic competitors are said to have excess capacity.

- explain why it is so difficult to make a formal analysis of an oligopolistic market structure.

- describe briefly the alternative approaches to modeling oligopolistic behavior.

- explain why most economists believe it is difficult to maintain the discipline necessary to sustain a cartel.

- use marginal cost and marginal revenue curves to derive the implications for price and quantity of sales maximization as opposed to profit maximization.

- use marginal cost and marginal revenue curves to explain how a kinked demand curve can imply sticky prices.

- analyze a payoff matrix to see if there is a dominant strategy.

- use the maximin criterion to determine the final outcome in a game-theory setting.

- analyze Nash equilibrium, zero-sum games, and repeated games.

- understand how credible threats could be used as entry-blocking strategies.

- explain how the concept of contestable markets means that even in an industry with few firms, no firm will earn long-run profits in excess of the opportunity cost of capital, and inefficient firms will not survive if entry and exit are costless.

- compare different attributes of the four market forms.

CHAPTER REVIEW

Pure competition and pure monopoly are the polar examples of market structure most easily analyzed in textbooks. Actual markets tend more toward *monopolistic competition* and *oligopoly*, which are the subjects of this chapter. It is harder to model firm behavior in these market structures, especially in the case of oligopoly. However, profit maximization remains a dominant objective for most firms and marginal cost and marginal revenue curves still are important tools when analyzing the decisions firms make.

(1) A market structure in which there are numerous participants, freedom of entry and exit, perfect information, and product heterogeneity is referred to as _____ competition. Because each seller is able to partially differentiate his product, individual firms will face a demand curve with a (negative/positive/zero) slope. At each point in time, profit-maximizing firms will try to produce at the output level where _____ _____ equals _____. The assumption of freedom of entry and exit implies that in the long run under monopolistic competition firms will earn (negative/positive/zero) economic profit. If existing firms are earning positive economic profits, the (entry/exit) of new firms will shift the demand curve down (and may raise costs) until the demand curve is just tangent to the (average/marginal) cost curve.

(2) A market structure with only a few firms producing a similar or identical product, and in which some firms are very large, is called a(n) _____. Formal analysis of such market structures is difficult; when considering the decisions of one firm, one must also take into account the possible reactions of competitors. No single model describes all the possible outcomes under oligopoly, and economists have found it useful to consider a number of possible models and outcomes. If firms in an oligopolistic market band together and act like a single profit-maximizing monopolist, the resulting group is called a(n) _____. If most firms look to pricing decisions made by a dominant firm, economists refer to the outcome as one of _____ _____.

Oligopolistic firms tend to be large corporations with professional managers. Some argue that managers are likely to be more interested in maximizing total revenue than in maximizing profits. This outcome is more likely if the compensation of managers depends more upon the size of the firm than upon its profitability. A firm interested in maximizing sales revenue will increase output until marginal revenue equals

(3) _____. Compared with profit maximization, sales maximization will mean a (higher/lower) price and a(n) _____ quantity.

Another traditional element of the analysis of oligopoly is the concept of a kinked demand curve. Such a demand curve comes from assuming that your competitors (<u>will/will not</u>) match any decrease in your price (4) but (<u>will/will not</u>) match any increase in your price. As a result, there is a gap in the (<u>marginal/average</u>) revenue curve, and profit-maximizing prices may not change unless there is a significant shift in the marginal _____ curve.

Game theory has been used productively by a number of economists to study oligopolistic behavior. Game theory involves listing the possible outcomes of your moves and your opponents' countermoves in a(n) _____ matrix and then choosing an appropriate _____. If there is one strategy (5) that always yields the highest return regardless of what your competitors do, that strategy is referred to as a(n) _____ strategy. If firms choose a strategy that protects them against the worst possible outcome, they are choosing a(n) _____ strategy. If firms choose strategies to maximize payoffs assuming competitors stick to their announced strategies, the result is called a(n) _____ equilibrium. If one firm's gain is the other firm's loss, the set of strategic choices are called a(n) _____ - _____ game. In repeated games, _____ becomes important and may lead to higher long-run profits. Threats are likely to be most effective if they are _____.

The concept of perfectly contestable markets suggests that even oligopolists may be limited in their ability to earn monopolistic profits. The crucial condition for perfect contestability is that _____ and (6) _____ are costless and unimpeded. In such a case, competitors would get into and out of the market whenever profits exceeded the _____ _____ of _____. While no market may be perfectly contestable, the extent to which markets are contestable will limit the ability of firms to charge monopolistic prices.

IMPORTANT TERMS AND CONCEPTS QUIZ

Choose the best definition for each of the following terms.

1. _____ Monopolistic competition

2. _____ Oligopoly

3. _____ Cartel

4. _____ Price leadership

5. _____ Price war

6. _____ Sales maximization

7. _____ Kinked demand curve

8. _____ Sticky price

9. _____ Payoff matrix

10. _____ Dominant strategy

11. _____ Maximin criterion

12. _____ Nash equilibrium

13. _____ Zero-sum game

14. _____ Repeated game

15. _____ Credible threat

16. _____ Perfectly contestable markets

a. Group of sellers who join together to control production, sales, and price

b. Listing of outcomes linked to the strategic choices of competitors

c. Selling at a lower price than your competitor without regard to cost

d. Market in which entry and exit are costless and unimpeded

e. Price does not change even if there are changes in cost

f. Threat that would not harm threatener if carried out

g. Many firms selling slightly different products

h. Selecting the strategy that yields the maximum profit, assuming your opponent tries to damage you as much as possible

i. Situation where one firm sets the price and other firms follow

j. Situations that are played out again and again

k. Situation where price declines are matched by competitors while price increases are not

l. Best result when one assumes opponents will stick to their chosen strategy

m. Industry composed of a few large rival firms

n. Expanding output to the point where marginal revenue equals zero

o. Operating independently, players choose strategies that lead to a worse outcome than would be chosen if players could coordinate strategies

p. A single strategy yields the highest payoff regardless of the strategy chosen by your competitor

q. One competitor's gain is the other's loss

BASIC EXERCISES

These problems explore several important issues in the analysis of monopolistic competition and oligopoly.

1. Our discussion of monopolistic competition argued that long-run equilibrium implies the firm's demand curve will be tangent to its average cost curve. We have also argued that profit maximization requires that marginal revenue equal marginal cost (or, alternatively, that firms should expand output as long as marginal revenue exceeds marginal cost). How do we know that marginal revenue equals marginal cost at the quantity given by the tangency between the demand curve and the average cost curve?

Table 12-1

Alice's Restaurant

Quantity	Average Revenue	Average Cost	Total Revenue	Total Cost	Total Profit
600	$19	$21.67	$11,400	$13,000	$–1,602
800	17	17.50	13,600	14,000	–400
1,000	15	15.00	15,000	15,000	0
1,200	13	13.33	15,600	16,000	–396
1,400	11	12.14	15,400	17,000	–1,596

Figure 12-1

Alice's Restaurant: Profit, Cost, and Demand

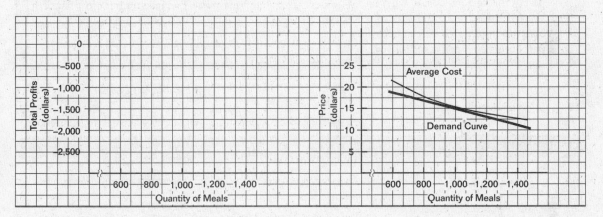

a. **Table 12-1** contains data on weekly costs and revenue for Alice's Restaurant. Average revenue and average cost are plotted in **Figure 12-1.** Note that the demand curve is tangent to the average cost curve. Plot total profits in the left half of Figure 12-1. What output level maximizes profits?

b. Use the data in Table 12-1 to compute marginal revenue and marginal cost in **Table 12-2.** According to Table 12-2, what level of output maximizes profits? Why?

Table 12-2

Alice's Restaurant: Marginal Revenue and Marginal Cost

Quantity	Marginal Revenue	Marginal Cost
800	_____	_____
1,000	_____	_____
1,200	_____	_____
1,400	_____	_____

2. **Figure 12-2** shows the kinked demand curve for a profit-maximizing firm that produces TV sets in an oligopolistic situation.

a. What is the profit-maximizing level of output and the corresponding price if TVs can be produced at a marginal cost of $100?

Quantity _____

Price _____

b. Assume that marginal cost increases by 25 percent to $125 per TV. Describe what happens to the profit-maximizing levels of price and quantity following this increase in marginal cost.

c. What increase in marginal cost would be necessary to induce a change in behavior on the part of this oligopolist and why?

d. What decrease in marginal cost would be necessary to induce a change in behavior on the part of this oligopolist and why?

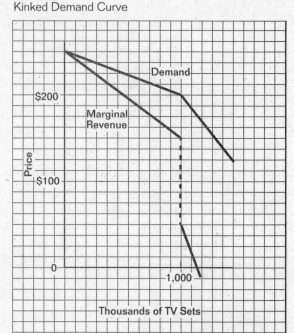

Figure 12-2

Kinked Demand Curve

SELF-TESTS FOR UNDERSTANDING

TEST A

Circle the most appropriate answer.

1. Which of the following is the important difference between perfect and monopolistic competition?
   a. few sellers rather than many
   b. heterogeneous rather than homogeneous product
   c. barriers to entry rather than freedom of entry
   d. long-run positive economic profits rather than zero economic profits

2. Monopolistic competition would be most appropriate when describing which of the following?
   a. collusion between contractors when bidding for government contracts
   b. the production of automobiles in the United States
   c. much retail trade in the United States
   d. the production of wheat

3. Under monopolistic competition the heterogeneity of output implies that
   a. individual firms face downward-sloping demand curves.
   b. both marginal cost and marginal revenue will increase with additional units of output.
   c. individual firms can make positive economic profits even in the long run.
   d. in the long run, individual firms will produce at minimum average cost.

4. Free entry and exit under monopolistic competition means that in the long run
   a. firms will earn economic profits.
   b. a firm's demand curve will be tangent to its average cost curve.
   c. a firm will operate where marginal cost exceeds marginal revenue.
   d. only one firm can survive.

5. Under monopolistic competition, firms are likely to produce
   a. to the left of the point of minimum average cost.
   b. at the point of minimum average cost.
   c. to the right of the point of minimum average cost.

6. Which of the following is most likely an example of monopolistic competition?
   a. the airline industry
   b. restaurants in Denver
   c. competition between automobile manufacturers
   d. cable television in Atlanta

7. Which of the following characterizes a firm's short-run equilibrium under monopolistic competition?
   a. production where average cost equals price
   b. production at minimum average cost
   c. production where marginal revenue equals marginal cost
   d. zero economic profits

8. Which of the following does not characterize a firm's long-run equilibrium under monopolistic competition?
   a. production where average cost equals price
   b. production at minimum average cost
   c. production where marginal revenue equals marginal cost
   d. zero economic profits

9. If long-run economic profits are zero, we know that firms are producing where
   a. marginal cost equals average cost.
   b. marginal revenue equals average cost.
   c. marginal cost equals price.
   d. average cost equals price.

10. The situation where a few large firms produce similar products is referred to as
    a. monopolistic competition.
    b. an oligopoly.
    c. contestable markets.
    d. price leadership.

11. Oligopoly may be associated with all but which one of the following?
    a. price leadership
    b. collusive behavior
    c. advertising
    d. lots of firms

12. If oligopolistic firms get together to carve up the market and act like a monopolist, the result is called a
    a. cabal.
    b. contestable market.
    c. cartel.
    d. natural monopoly.

13. A firm interested in maximizing sales revenue will produce at a point where
    a. marginal revenue equals marginal cost.
    b. average cost is minimized.
    c. marginal revenue equals zero.
    d. average revenue equals average cost.

14. A firm that maximizes sales revenues instead of profits will charge
    a. a higher price.
    b. a lower price.
    c. the same price but will advertise more.

15. Game theory may be especially useful in analyzing a firm's behavior under conditions of
    a. pure competition.
    b. monopolistic competition.
    c. oligopoly.
    d. pure monopoly.

16. The term *payoff matrix* refers to
    a. bribes paid by cartels.
    b. the structure of winnings in an office pool on the NCAA basketball championship.
    c. the set of possible outcomes in a game theory situation.
    d. players' shares in the NFL playoffs.

17. The term *kinked demand curve* refers to
    a. economists' inability to draw straight lines.
    b. the demand for X-rated movies.
    c. industries with substantial economies of scale.
    d. a situation where competitors match price decreases but not price increases.

18. If a firm faces a kinked demand curve, the demand curve for price increases will likely
    a. be steeper than for price decreases.
    b. have a positive slope.
    c. be more elastic than for price decreases.
    d. be less elastic than for price decreases.

19. Markets can be perfectly contestable if
    a. products are identical.
    b. entry and exit are free and easy.
    c. only two firms are bidding against each other.
    d. long-run economic profits are zero.

20. All but which one of the following market structures are likely to result in a misallocation of resources?
    a. perfect competition
    b. monopolistic competition
    c. oligopoly
    d. monopoly

TEST B

Circle T or F for true or false.

T F 1. Firms that operate under conditions of oligopoly are likely to engage in lots of advertising.

T F 2. Heterogeneity of output is an important feature of monopolistic competition.

T F 3. Under monopolistic competition, freedom of entry and exit will guarantee that a firm always earns zero economic profit, in both the short run and the long run.

T F 4. For profit-maximizing firms under monopolistic competition, marginal revenue equals marginal cost in the short run but not in the long run.

T F 5. There would be an unambiguous social gain if in a market with monopolistic competition some firms were forced by regulation to stop producing.

T F 6. Oligopoly is characterized by a small number of firms, some very large, producing an identical or similar product.

T F 7. Arrangements such as price leadership and tacit collusion can be important in oligopolistic markets.

T F 8. A firm that maximizes sales revenue will typically charge a higher price than a firm that maximizes profits.

T F 9. An oligopolist facing a kinked demand curve will see a more elastic demand curve for price increases than for price decreases.

T F 10. Perfectly contestable markets are only possible when there are a large number of competing firms.

SUPPLEMENTARY EXERCISES

1. The equations below for demand and total cost underlie the first problem in the Basic Exercises. Use these equations to derive explicit expressions for marginal cost, marginal revenue, and average cost. Now solve for the level of output that maximizes profits. Compare your answer with the results you obtained in the Basic Exercises.

$$Q = 2,500 - 100P \text{ (demand curve)}$$

$$TC = 10,000 + 5Q \text{ (total cost curve)}$$

where Q = total quantity, P = price, and TC = total cost.

2. This problem illustrates the difference between maximizing profits and maximizing sales. Demand and total cost are given by the equations below.

Demand

$$Q = 16,000 - 200P$$

Total Cost

$$TC = 0.00000015625Q_3 - 0.003125Q_2 + 40.625Q$$

a. If the firm maximizes profits, what are output, price, and profits?
b. If the firm maximizes sales revenue, what are output, price, and profits?
c. Is it true that maximizing sales revenue involves a higher quantity, lower price, and lower profits?

3. For an interesting discussion of apparent tacit collusion in practice and how academic research along with the resulting publicity changed behavior, see William G. Christie and Paul H. Schultz, "Policy Watch: Did Nasdaq Market Makers Implicitly Collude?" *Journal of Economic Perspectives* (Vol. 9, Number 3) Summer 1995, pp. 199–208. Figure 1 is a dramatic piece of evidence.

ECONOMICS IN ACTION

COMPETITION OR COLLUSION?

What do the latest mergers of telecommunications companies mean—more or less competition?

There was a time when there was no Internet, no cable television and only one telephone company, AT&T, known to many as Ma Bell. The reason there was only one telephone company was the belief that telephone service was a natural monopoly. In many ways AT&T was very successful. It grew to employ more than a million people, and its stock was the epitome of a safe investment for widows and orphans.

People did not own their telephones, AT&T did, and monthly telephone bills included a rental charge for the phone. The AT&T monopoly began to unravel in the 1960s when MCI entered the long-distance market using microwave technology.

The emergence of cell phone networks eliminated the distinction between local and long-distance calls, undermining earlier regulation that attempted to separate the two. Cable companies, originally formed to bring high-quality television service to people's homes, now offer Internet access with high quality Internet phone service, a new emerging technology.

In late 2004 and early 2005, it almost seemed like there was a new telecom merger everyday as first Sprint and Nextel announced plans to merge, SBC bought out AT&T, and Verizon moved to acquire MCI. Will the result be increased competition among a small number of surviving giants or will consumers lose as a small number of companies conspire to act as a monopolist?

Surviving firms argue that mergers are necessary to take advantage of new technologies to improve customer service and competitive positioning. They argue that they are not competing among themselves but competing against cable companies and the Internet. Others are not so sure and expect consumers will be faced with limited choice of costly bundled services many do not want. "Companies always say that the next merger will be the one to unleash competition," according to Mark Cooper, research director for the Consumer Federation of America. "The reality is that these are consolidations. They take alternatives away from consumers."

Steven Pearlstein is more optimistic and argues that "(T)he traditional distinctions between local and long distance, voice and data, Internet and television are increasingly irrelevant." At the same time Pearlstein argues that the big question for regulators is whether to permit emerging companies to retain exclusive control over their own networks or whether they should be required to grant access to competitors to ensure a competitive market.

1. Who was right, Cooper or Pearlstein? What has happened to the price of cell phone service? Have telecom consolidations meant an increase in price or a reduction?

2. Were consumers better off dealing separately with their local phone service, a cell phone provider, a cable company, and an Internet service provider, or have consolidations offered consumers better options at better prices?

Source: Steve Pearlstein, "Calling for Real Competition," *Washington Post*, February 16, 2005. David Lazarus, "Verizon reduces choices," *San Francisco Chronicle*, February 15, 2005.

STUDY QUESTIONS

1. How does monopolistic competition differ from perfect competition?

2. What is meant by the notion that monopolistic competition leads to excess capacity?

3. "As monopolistic competition leads to excess capacity, there will be an unambiguous social gain if government regulation reduces the number of firms and eliminates the excess capacity." Do you agree or disagree? Why?

4. What difference would it make if a firm acts to maximize profits or to maximize sales?

5. As a cartel is assumed to act to maximize profits, why do economists believe that cartels are difficult to establish and tend to self-destruct?

6. How can a kinked demand curve help explain price stickiness in an oligopolistic setting?

7. "Even if there are few firms in a market, the power of these firms to charge high prices will be limited if markets are contestable." Why is free and easy exit as important to contestable markets as free and easy entry?

8. What is the maximin criterion for choosing among strategies in a game theory setting?

9. Why is reputation an important element in repeated games?

Limiting Market Power: Regulation and Antitrust

13

Important Terms and Concepts

Economies of scale

Monopoly power

Antitrust policy

Concentration of industry

Concentration ratios

Herfindal-Hirschman index

Predatory pricing

Bundling

Regulation

Economies of scope

Cross-subsidization

Price cap

Learning Objectives

After completing this chapter, you should be able to:

- explain why monopoly power is undesirable.

- analyze how the various antitrust laws help in protecting competition.

- describe how concentration ratios are calculated and how, in the United States, they have changed.

- describe how concentration may or may not be related to market power.

- describe what is meant by predatory pricing and how one might identify it.

- explain how antitrust laws can be used to thwart competition.

- describe the major purposes of regulation.

- discuss arguments for and against bigness per se.

- evaluate the arguments supporting regulation.

- explain why marginal cost pricing may be infeasible in an industry with significant economies of scale.

- explain why allowing a firm to earn profits equal to the opportunity cost of its capital provides little incentive for increased efficiency.

- summarize recent experience under deregulation of several industries.

CHAPTER REVIEW

Economists and others have long argued whether bigness per se is good or bad. Opponents contend that the flow of wealth to firms with significant market power is socially undesirable and should be restrained. Profit-
(1) maximizing monopolists are likely to lead to a misallocation of resources as they produce (less/more) output than is socially desirable, and large firms with significant market power have (less/more) inducement for innovation.

(2) Proponents counter that large firms are necessary for successful innovation. They maintain that many big firms, because of (increasing/decreasing) returns to scale, can yield benefits to the public as a result of the associated (reduction/increase) in unit cost that accompanies large-scale production. To break up these firms into smaller units would (increase/decrease) costs. The United States has chosen to deal with potential monopolies through the use of regulation and antitrust policy.

ANTITRUST POLICY

Antitrust policy is designed to control the growth of monopolies and prevent undesirable behavior from powerful firms. Reducing your price to destroy your rivals and become a monopolist is
(3) called _____ _____. Economists argue that a price below average cost (is/is not) by itself evidence of predatory pricing. Remember that setting price below average cost may maximize profits by minimizing losses. Only if price is below marginal or average _____ cost might there be evidence of predatory pricing. Even then the courts have held that there must be evidence that such prices were adopted to harm rival firms and that the predatory firm could subsequently raise prices to monopoly levels.

There is no perfect measure of how concentrated an industry is. One widely used gauge looks at the percent of industry output accounted for by the four largest firms. This measure is called a four-firm
(4) _____ ratio. The _____ - _____ index gives greater weight to large firms by squaring and summing the market share of firms. In this century, concentration ratios in the United States have shown (much/little) change.

REGULATION

Regulatory procedures have been adopted for several reasons including:

(5)   A. To regulate the actions of natural monopolies in industries where economies of _____ and economies of _____ mean that free competition between a large number of suppliers (is/is not) sustainable.

B. To ensure service at reasonable prices to isolated areas. It is argued that regulation is necessary so that suppliers can offset (<u>above/below</u>)-cost prices in isolated areas with (<u>above/below</u>)-cost prices elsewhere and thus be protected from competitors who concentrate only on the profitable markets.

Regulation of prices is a very complicated undertaking. Established to prevent abuses of monopoly such as charging prices that are "too high," the regulatory agencies have, in many cases, actually raised prices. In these cases, regulation preserves the shadow of competition only by protecting (<u>high/low</u>)-cost, inefficient firms. (6) Economists typically argue for the use of marginal cost as a more appropriate basis for regulated prices.

The application of marginal cost pricing is difficult in an industry with significant economies of scale. In this case, average cost will (<u>decline/increase</u>) as output increases. When average cost declines, marginal cost is (7) (<u>greater/less</u>) than average cost and setting price equal to marginal cost will mean (<u>losses/profits</u>).

Sometimes regulation limits overall profitability rather than prices. For example, a firm's rate of return might be limited to 10 percent. While rate of return regulation might seem to limit the ability of firms to exercise monopoly power, it also (<u>enhances/reduces</u>) the incentive for firms to be efficient. In the absence of profit regula- (8) tion, successful efforts to reduce costs will be rewarded with higher profits. If profits are regulated, there is less incentive to seek out the most efficient means of production. To solve this problem, some advocate the use of price ceilings that decline over time and leave firms free to earn higher profits through even greater efficiency. Experience with deregulation, especially in airline, transportation, and telephone service, is now close to two decades old, and a number of trends have emerged.

a. Adjusted for inflation, prices have generally declined.

b. Local airline service has not suffered, as was feared, due to the establishment of specialized commuter airlines.

c. New firms have entered previously regulated industries, although not all have survived.

d. Unions in previously regulated industries have been under significant pressure to reduce wages and adjust work rules.

e. Some have argued that product quality has declined while others argue that consumers prefer lower prices.

f. In industries like airlines there is a legitimate concern about safety, but evidence to date shows no adverse impact.

165

IMPORTANT TERMS AND CONCEPTS QUIZ

Choose the most appropriate definition for each of the following terms.

1. _____ Economies of scale
2. _____ Monopoly power
3. _____ Antitrust policy
4. _____ Concentration of industry
5. _____ Concentration ratios
6. _____ Herfindahl-Hirschman Index
7. _____ Predatory pricing
8. _____ Bundling
9. _____ Regulation
10. _____ Economies of scope
11. _____ Cross-subsidization
12. _____ Price cap

a. Losses on one product balanced by profits on another
b. Discounts to customers who buy a set of products as a group
c. Legal restrictions or controls on business decisions of firms
d. Pricing to destroy rivals
e. Ability of a firm to affect the price of its output for its own benefit
f. Sum of the square of market share for firms within an industry
g. Percentage of an industry's output produced by the largest firms
h. Temporary monopoly for the initial use of an innovation
i. Pre-assigned price ceilings that decline in anticipation of future productivity growth
j. Savings acquired through simultaneous production of different products
k. Policies designed to control growth of monopoly and to prevent powerful firms from engaging in "anti-competitive" practices
l. Savings acquired through increases in quantities produced
m. Share of the total sales or assets of the industry in the hands of its largest firms.

BASIC EXERCISES

1. **Economies of Scale**

This exercise illustrates the difficulty of marginal cost pricing when average cost declines.

Imagine that the efficient provision of telephone calls in a medium-sized city involves an initial investment of $100 million financed by borrowing at 6.00 percent and variable cost of 5 cents a phone call. The phone company's annual fixed cost would be $6.0 million (6.00 percent of $100 million).
a. Use this information about costs to plot marginal cost and average total cost in **Figure 13-1.** (Use the $6.00 million figure for annual fixed cost.)
b. Assume that regulators set price at 5 cents, the level of marginal cost. What is the firm's profit position if 60 million calls a year are demanded at that price? 90 million? 150 million?
c. Is setting price equal to marginal cost a viable option in this case? Why or why not?

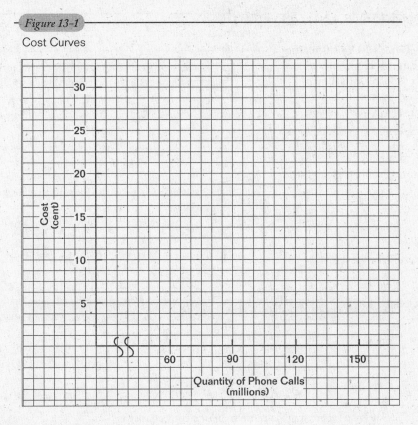

Figure 13-1

Cost Curves

2. Predatory Pricing

Michelle owns a company that manufactures Yuk, a gooey substance that drips down the wall in a horrible mess but can be peeled off without damaging paint or wallpaper. While Michelle thought that Yuk would appeal to grade school children, she has found that her strongest market is college students. Michelle is concerned about plans by a rival firm to introduce Splat, a similar product. Yuk can be produced with a fixed cost of $50,000 and a variable cost of 75¢ a pound. Michelle hopes to produce and sell 100,000 pounds of Yuk at an average cost of $1.25 a pound.

a. If average variable cost is taken as an indicator of predatory pricing, how far could Michelle lower her price without fear of losing a court case over possible predatory pricing?

b. As argued in Chapter 7, while it can be "profitable" for firms to continue production even if price is less than average cost, once price has dropped below average variable cost, the firm would be better off shutting down production. The discussion in this chapter suggested that predatory pricing requires a firm to set price below average variable cost. How can it ever be in Michelle's or any company's interest to sell at a price below average variable cost?

3. **Concentration Ratios**

Complete **Table 13-1** by calculating the four-firm concentration ratio and the Herfindahl-Hirschman index for each industry. Do the rankings always agree? Can you explain why they differ? Which industry do you think shows the most concentration?

■ Table 13-1

Concentration Ratios

Firm	Market Share	Market Share	Market Share
A	50	22.5	75
B	10	22.5	5
C	10	22.5	5
D	10	22.5	5
E	10	5	5
F	10	5	5
Four-Firm Concentration Ratio	_____	_____	_____
Herfindahl-Hirshman Index	_____	_____	_____

SELF-TESTS FOR UNDERSTANDING

TEST A

Circle the most appropriate answer.

1. Antitrust policy seeks to (there may be more than one correct answer)
   a. force firms to set price equal to marginal cost.
   b. prevent the acquisition of monopoly power.
   c. limit the maximum market share of firms to 25 percent.
   d. ban anticompetitive practices.

2. Monopoly power is undesirable because (there may be more than one correct answer)
   a. monopolists face less pressure to innovate than competitive firms.
   b. monopoly prices have adverse impacts on the distribution of wealth.
   c. monopolies will set price equal to marginal cost.
   d. prices charged by monopolists typically result in a misallocation of resources.

3. Antitrust policy should be most concerned with industries where (there may be more than one correct answer)
   a. there are substantial economies of scale.
   b. entry is cheap and easy.
   c. the Herfindahl-Hirschman index is low.
   d. entry requires significant upfront fixed costs.

4. Regulations that limit market power and economic behavior affect industries producing about _____ percent of GDP.
   a. 5
   b. 10
   c. 25
   d. 40

5. Which of the following is an example of economies of scale?
   a. Anna finds her costs increasing as she tries to increase the production of her custom designed clothes.
   b. Jim discovers that a 15 percent reduction in price leads to a 30 percent increase in sales.
   c. Sarah realizes that her firm's expertise and experience in producing specialized medical equipment will be useful in the production of testing equipment for physicists.
   d. Intel is able to reduce unit costs when it doubles production of computer chips.

6. Which of the following is an example of economies of scope?
   a. An increase in circulation for the Daily Planet would involve only printing costs and require no increase in the editorial staff.
   b. Ramona and Ricardo have invested their wealth in a portfolio of stocks, bonds, and real estate.
   c. In an effort to keep production lines busy all year, Arctic Enterprises produces a variety of small-engine home and garden tools in addition to its successful line of snowblowers.
   d. AT&T used profits from long-distance calls to reduce monthly charges for local phone service.

7. Significant economies of scale and economies of scope are examples of a
   a. nationalized industry.
   b. natural monopoly.
   c. regulated industry.
   d. competitive industry.

8. Regulation that sets prices at a level that just covers costs and allows for a fair rate of return
   a. provides a strong incentive for efficiency and innovation.
   b. provides little incentive for efficiency and innovation.

9. The term cross-subsidy refers to
   a. an angry firm that does not receive a subsidy.
   b. higher prices on some products/services that help to cover costs on other products/services.
   c. congressional subsidies for agriculture.
   d. the financing of Christian churches.

10. Regulation has promoted cross-subsidization as a way of
    a. dealing with universal service to isolated, high-cost locations.
    b. protecting the economy.
    c. promoting efficiencies from synergetic business combinations.
    d. addressing the effects of self-destructive competition.

11. If regulators want existing firms to engage in extensive cross-subsidization they
    a. should encourage entry of new firms.
    b. will need to pursue privatization as a long-run strategy.
    c. will need to restrict entry.
    d. prevent firms from taking advantage of economies of scale.

12. Marginal cost pricing is not feasible in industries characterized by
    a. an elastic demand curve.
    b. constant returns to scale.
    c. rising average costs.
    d. significant economies of scale.

13. Concerns about marginal cost pricing in industries with significant economies of scale arises because
    a. demand is typically inelastic.
    b. marginal cost will be below average cost.
    c. fixed costs are likely to be small.
    d. average revenue declines as firms try to sell more.

14. The term price caps refers to
    a. price floors.
    b. price ceilings that decline in anticipation of future efficiencies.
    c. limits on a firm's overall profits.
    d. attempts to control inflationary increases in prices.

15. To serve customers, competitors must sometimes share a common facility, often owned by one of the competitors. This common facility is called a(n)
    a. essential link.
    b. keystone facility.
    c. marginal unit.
    d. bottleneck facility.

16. If a firm lowers its price below average variable cost to drive out rivals, it is said to be engaging in
    a. predatory pricing.
    b. price discrimination.
    c. tying contracts.
    d. tacit collusion.

17. If an industry is composed of ten firms, each the same size, then the four-firm concentration ratio would be
    a. 4.
    b. 10.
    c. 40.
    d. 100.

18. In the case of a pure monopoly the Herfindahl-Hirschman index would be
    a. 100.
    b. 1,000.
    c. 10,000.
    d. 100,000.

19. Deregulation of the airline industry in the United States has
    a. resulted in higher prices for airline tickets.
    b. led to widespread abandonment of service to smaller towns.
    c. depressed profits and wages in the airline industry.
    d. increased the monopoly power of established airlines like Delta and United.

20. Studies of concentration and market power conclude that
    a. any increase in concentration ratios tends to increase prices.
    b. contestable markets are the most susceptible to the exercise of market power.
    c. a strong correlation exists between concentration and the use of market power.
    d. whether increases in concentration will allow firms to exercise more market power depends upon whether other factors favor collusion.

TEST B

Circle T or F for true or false.

T F   1. Regulators are exclusively concerned with getting regulated industries to lower prices.

T F   2. The term economies of scope refers to the reduction in average costs that come from large-scale production.

T F   3. Fair-rate-of-return regulations—that is, price controls that allow firms in an industry to earn profits sufficient to cover the opportunity cost of their capital—offer strong incentives for efficiency and innovation.

T F   4. Setting price equal to marginal cost is not a viable strategy in industries subject to increasing returns to scale.

T F   5. In the absence of regulation, firms required to provide service to isolated communities at high cost might find their more profitable low-cost markets taken over by competitors through a process called cream skimming.

T F   6. If price is less than average cost, this is strong evidence of predatory pricing.

T F   7. Any price discount for buying a bundle of goods and services is strong evidence of anticompetitive behavior.

T F   8. Four-firm concentration ratios show a significant increase in concentration of American business during the last 100 years.

T F   9. Evidence clearly shows that any increase in concentration leads to an increase in market power.

T F 10. Research by economists suggests that only the largest firms can afford to engage in research and development.

SUPPLEMENTARY EXERCISE

The two lists in **Table 13-2** identify the 25 largest industrial firms in the United States in 1929 and 1955, ranked by assets. The list for 1955 comes from the first *Fortune*[1] list of the 500 largest industrial companies. The list for 1929 comes from work by two economists, Norman Collins and Lee Preston.[2]

See if you can list the largest firms today. Then look up the most recent list of the *Fortune* 500. It is usually in the May issue of *Fortune* and can be found on the Web at http://www.fortune.com. Beginning in 1995 the *Fortune* list was modified to include the 500 largest corporations, not just the 500 largest industrial corporations. Of the original 500 industrial firms included in the 1955 list, only 116 appear in the 1995 list. How many of the corporations listed in Table 13-2 are still in the top 25 or even the top 500? How many corporations have slipped in ranking? How many have gained?

In 1955 the companies listed in Table 13-2 had sales that totaled $46.8 billion. Their sales equaled 12 percent of GDP. What are comparable figures today?

Fortune also publishes a list of the 500 largest corporations in the world. How big are the biggest American firms when compared to their international competition?

Table 13-2

Largest Firms

1929	Rank	1955
U.S. Steel	1	Standard Oil (N.J.)
Standard Oil (N.J.)	2	General Motors
General Motors	3	U.S. Steel
Bethlehem Steel	4	Du Pont
Anaconda	5	Mobil Oil
Ford Motor Company	6	Standard Oil (Ind.)
Mobil Oil	7	Gulf Oil
Standard Oil (Ind.)	8	Texaco
Gulf Oil	9	General Electric
Shell Oil	10	Standard Oil (Cal.)
Texaco	11	Bethlehem Steel
Standard Oil (Cal.)	12	Westinghouse
Du Pont	13	Union Carbide
General Electric	14	Sinclair Oil
Armour	15	Phillips Petroleum
Sinclair Oil	16	Western Electric
Allied Chemical	17	Cities Service
International Harvester	18	Shell Oil
Western Electric	19	Chrysler
Union Oil	20	International Harvester
Union Carbide	21	Alcoa
Swift	22	Anaconda
Kennecott Copper	23	American Tobacco
International Paper	24	Republic Steel
Republic Steel	25	Kennecott Copper

ECONOMICS IN ACTION

PREDATORY PRICING

In May 1999 the federal government filed an antitrust suit accusing American Airlines of engaging in predatory pricing. The Justice Department reported, after an 18-month investigation, that company documents titled "Dallas-Ft. Worth Low Cost Carriers Strategy," showed that American had deliberately incurred short-term losses to eliminate three low-cost competitors—Vanguard Airlines, Sun Jet International, and Western Pacific—from the Dallas-Fort Worth airport. The Justice Department suit cited internal memos that said American "would like to 'drive [Vanguard] from the market' and 'get [Western Pacific] out.'"

172

According to Joel Klein, head of the Justice Department's antitrust division, "American adopted a predatory responsive strategy, saturating the market in which the start-up carriers had begun service with as much new, low-fare service of its own as was necessary to drive out the start-ups." In announcing the suit, the Justice Department released the following data, which they said illustrated how American Airlines implemented a policy of predatory pricing.

	Colorado Springs	Kansas City	Wichita, KA
Average nonstop one-way fare			
Before competition	$158	$113	$110
With competition	$88	$83	$57
Post-competition	$133	$125	$96
Average number of passengers per month			
Before competition	3,723	22,423	4,465
With competition	19,909	31,228	11,246
Post-competition	9,237	23,460	8,540

American, which controls about 70 percent of scheduled seats out of Dallas-Fort Worth, was willing to risk losing money to drive out the three actual competitors and to discourage future potential competitors. According to the Justice Department, American's dominant position at the airport would allow it to earn back any losses by exercising market power.

American Airlines officials rejected the argument that it had engaged in predatory pricing or flooded the market with extra flights. They called the suit sour grapes on the part of airlines that had been unable to compete successfully and said there was nothing illegal about "tough talk." Spokesperson Chris Chiames argued that American simply matched the competition with regard to price and added flights when the lower prices attracted additional customers. "It would have a chilling effect on the marketplace if companies felt they could not match prices of competitors," said Chiames.

A major issue is whether the new prices were below variable cost. American asserted they were not while the Justice Department argued that they were below American's established measures of acceptable profits and thus predatory.

Seasoned court observers said it would be difficult for the government to win its case, citing a 1986 decision in which the Supreme Court said, "Cutting prices in order to increase business often is the very essence of competition." Mistaken conclusions of predatory pricing "chill the very conduct the antitrust laws are designed to protect."

1. Has the government proven that American priced flights below cost and that American had plausible means for recouping losses? Or is American right and is the lawsuit just a way for competitors to win in court what they could not win in the marketplace?

Sources: Stephen Labaton and Laurence Zuckerman, "Airline is Accused of Illegal Pricing: U.S. Says American Was Trying to Drive Out Competitors," *The New York Times*, May 14, 1999. Laurence Zuckerman, "Airline Suit: 70's Revival in Antitrust," *The New York Times*, May 15, 1999. Anna Wilde Matthews and Scott McCartney, "U.S. Sues American Air in Antitrust Case," *The Wall Street Journal*, May 14, 1999; Keith L. Alexander, "American Airlines Ruling Appealed," *The Washington Post*, January 17, 2002.

STUDY QUESTIONS

1. What is the difference between economies of scale and economies of scope?

2. Why do regulators often work to increase rather than limit prices?

3. Why does the text say that not all big firms have monopoly power?

4. What is meant by the term cross-subsidy?

5. Why aren't prices based on marginal cost a feasible alternative in cases of natural monopolies arising from economies of scale?

6. How do price caps provide an incentive for efficiency?

7. What is your evaluation of the American experience with deregulation?

8. Why regulate at all? Why not let the free market work without regulation?

9. How are concentration ratios measured?

10. Has American business become more or less concentrated over the last 50 years? 100 years?

11. What does the evidence suggest about increasing concentration and the use of market power?

12. Consider antitrust policy that divided the largest firms whenever the four-firm concentration ratio in any industry exceeded 50 percent. Would such a policy be good for the country? Why or why not?

13. Should American antitrust laws include an explicit exclusion for cooperative research and development activities? Why?

14. How effective do you believe American antitrust laws have been?

ECONOMICS ONLINE

The Antitrust Division of the U.S. Department of Justice maintains its own homepage.

http://www.usdoj.gov/atr

Concentration ratios for many industries from the 1997 as well as the 2002 Economic Census are posted at this site. Concentration ratios are calculated for the largest 4, 8, 20, and 50 companies. Information from the 2007 Economic Census is scheduled to be posted during 2009 and 2010.

http://www.census.gov/epcd/www/concentration.html

ECONOMICS IN ACTION

In June 2001, the Justice department's case was dismissed by Judge J. Thomas Marten who said, "There is no doubt that American may be a difficult, vigorous, even brutal competitor, but here, it engaged only in bare, but not brass, knuckle competition." In January 2002, the Justice Department appealed.

The government lost its appeal.

The Case for Free Markets: The Price System

14

Important Terms and Concepts

Efficient allocation of resources	Input-output analysis	Producer's surplus
Laissez-faire	Consumer's surplus	

Learning Objectives

After completing this chapter, you should be able to:

- explain the difference between an efficient and inefficient allocation of resources.

- explain how competitive markets, in which all producers and consumers respond to common market prices, can allocate resources efficiently.

- describe situations in which price increases may be in society's best interest.

- list the three coordination tasks that must be solved by any system of resource allocation.

- explain input-output analysis and the near impossibility of central planning.

- explain how prices play a critical role in determining both the allocation of resources and the distribution of income.

- explain how competitive markets maximize the sum of consumer's surplus plus producer's surplus.

- use marginal analysis to show how perfect competition achieves optimal output.

- describe the conditions under which an inefficient allocation of resources might be preferred to an efficient allocation.

CHAPTER REVIEW

This chapter discusses how prices work to allocate resources and how they affect the efficiency of the economy. In particular, it is shown that in a competitive economy, the self-serving actions of utility-maximizing individuals and profit-maximizing firms can lead to an efficient allocation of the economy's resources. The complete, rigorous proof of this proposition is usually discussed only in graduate courses in economic theory and involves the use of some fairly advanced mathematics. This chapter offers a simpler introduction to this material.

The efficiency implications of a laissez-faire, competitive economy are important reasons why economists have great respect for the workings of the price system. But the proof of this abstract proposition is not a proof that we should dismantle the government and that all markets should be unregulated. The proposition refers to

(1) the efficiency of a perfectly competitive economy. Many aspects of the American economy (are/are not) consistent with the requirements for a competitive economy. The implications of these real-world imperfections are an important part of Chapters 15 through 21. Also, efficiency is not the only way to judge the workings of an economy. Notions of fairness, or equity, are also important and may at times lead to a preference for less efficient, but fairer, nonmarket procedures.

Sometimes proposals to change prices for efficiency reasons are opposed because of their potentially adverse impact on a particular group. For example, higher taxes on energy to foster conservation and the development of alternative energy sources to reduce our dependence on foreign energy are often opposed because it is believed they will increase the cost of living for poor households. These equity considerations are an important part of any final decision. However, many economists argue that it is preferable to address the issue of income distribution through general taxes or transfers rather than by limiting changes in prices that promote efficiency. For example, changes in income tax credits, personal exemptions, or the standard deduction could be used to provide protection to lower income households while letting higher energy prices provide an incentive for all households, rich and poor, to reduce their use of energy.

(2)   All economies must answer three questions. First is the question of output _____: How much of each type of good and service should be produced? Next, there is the question of production _____: How should various productive inputs be allocated among the millions of firms and plants in order to meet the original output decisions? Finally, there is the question of the _____ of goods and services: How are the available goods and services to be divided among consumers? How do we evaluate the job that an economy does in answering these questions? Economists typically use two yardsticks: efficiency and equity. This chapter concentrates on efficiency.

Economic efficiency is an important but relatively abstract concept. If by redistributing the commodities that are produced we can make everyone better off in his or her own estimation, we would say that the initial alloca-

(3) tion of commodities (was/was not) efficient. It is only when there are no more opportunities to make some individuals better off while not worsening the situation of others that economists would characterize the economy as _____.

There are usually many efficient allocations of resources. For example, each point on an economy's production possibilities frontier is (efficient/inefficient) in terms of the production of output. If an economy is operating on (4) this frontier, it is impossible to increase the output of one good without _____ the output of one or more other goods.

Let us consider in more detail how a competitive economy achieves efficiency in the selection of output. (The Supplementary Exercises to this chapter discuss efficiency in production and output distribution.) Efficiency in the selection of output requires that, for the quantity produced, the marginal utility of the last unit to consumers must equal the marginal cost of producers.

Why is this condition necessary for an efficient output selection? Remember that the definition of efficiency refers to consumers' evaluations of their own well-being, an evaluation that economists assume consumers are making when they maximize the difference between total utility and spending. If the marginal utility of some good exceeds the marginal cost of producing more units, then the production of at least one more unit of output will result in a net (increase/decrease) in consumer well-being. Consumers benefit by the increase in their utility (5) while the cost to society of additional production is given by the marginal _____. If marginal utility exceeds marginal cost, the benefit to consumers from increased production will be (greater/less) than the cost to society, and the initial output selection (is/is not) efficient. It is only when marginal utility (exceeds/equals/is less than) marginal cost that there are no more opportunities for net gains.

It is one of the beauties of a competitive economy that utility-maximizing individuals and profit-maximizing firms will, while pursuing their own self-interests, make decisions that result in marginal utility being equal to marginal cost. Our optimal purchase rule of Chapter 5 showed that utility-maximizing consumers will purchase additional units until the marginal utility of the last unit consumed equals the _____ of the (6) commodity. The discussion in Chapter 8 showed that profit-maximizing firms will equate marginal revenue and _____ _____. The discussion in Chapter 10 showed that for a firm under perfect competition, marginal revenue is equal to _____. Thus a profit-maximizing firm under perfect competition, producing where marginal cost equals marginal revenue, will be producing where the marginal cost of the last unit produced equals the _____ of the commodity.

To summarize, utility-maximizing consumers set marginal _____ equal to price, and prof- (7) it-maximizing competitive firms set marginal _____ equal to price. The result is that marginal utility (exceeds/equals/is less than) marginal cost, our condition for efficiency in the selection of output.

Consumer's surplus is the difference between the maximum amount a consumer would be willing to pay for an item and the market price she has to pay. Any consumer who is unwilling to pay the market price does not and receives no consumer surplus. Producer's surplus is the difference between the market price and the lowest price at which a supplier would be willing to supply the item. The virtue of competitive market prices determined by the intersection of the demand and supply curves is that this price and the resulting quantity (maximize/minimize) the sum of consumer's and producer's surplus. (8)

A centrally planned economy would attempt to answer the three basic questions of output selection, production planning, and product distribution by direct decree, without the use of prices. Often in these economies, decisions about output selection were made with little attention to individual consumer preferences. More weight was typically given to the planners' preferences for such things as increased production of steel and electricity, although periodic newspaper accounts of a readjustment of production goals in response to consumer unrest and the final collapse of central planning in Eastern Europe and the former Soviet Union showed that even planners cannot forget entirely about consumers.

Once decisions about output levels have been made, a central planner must be sure that productive inputs are allocated to ensure that the production goals can in fact be achieved. One type of analysis that takes account
(9) of the interindustry flows of inputs necessary for the production of goods for final use is _____ - _____ analysis. A major limitation of this type of analysis is the enormity and complexity of the required information. It is a major conceptual advantage that the price system in a competitive economy does not require that this information be centralized.

IMPORTANT TERMS AND CONCEPTS QUIZ

Choose the best definition for each of the following terms.

1. _____ Efficient allocation of resources
2. _____ Laissez-faire
3. _____ Input-output analysis
4. _____ Consumer's surplus
5. _____ Producer's surplus

a. Situation in which one person's welfare can be improved without injury to anyone else
b. Technique of simultaneously solving equations that link necessary inputs to output for all industries
c. Situation that takes advantage of every opportunity to make some individuals better off without harming others
d. Difference between what a consumer would pay and must pay
e. Minimal interference with the workings of the free market
f. Difference between what a firm gets from selling at the market price and what it would accept

BASIC EXERCISE

This problem is designed to illustrate the logic of the rule for efficiency in output selection.
Discussion in the chapter indicated that efficiency in the selection of output requires marginal utility to equal marginal cost for all commodities. If not, it is possible, by changing the selection of output, to improve consumers' well-being.

Consider an economy's production of shirts. Assume that at the current level of shirt output, the marginal utility of shirts is $25 and the marginal cost is $15.

1. The production of one more shirt will increase total utility by $ _____. The production of one more shirt will cost society $ _____.

2. In Chapter 5 we saw that utility-maximizing consumers will maximize the difference between total utility and total spending. This difference equals the money value of their well-being. Looking at the change in utility and assuming that the price of shirts is equal to their marginal cost of $15, we can see that the production of one more shirt will increase consumer well-being by $ _____. Efficiency in the production of shirts requires (<u>more/fewer</u>) shirts.

3. What if the marginal utility of an additional shirt is $15 and the marginal cost is $18? Then the production of an additional shirt will (<u>increase/decrease</u>) consumer well-being by $ _____ and efficiency in the production of shirts will call for (<u>more/fewer</u>) shirts.

4. If the marginal cost of additional shirts is constant at $18, then in order that there be no opportunity for a change in the production of shirts to increase consumer well-being, enough shirts should be produced so that the marginal utility of an additional shirt is $ _____.

SELF-TESTS FOR UNDERSTANDING

TEST A

Circle the most appropriate answer.

1. For any economy that uses the price system, which of the following is not necessarily true?
   a. Prices play an important role in shaping the allocation of resources.
   b. Prices play an important role in shaping the distribution of income and wealth.
   c. Prices will reflect consumer preference and income.
   d. Prices of necessities will be low, and prices of luxuries will be high.

2. The price system distributes goods and services on the basis of income and
   a. scarcity.
   b. consumer preferences.
   c. education.
   d. planner preferences.

3. The three basic coordination tasks for resource allocation that economies may solve by markets or planning include all but which one of the following?
   a. the distribution of output among consumers
   b. how much of different goods to produce
   c. the allocation of available resources to the production of different goods
   d. the amount of money that the government will print

4. The use of prices to allocate goods among consumers means that
   a. all consumers will be able to buy an equal share of all outputs.
   b. the resulting allocation must necessarily be inefficient.
   c. wealthy consumers will be able to command a greater amount of output.
   d. there must be persistent inflation in order to choke off consumer excess demand.

181

5. Prices in competitive markets affect all but which one of the following?
   a. the allocation of inputs among competing producers
   b. the allocation of output among consumers
   c. the distribution of income
   d. the location of the production possibilities frontier

Figure 14-1

Production Possibilities Frontier

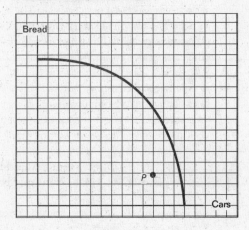

6. Consider the production possibilities frontier shown in **Figure 14-1**. Efficiency in production is given by
   a. all of the points inside the frontier.
   b. all of the points on or inside the frontier.
   c. all of the points on the frontier.
   d. the point of equal output of all goods.

7. Consider production at point P in Figure 14-1. If the economy produces at point P, one would say that output selection is
   a. efficient.
   b. inefficient.
   c. efficient or inefficient depending upon consumers' preferences.

8. Under conditions of perfect competition, firms will choose to produce the quantity of output such that
   a. MC = AC.
   b. MU = total utility.
   c. MC = P.
   d. AC = P.

9. In competitive markets consumers will demand particular commodities up to the point where
   a. MU = MC.
   b. MU = P.
   c. MC = P.
   d. MU = 0.

10. The condition for optimal output selection is
    a. MC = P.
    b. MC = MU.
    c. MRP = P.
    d. MU = P.

11. Competitive markets can meet the criterion for efficiency in production planning
    a. through the use of input-output tables.
    b. only after Congress approves the president's budget proposal.
    c. automatically.
    d. less efficiently than centrally planned economies.

12. If the marginal utility of color television sets is $300 and the marginal cost is $200, then efficiency in output selection requires that the production of color television sets should
    a. increase.
    b. decrease.
    c. neither increase nor decrease.

13. The change in the production of color television sets from question 12 will likely
    a. increase marginal cost and marginal utility.
    b. increase marginal cost and decrease marginal utility.
    c. decrease marginal cost and marginal utility.
    d. decrease marginal cost and increase marginal utility.

14. An efficient allocation of resources
    a. will always be fair.
    b. is the best allocation possible.
    c. means the economy is operating somewhere on its production opportunity frontier.
    d. is always better than an inefficient allocation.

15. Leon does not now own a motorcycle. He would pay up to $2,000 for one. Motorcycles produced by competitive firms in long-run equilibrium, earning zero economic profit, cost $4,000 to produce. Which of the following is false?
    a. Leon is not likely to buy a motorcycle.
    b. Since Leon's marginal utility is less than the marginal cost of production, there would be a social gain if direct government controls reduced the price of motorcycles.
    c. The marginal utility of a motorcycle to someone must be at least $4,000.

16. If resources have been allocated in a way that meets the requirements of economic efficiency, then we know that
    a. output is being produced in accordance with the preferences of the Council of Economic Advisers.
    b. production occurs at a point inside the economy's production possibilities frontier.
    c. there is no reallocation of resources that can make some individuals better off without making others worse off.
    d. the marginal cost of producing every commodity has been minimized.

TEST B

Circle T or F for true or false.

T F 1. The term laissez-faire refers to an economy with minimal economic regulation by government.

T F 2. If resources are being allocated efficiently, we know that there is no better allocation possible.

T F 3. Efficient resource allocation always requires the intervention of a central planner to set prices correctly.

T F 4. Efficiency in the selection of output requires that the marginal utility of every commodity be equal to its marginal cost.

T F 5. An unregulated competitive economy is incapable of achieving appropriate efficiency conditions for all commodities.

183

T F   6. Input-output analysis is a mathematical tool to aid in the distribution of output among consumers without using the price system.

T F   7. Charging higher prices on public transportation during rush hours can be an example of using the price system to increase efficiency.

T F   8. Considerations of fairness may sometimes lead a society to prefer an inefficient allocation to an efficient one.

T F   9. Efficiency in the distribution of goods implies that everyone will get an equal share of all goods.

T F 10. Competitive markets promote efficiency in output selection because both firms and consumers respond to the same price.

SUPPLEMENTARY EXERCISES

The first two exercises illustrate the implications of the rules for efficiency in the allocation of output among consumers and in the allocation of productive inputs.

1. **Efficiency in the Distribution of Output Among Consumers**

    The rule for efficiency in the distribution of output among consumers is that for every commodity every consumer must have the same marginal utility. If not, it would be possible to redistribute output among consumers in a way that makes at least one person better off without harming anyone else.

    Imagine that Todd and Nicole both consume steaks and pizzas. The initial allocation of steak and pizza has resulted in the following marginal utilities:

	Marginal Utility	
	Todd	Nicole
Steaks	$ 9.00	$ 6.00
Pizza	4.00	4.00

   a. Is the condition for efficiency in the distribution of output satisfied? _____ If not, there should be some, possibly many, reallocations of output that will increase either Todd's or Nicole's total utility (or both) without reducing total utility for the other.

   b. Imagine that Nicole gives Todd one steak in exchange for two pizzas. On net, considering the full effects of the trade, what is the change in Todd's utility? (increase/decrease) $ _____ Nicole's utility? (increase/decrease) $ _____ An implication of the utility changes of the reallocation is that the initial allocation was (efficient/inefficient).

   c. How do competitive markets work to ensure that uncoordinated individual demands will satisfy the condition for efficiency in the distribution of output among consumers?

2. **Efficiency in Production Planning**

    The rule for efficiency in Production Planning says that if two inputs, labor and land, are both used to produce two outputs, then inputs should be assigned to each output until the ratio of marginal physical product for two inputs is the same in all uses. If not, it will be possible to reallocate resources and increase the production of at least one commodity without decreasing the production of other commodities.

a. We know from Chapter 8 that this condition will be automatically satisfied under perfect competition for profit-maximizing firms that buy inputs at given prices. Perhaps less clear is that if this condition is not satisfied, then it would be possible to reallocate inputs among firms and produce more total output— with the same quantity of inputs. Consider the following table showing the initial marginal physical products of land and labor in the production of corn and tomatoes. Note that the ratio of marginal physical products in the production of corn (120/40) is less than the ratio in the production of tomatoes (1,200/200).

Marginal Physical Product of Labor and Land in the Production of Corn and Tomatoes

	Corn (bushels)	Tomatoes (pounds)
Labor (person)	120	1,200
Land (acre)	40	200

Consider the reallocation of one worker from corn production to tomato production. As a result of this reallocation of labor, the production of corn will fall by _____ bushels and the production of tomatoes will rise by _____ pounds. Now consider moving four acres of land from tomato production to corn production. As a result of the reallocation of land, the production of corn will rise by _____ bushels and the production of tomatoes will fall by _____ pounds. Counting the reallocation of both land and labor, the production of corn changes by _____ bushels and the production of tomatoes changes by _____ pounds.

b. How do competitive markets work to ensure that the uncoordinated decisions of firms satisfy the condition for efficiency in the allocation of productive inputs?

Efficiency in the selection of inputs helps to achieve efficiency in the choice of outputs. We have seen that efficiency in the selection of outputs requires that MU = MC. In competitive markets, MU = MC because utility-maximizing individuals see to it that MU = P. The discussion below shows how efficiency in the selection of inputs helps to ensure that competitive firms produce where MC = P.

We saw in Chapter 6 that our rule for optimal use of inputs could also be expressed in terms of marginal revenue product. Using symbols, our optimal input rule says

$$P_Q \times MPP_X = P_X$$

where P_Q is the product price, P_X is the input price, and MPP_X is the marginal physical product of input X in the production of Q. If we divide both sides of the equation by MPP_X we get

$$P_Q = P_X/MPP_X$$

Note that P_X/MPP_X is the marginal cost of producing more output by using more of input X. If we buy one more unit of input X, we spend P_X and get MPP_X more units of output at a cost of P_X/MPP_X per unit of additional output. A profit-maximizing firm will use the optimal input rule for all its inputs. Thus, the marginal cost of an output expansion by the use of any single input, of the many that a firm may use, will be equal to the marginal cost from the additional use of any other input.

3. You can look up information about the most recent input-output table for the U.S. economy on the Web at http://www.bea.gov/industry/io_annual.htm. The most detailed input-output tables, the

benchmark tables are organized with information for almost 500 industries. These tables are available for 1982, 1987, 1992, and 1997 to 2002.

There are several input-output tables. One table indicates which industries use which commodities. Another table indicates which industries produce which commodities. The table of direct requirements shows what direct inputs are necessary per unit of output of each industry. The table of direct and indirect requirements solves all the input-output relationships and shows how the output of every industry must adjust in order to increase the output of any one industry. It is this table that takes into account such indirect requirements as increased electricity to make more steel in order to increase the output of cars.

a. How many separate pieces of information do these input-output tables contain? How long do you think it would take you to solve all the interrelationships and produce a table of direct and indirect requirements without the help of a computer?

b. Which industries produce mainly for final uses and which produce mainly intermediate outputs, that is, inputs for other industries?

c. You can find input-output information on the web as far back as the 1982 benchmark tables. Pick one or two favorite industries and see how total and direct requirements from the most recent input-output table have changed over time.

d. If you are a planner concerned with the year 2012, how would you determine what input-output requirements are relevant?

ECONOMICS IN ACTION

HI-HO, HI-HO, IT'S OFF TO WORK WE GO

It's not only bridges that get congested. On Sunday morning, additional cars do not seem to interfere with the traffic flow on most urban highway systems, but on Monday morning or Friday afternoon each additional driver adds to congestion, makes every other driver's commute take longer, and seems to turn many highways into linear parking lots.

The highway and road systems of most large cities seem to be a clear case of too many vehicles and too few roads. Yet building more roads seems only to increase the traffic without solving the problem. Economist Kenneth A. Small, writing in *The Brookings Review,* talks of a reservoir of potential drivers, deterred from driving by existing congestion, who quickly fill up new roads as they are completed. Small is skeptical that policies such as campaigns to promote ride-sharing, mass transit, staggered work hours, or high-occupancy-vehicle lanes will have more than a temporary impact on urban congestion. Are there market mechanisms that would improve the situation? Small believes there are, specifically congestion pricing— "charging motorists a very high premium for using the most popular roads during peak hours."

Small argues that congestion pricing provides an incentive for drivers to consider alternative routes, alternative times, and/or alternative means of transportation. The other policies listed above focus on only a subset of travelers while providing no incentive for the vast majority of drivers to change their behavior. While no one likes paying tolls, not many of us like being stuck in traffic, either.

186

To be successful, Small argues that congestion pricing must impose tolls that vary widely by time of day and are sufficiently high at peak demand to have a measurable impact. Although not its primary purpose, Small believes congestion pricing also would improve air quality by reducing both the volume of traffic and the higher emissions associated with congestion.

Small is concerned that congestion prices might be a burden for lower income families and argues that a portion of the revenues collected should be used in ways that benefit low-income households. He proposed using one-third for reimbursements to travelers through an employee commuting allowance and fuel tax reduction; another third for reductions of the portion of sales and property taxes that subsidize highways and transportation; and the remaining third for improvements to transportation services, including mass transit and critical highway projects.

1. What is your evaluation of Small's proposal?

2. The Orange County Express Lanes described in this chapter of the text are a form of congestion pricing. Why do you think there are not more examples?

3. Would you be willing to pay $1 to save thirty minutes in traffic? Would you be willing to pay $6.75?

Source: Kenneth A. Small, "Urban Traffic Congestion: A New Approach to the Gordian Knot," *Brookings Review,* Spring 1993, pp. 6–11.

STUDY QUESTIONS

1. What are the three coordination tasks that must be solved by any system of resource allocation?

2. Why is the determination of efficient allocations a largely technical exercise with many potential solutions rather than a method for determining the best allocation for the economy?

3. Why isn't point P in Figure 14-1 an example of efficiency in output selection? Starting at point P, show what other possible points of production dominate point P in terms of efficiency considerations. Is there only one such point or a set of points? If a set, how can there be more than one?

4. Is it ever possible that society would be better off with higher rather than lower prices? Explain.

5. Should an economy always prefer an efficient allocation to an inefficient allocation? Explain.

6. How can a price system (market mechanism) hope to solve the large number of coordination decisions that are included in the mathematics of an input-output table for the entire economy?

The Shortcomings of Free Markets

15

Important Terms and Concepts

Production possibilities frontier

Resource misallocation

Beneficial Externality

Detrimental Externality

Marginal social cost (MSC)

Marginal private cost (MPC)

Marginal social benefit (MSB)

Marginal private benefit (MPB)

Public good

Private good

Depletability

Excludability

Rent seeking

Moral hazard

Principals

Agents'

Stocks options

Cost disease of the personal services

Learning Objectives

After completing this chapter, you should be able to:

- list the major shortcomings of free markets.

- explain why detrimental externalities mean that marginal private costs will understate marginal social costs.

- explain why beneficial externalities mean that marginal private benefits will understate marginal social benefits.

- explain why the existence of externalities, whether beneficial or detrimental, will result in an inefficient allocation of resources.

- describe the important characteristics of public goods.

- explain why these characteristics mean that private profit-maximizing firms will not supply public goods.

- explain why some people believe that free markets are unlikely to result in an appropriate allocation of resources between the present and the future.

- explain when individuals or firms will engage in rent-seeking behavior.

- explain why insurance companies worry about moral hazard.

- explain why information might be asymmetric as between principals and agents, and why stock options have often been ineffective.

- explain how uneven productivity growth results in the cost disease of personal services.

CHAPTER REVIEW

This chapter lists seven issues often seen as shortcomings of unregulated markets. Some have been discussed in previous chapters, and several others will receive a more complete treatment in later chapters. The discussion here focuses on four of the seven: externalities, public goods, the trade-off between present and future consumption, and the cost disease of personal services.

Chapter 3 introduced the concept of an economy's *production possibilities frontier*. We saw that the slope of the frontier measured how much the output of one commodity must decrease in order to increase the production of another commodity. In other words, the slope of the production possibilities frontier measures the

(1) _____ cost of increasing the output of any one commodity.

Chapter 14 explained how a market economy can lead to an *efficient allocation of resources*, one where marginal utilities and marginal costs are equal. If the marginal utility of the last unit of some good is not equal to the marginal cost of producing that last unit, the result is a *misallocation of resources*. The virtue of competitive

(2) markets is that firms maximize profits by producing where price equals _____ _____ and individuals maximize by consuming where price equals _____ _____. Thus, our condition for an efficient allocation is automatically satisfied. An economy that satisfies all of the assumptions necessary for perfect competition will automatically result in an efficient allocation of resources. The economy will operate (on/inside) the production possibilities frontier.

For reasons mentioned at the beginning of the chapter the wrong prices may get established, leading to an inefficient allocation of resources. For example, if price is greater than marginal cost, the economy will tend to

(3) produce too (much/little) of a good to maximize consumer benefits. There may be a case for government intervention to help establish prices that will lead to an efficient allocation.

EXTERNALITIES

Many economic activities impose incidental burdens or benefits on other individuals for which there is

(4) no compensation. These sorts of activities are said to involve _____. If an activity, such as pollution, harms others and there is no compensation, we say that there are _____ externalities. If an activity benefits others who do not pay for the benefits they receive, we say that there are

_____ externalities.

Externalities imply that many activities are likely to have private benefits and costs that are different from

(5) social benefits and costs. In the case of detrimental externalities, social costs will be (higher/lower) than private costs, while in the case of beneficial externalities, social benefits will be _____ than private benefits.

(6) Private, profit-maximizing firms will base their production decisions on (private/social) costs. When externalities are important the result will be an (efficient/inefficient) use of resources. In the case of detrimental externalities, too (much/little) of the commodity in question will be produced. In the case of beneficial

externalities, unregulated markets are likely to produce (less/more) output than is socially desirable. Schemes for taxes and subsidies are in principle capable of adjusting private costs and benefits to more adequately reflect social costs and benefits.

PUBLIC GOODS

Most goods provided by private, profit-maximizing firms have two primary characteristics. The first is that the more of a good you use, the less there is for someone else. This characteristic is called _____. The second is that you must pay for goods in order to use them. This charac- (7) teristic is called _____. Goods that have neither of these characteristics are called _____ goods. Things like national defense, police protection, beautiful parks, and clean streets are examples of such goods.

Once public goods are provided to one individual, their benefits are available to all and cannot easily be restricted to just a few people. It is (difficult/easy) to exclude nonpayers. As a result, it is difficult to get indi- (8) viduals to pay for the goods they can enjoy for free when someone else is paying for them. This is sometimes referred to as the free-_____ problem.

Besides the problem of lack of excludability, one person's use of public goods, such as enjoying a park, does not usually deplete the supply for others. In technical language, the marginal cost of serving additional users is _____. This contrasts with private goods, where providing additional units of output requires addi- (9) tional resources and entails a positive marginal cost. An efficient allocation of resources requires that price equal marginal social cost. The clear implication is that from an efficiency standpoint, public goods should be priced at _____. One should not be surprised if profit-maximizing firms fail to provide public goods.

PRESENT AND FUTURE CONSUMPTION

The productive use of resources is time specific. Loafing today will not make tomorrow twice as long. A machine that is idle one week does not mean that twice as many machine hours will be available the next week. While the use of resources is time specific, the consumption of output is not. Output can be saved, either directly by adding to inventories in warehouses or indirectly by building plants and machines that increase future production possibilities. Thus, an economy does have the ability to transfer consumption through time by acts of saving and investment.

The rate of interest is an important determinant of how much investment will take place. A number of observers have questioned whether the private economy will result in interest rates and investment spending that are socially optimal. In the real world, monetary and fiscal policies can be used to manipulate interest rates and will influence investment in ways that may not correspond to the best plans for the future. Some observers, such as the English economist A. G. Pigou, have argued that people are simply shortsighted when it comes to saving for the future.

Individual investment projects often entail great risk for the individual investors but little risk for society.

(10) Bankruptcy may wipe out an investor's financial investment, but it (<u>does/does not</u>) destroy buildings and machines. These capital goods will still be around for others to use. It has been argued that the high individual risk will result in a level of investment that is (<u>less/more</u>) than socially optimal.

(11) Many decisions, such as damming a canyon, are essentially _____, and there is concern that in these cases decisions in unregulated markets may not adequately represent the interests of future generations. These arguments suggest that even competitive markets may result in inappropriate decisions about savings and investments.

COST DISEASE OF PERSONAL SERVICES

Many services—doctor visits, education, police protection—require significant labor input and offer

(12) (<u>limited/substantial</u>) opportunities for increases in labor productivity. By contrast, increasing mechanization and technological innovations have resulted in substantial increases in labor productivity in the production of many commodities. Increased labor productivity has led to higher wages for workers in these industries. Since workers can move among occupations, the wages of teachers, nurses, and police, for example, have had to increase to remain competitive with job opportunities in other industries. In manufacturing industries, increased labor productivity helps offset the cost pressures from higher wages. In many service industries, limited opportunities exist for increases in labor productivity to help contain cost pressures. The result is that many personal services have become more expensive over time because of the uneven pattern of increases in labor productivity. Increases in productivity always make an economy better off in the sense that it can now produce more of all goods, including personal services. But at the same time, society will find that lagging productivity in service industries means that the cost of these services has increased. Concerns about controlling costs may be misdirected if the major problem is the natural market response to differential productivity growth.

IMPORTANT TERMS AND CONCEPTS QUIZ

Choose the best definition for each of the following terms.

1. _____ Production possibilities frontier
2. _____ Resource misallocation
3. _____ Externalities
4. _____ Marginal social cost
5. _____ Marginal private cost
6. _____ Marginal social benefit
7. _____ Marginal private benefit
8. _____ Public good
9. _____ Private good
10. _____ Depletability
11. _____ Excludability
12. _____ Rent seeking
13. _____ Moral hazard
14. _____ Principals
15. _____ Agents
16. _____ Stock options
17. _____ Cost disease of personal services

a. Tendency of clients who have the lowest risks to be the most likely insurance customers
b. Results of activities that provide incidental harm or benefit to others
c. Tendency for the real cost of services to increase because of difficulty of increasing productivity
d. Portion of marginal benefit that accrues to those who engage in activity
e. Total marginal benefit, marginal private benefit plus benefits to others
f. Commodity or service whose benefits are not depleted by an additional user and for which it is difficult to exclude people from enjoying its benefits
g. Unproductive activity in pursuit of profit
h. Utility of a change in output differs from its opportunity cost
i. Parties to a transaction know different things about the item to be exchanged
j. Marginal private cost plus costs imposed on others
k. Commodity or service whose benefits are depleted by an additional user and for which people are excluded from its benefits unless they pay
l. The ability to keep someone who does not pay from enjoying a commodity
m. Tendency of insurance to discourage risk-avoiding behavior
n. Portion of marginal cost paid by those who engage in the activity
o. Those to whom decision-making authority is delegated
p. Commodity is used up when consumed
q. Curve that shows the maximum quantities of outputs it is possible to produce with the available resources and technology
r. Decision makers who delegate their power to others
s. Option to buy stock at predetermined price

BASIC EXERCISES

This exercise is designed to illustrate the cost disease of personal services.

Table 15-1 has spaces to compute the costs of producing both widgets and police services; both are assumed to be produced with only labor input. (Wages for police officers and for workers in the widget factory are assumed to be equal, as individuals can choose between these occupations.)

Table 15-1

Costs of Producing 240,000 Widgets	(1)	(2)	(3)
Widgets per worker	1,920	2,000	3,000
Number of workers[a]	125	_____	_____
Annual earnings per worker	$21,120	$22,000	$33,000
Total labor costs (total cost)	_____	_____	_____
Cost per widget	_____	_____	_____
Costs of Producing 200,000 Hours of Police Services			
Hours per police officer	2,000	2,000	2,000
Number of police officers[b]	100	_____	_____
Annual earnings per police officer	$21,120	$22,000	$33,000
Total labor cost (total cost)	_____	_____	_____
Cost per hour of police services	_____	_____	_____

[a]240,000 ÷ widgets per worker
[b]200,000 ÷ hours per police officer

1. Fill in the missing spaces in the first column to determine the cost per widget of producing 240,000 widgets and the cost per hour of 200,000 hours of police services.

2. The first entry in the second column assumes that labor productivity in the production of widgets has risen by 4.17 percent. The earnings of widget workers and police officers are assumed to increase by the same percentage as productivity. Now fill in the rest of the second column. What has happened to the average cost of producing one widget? What about the cost of producing one hour of police services?

3. The first entry in column 3 assumes that the growth in average labor productivity continues for another ten years. Again, the growth in earnings is assumed to match the growth in productivity. Fill in the rest of column 3. What is the increase in the cost of producing one widget? _____. What about the cost of one hour of police services? _____.

4. One way to hold the line on police costs is to refuse to increase salaries for police officers. Another way is to reduce the number of police officers. What are the long-run implications of both these policies?

SELF-TESTS FOR UNDERSTANDING

TEST A

Circle the most appropriate answer.

1. The condition for efficient resource allocation is
   a. MC = MR.
   b. *P* = Average Revenue.
   c. MU = MC.
   d. MU = Price.

2. Which of the following is a clear indicator of a misallocation of resources?
   a. Barney and Michelle, who subscribe to *Gourmet* magazine, despair over the increasing number of fast-food outlets.
   b. In the long run, farmer Fran makes zero economic profit.
   c. After careful study, economists have concluded that the economy of Arcadia is operating at a point inside its production possibilities frontier.
   d. The latest census survey indicates that the top 10 percent of the income distribution has an average income that is more than fifteen times that of the bottom 10 percent.

3. The term *externalities* is used by economists to describe
   a. economic decisions by foreign governments.
   b. occupants of extraterrestrial spaceships.
   c. all economic activity that takes place outside the classroom.
   d. activities that impose costs or benefits on third parties.

4. Economists expect profit-maximizing competitive firms to expand production as long as price exceeds
   a. marginal social cost.
   b. marginal utility.
   c. marginal private cost.
   d. average cost.

5. Which of the following is an externality?
   a. imperfect information
   b. your pride in the new home entertainment system you just purchased at a bargain price
   c. natural monopolies, such as the local electric utility
   d. the new road built for the NASA tracking station that has substantially reduced transportation costs for local farmers

6. A detrimental externality arises when
   a. the actions of a firm provide unintended benefits for third parties.
   b. having bought insurance, Jason figures he doesn't need to buy as sturdy a bike lock.
   c. a firm's managers cannot be closely monitored by stockholders.
   d. the actions of a firm impose costs on families living near the firm's plants.

7. In the presence of detrimental externalities, marginal private cost is usually
   a. less than marginal social cost.
   b. equal to marginal social cost.
   c. greater than marginal social cost.

8. Economists argue that if the production of paper is associated with detrimental externalities, a free market will likely
   a. produce less paper than is socially desirable.
   b. produce the socially optimal quantity of paper in spite of the detrimental externality.
   c. produce more paper than is socially desirable.

9. If the production of gizmos involves beneficial externalities, then it is likely that
   a. a free market will produce too many gizmos.
   b. marginal private benefits are less than marginal social benefits.
   c. a tax on the production of gizmos will lead to a more efficient allocation.
   d. the use of gizmos does not involve depletion.

10. Economists define public goods as
    a. all things the government spends money on.
    b. economic activities that impose costs or benefits on third parties.
    c. goods and services that many people can enjoy at the same time and from which it is difficult to exclude potential customers who do not want to pay.
    d. goods and services that should receive public subsidy such as improved health care and better housing for poor families.

11. Economists expect that profit-maximizing firms in competitive markets will produce _____ public goods.
    a. too few
    b. too many
    c. about the right quantity
    d. no

12. For a pure public good, the marginal cost of serving an additional user is equal to
    a. $1,000.
    b. $100.
    c. $10.
    d. $0.

13. Which of the following does not have the characteristics of a public good?
    a. clean rivers
    b. visits to the doctor
    c. police and fire protection
    d. unscrambled radio and television signals

14. The "free-rider" problem refers to
    a. the difficulty of stopping kids from sneaking onto the local merry-go-round.
    b. using subsidies to encourage the production of goods with beneficial externalities.
    c. the difficulty of getting people to voluntarily contribute to pay for public goods.
    d. increasing problems with hitchhikers on the interstate highways.

15. Which of the following is an argument that free markets may result in an inappropriate amount of saving and investment? (There may be more than one correct answer.)
    a. Investment projects are often riskier to individuals than to the community.
    b. Government policy may manipulate interest rates for reasons of short-term macroeconomic policy.
    c. Due to "defective telescopic faculties," people do not give enough consideration to the future.
    d. Many decisions concerning natural resources are made without enough consideration given to their irreversible consequences.

16. Which of the following explains the cost disease of personal services?
    a. the supply effects of price controls, such as rent control
    b. the existence of monopoly elements in the economy
    c. detrimental externalities
    d. the uneven prospects for improved labor productivity in different sectors of the economy

17. Which of the following is *not* likely to suffer from the cost disease of personal services?
    a. individual piano lessons
    b. the production of television sets
    c. colleges and universities that strive to maintain an unchanged student-faculty ratio
    d. orchestras and symphonies

18. Which of the following is an example of rent seeking?
    a. the efforts of lobbyists to get Congress to restrict the import of foreign steel
    b. Cleon's efforts to find an inexpensive apartment before school starts
    c. the hours Juan and Ramona spend working in their own restaurant
    d. the time and effort Julie spends studying to be a doctor

19. As used by economists, the term *moral hazard* refers to the
    a. temptations of large cities on impressionable teenagers.
    b. state of much television programming.
    c. tendency of insurance to make people less concerned about risky behavior.
    d. dangers of sexually transmitted diseases among single men and women.

20. Decisions by company managers that make their own lives more comfortable at the cost of reducing stockholder profits are examples of
    a. moral hazards.
    b. principal-agent problems.
    c. detrimental externalities.
    d. public goods.

TEST B

Circle T or F for true or false.

T F 1. An unregulated market economy would never have business cycles.

T F 2. Externalities, whether beneficial or detrimental, imply that marginal social cost is always less than marginal private cost.

T F 3. An activity that causes damage to someone else and for which there is no compensation is said to involve a detrimental externality.

T F 4. A beneficial externality is likely to result in marginal private benefits exceeding marginal social benefits.

T F 5. Economists define public goods as anything for which the government spends money.

T F 6. The fact that it is difficult to restrict the use of public goods to those who are willing to pay is the problem of depletability.

T F 7. The provision of public goods is complicated by the "free-rider" problem.

T F 8. The fact that public goods are not depleted by use implies that the marginal cost of providing the goods to one more consumer is zero.

T F 9. The interest rate plays an important role in the allocation of resources between the present and the future because it affects the profitability of investment projects.

T F 10. Many investment projects will entail less risk for the individual investor than for the community as a whole.

SUPPLEMENTARY EXERCISES

1. Consider the economy of Beethovia, which produces two goods: widgets and music recitals. Widgets are manufactured with capital and labor according to the following production function:

$$W = 60L^{1/2}K^{1/2},$$

where L = number of workers producing widgets and K = number of machines. Music recitals are labor intensive and produced according to the following production function:

$$M = 50 \times L.$$

There are 40,000 workers in Beethovia, meaning that the sum of labor allocated to the production of widgets and recitals cannot exceed 40,000, and initially there are 22,500 machines, or $K = 22,500$.

a. Draw the production possibilities frontier for Beethovia showing the trade-off between the production of widgets and recitals. (It is probably easiest to arbitrarily fix the number of recitals, calculate how many workers it will take to produce that many recitals, and then calculate the maximum production of widgets with the remaining labor and all the machines.)

b. Competitive markets have initially resulted in 39,601 widget workers and 399 musicians. At this allocation, what is the marginal product and average product of labor in the production of widgets? In the production of recitals?

c. Assume that saving and investment by the people of Beethovia increase the number of machines to 28,900. At the initial allocation of labor, but with the new number of machines, what is the marginal and average product of labor in the production of widgets? What has happened to the productivity of workers in the production of recitals?

d. What has happened to the opportunity cost of music recitals; that is, what is the new slope of the production possibilities frontier at the allocation of workers specified in question b? To answer this question, either draw a new production possibilities frontier or derive a mathematical expression for the slope of the frontier.

e. If you have answered question d correctly, you should have determined that the cost of recitals has increased. Recitals suffer from the cost disease of personal services. At the same time, how can you show that the increase in productivity has made Beethovia unambiguously richer?

2. Go to the library or bookstore and get a copy of *Encounters with the Archdruid* (New York: Farrar, Straus and Giroux, 1971) by John McPhee. The book reports on three encounters between David Brower, who was president of the Sierra Club, and other individuals who wanted to dam the Colorado River, build a copper mine in the Cascades, and develop Hilton Head Island. Many think that McPhee's description of the raft trip down the Colorado River with Brower and Floyd Dominy, who was head of the Bureau of Reclamation, is especially good.

a. Whose position do you favor?

b. Is Brower always right? Is he ever right?

ECONOMICS IN ACTION

STANDARDS OR TAXES?

In 1975, after the significant increase in international oil prices, the Energy Policy and Conservation Act mandated minimum corporate average fuel economy (CAFE) standards for new passenger cars sold in the United States. Originally established at 18.5 miles per gallon (mpg) for 1978, the CAFE standards are now 27.5 mpg for cars and 20.7 mpg for light trucks, a category that includes sport utility vehicles. Under the original policy, CAFE standards were to increase still further to reduce American dependency on foreign oil and to help reduce carbon dioxide emissions. Since the mid-1990s, Congress has frozen CAFE standards.

Following the terrorist attacks of September 11, 2001, there has been renewed interest in limiting America's dependence on imported oil. In late November 2001, Robert F. Kennedy, Jr., a lawyer for the Natural Resources Defense Council, argued for CAFE standards of 40 miles per gallon by 2012 and 55 miles per gallon by 2020. Kennedy argued that even modest increases in gas mileage would limit the need to import oil and had the potential to save more oil than could be found in the Arctic National Wildlife Refuge.

Columnist Virginia Postrel disagrees with Kennedy's approach. Citing work by economists Pietro S. Nivola and Robert W. Crandall, Postrel argues that increased gas taxes would be a more efficient means of reducing consumption. CAFE standards affect only new cars, which account for only a small proportion of total cars and miles driven. If higher CAFE standards increase the price of new cars, they may induce people to hold on to older, less fuel-efficient cars. By lowering the marginal cost of driving, higher CAFE standards might also in-

199

crease the number of miles driven by new car owners. In contrast, a fuel tax has opposite effects. It provides an incentive to get rid of older, less efficient cars for newer cars while increasing the marginal cost of driving for all drivers. If one is worried about the impact of higher gasoline taxes on low-income families, one could couple an increase in gas taxes with a reduction in income or payroll taxes targeted at low-income families.

It has been argued that CAFE standards were originally preferred by legislators because their cost is hidden in the price of new cars while an increased gasoline tax is quite visible. Postrel argues that increased CAFE standards might well come with exceptions that may have unintended consequences. She points out that the original standards had an exception for light trucks that was meant to reduce the cost of work vehicles, an exception that contributed to the proliferation of sport utility vehicles.

1. Which would you favor to reduce oil consumption, higher CAFE standards, higher gasoline taxes, or higher taxes on all uses of petroleum? Which do you think would be more effective? Which do you think is fairer? Why?

2. Do you think that reducing oil consumption should be a national priority?

Sources: Robert F. Kennedy, Jr., "Better Gas Mileage, Greater Security, *The New York Times*, November 24, 2001; Virginia Postrel, "Setting fuel-efficiency targets for vehicle fleets makes little sense," *The New York Times*, December 6, 2001.

STUDY QUESTIONS

1. Why do economists argue that externalities, whether beneficial or detrimental, are likely to lead to a misallocation of resources?

2. Why does a free market tend to overproduce goods with detrimental externalities?

3. Why does a free market tend to underproduce goods with beneficial externalities?

4. How can the price system help correct the problems of externalities?

5. What are the distinguishing characteristics of a public good as compared with a private good?

6. Why can't we leave the provision of public goods to profit-maximizing firms?

7. Do you believe that unregulated private markets will save too little or too much? Why?

8. Colleges and universities are often urged to hold tuition increases under the inflation rate. What does the concept of the cost disease of personal services suggest would happen if such a policy were followed for the next ten years?

9. What is rent-seeking behavior and why do people engage in it?

10. Is direct government regulation the appropriate response to all market failures?

The Market's Prime Achievement: Innovation and Growth

16

Important Terms and Concepts

Externality	GDP	Research and development (R&D)	Process innovation
Per capita income	Invention	High-tech	Basic research
Productivity	Innovation	Ratchet	Applied research
Industrial revolution	Entrepreneur	Product innovation	Technology trading
Capitalism			Cross licensing

Learning Objectives

After completing this chapter, you should be able to:

- explain why market economies have a stronger record of innovation than other forms of economic organization.

- explain the importance of innovation for economic growth.

- explain the role of innovative entrepreneurs in free-market innovation.

- understand why no firm in a high-tech industry can afford to fall behind its rivals in an innovation arms race.

- explain Schumpeter's Model and the initial entrepreneur's "monopolistic" earnings.

- explain how the concepts of marginal cost and marginal revenue can help a firm determine how much to spend on research and development.

- explain the difference between process and product innovation.

- analyze the impact of process innovations on price and output.

- explain the difference between basic and applied research.

- describe some of the arrangements firms might use to control the risk associated with specific R&D projects.

- evaluate the arguments about whether free economies invest enough in R&D.

CHAPTER REVIEW

This chapter reviews some of the microeconomic forces behind the process of innovation. Up to the Industrial Revolution, economic growth as we know it today hardly existed. Many products and processes at the beginning of the eighteenth century would have been familiar to Roman citizens. The past 200 years have seen a dramatic change. Labor at the beginning of the twenty-first century is much more productive than at the beginning of the nineteenth century. What explains this dramatic increase in labor productivity, and why have capitalist economies been so successful at it?

Major factors responsible for the growth in labor productivity include increased education and experience of the labor force, investment in plant and equipment, and the almost continuous development and introduction (1) of new products and production processes or _____. Today it seems that competition between firms in innovation is as important as price competition.

It is helpful to distinguish between invention and innovation. Research that focuses on fundamental scien- (2) tific ideas or entirely new products is an example of _____ while _____ refers to the entire process that prepares new ideas for practical use and marketing. Individuals who organize firms to exploit new products or production technologies are called _____. Breakthrough innovations come disproportionately from (small entrepreneurial/large) firms. At the same time one should not underestimate the cumulative impact of numerous incremental improvements to a wide range of consumer and industrial products.

Research and development activities are organized expenditures by firms to develop new products and processes. That is, rather than leaving innovation to chance, firms make clear decisions to invest in innovation. R&D budgets are like other business decisions and can be analyzed using the tools and concepts we have developed in earlier chapters. As with other business decisions, firms should expand R&D expenditures as long as (3) the expected marginal returns are greater than the marginal _____. While some individual innovations have been wildly profitable, the returns to innovation as a whole do not appear to offer above-normal profits, a result that should not be surprising under conditions of free _____.

Why is innovation such an important part of capitalist economies? Why has innovation become such an important part of competition? Some have suggested that the kinked revenue model is an important part of the explanation. If a firm does not keep up with the competition in terms of the attractiveness of its products or the efficiency of its production processes, it will lose out. As a result, a firm that spends less on R&D runs the risk of not keeping up. There is little incentive to spend more than the average, as your competitors will only match your efforts. However, when someone's efforts have made an important difference, competitors need to increase their R&D spending to keep up. This process that works to sustain R&D spending is called a (4) _____.

Innovations have important impacts for the economy as a whole. Many innovations enlarge the range of choices for consumers and producers; that is, they create cumulative change. Many innovations have characteristics of public goods in that repeated use of an innovation neither uses it up nor requires that the act of innovation be repeated.

Do firms spend enough on innovation? Those who are concerned that firms spend too little point out that most innovations have beneficial _____, that is new and enhanced products and production processes offer significant benefits to lots of people in terms of better commodities and lower prices. As a result, the social benefits to innovation may exceed the private returns and profit-maximizing firms may stop short of a social optimum. The _____ system is an attempt to overcome this problem as its provides exclusive monopoly or licensing rights for a period of time. Competitive pressures to match the innovative efforts of competitors also works to increase spending on innovations. Licensing and technology trading are ways that firms try to capture the external benefits of their investments in R&D. (5)

Individual R&D projects can be quite risky. Not all new products make it to market. Large firms can begin to reduce the risk of R&D by sponsoring numerous projects. Firms can also enter into arrangements to share the innovations of other firms through technology _____ and cross _____ of patents. (6)

Do consumers benefit from innovation? Product innovations mean new or enhanced products but at what cost? Process innovations that lower the marginal cost of production should mean an unambiguous gain for consumers through (higher/lower) output and _____ prices. (7)

IMPORTANT TERMS AND CONCEPTS QUIZ

Choose the best definition for each of the following terms.

1. _____ Externality
2. _____ Per capita income
3. _____ Productivity
4. _____ Industrial Revolution
5. _____ Capitalism
6. _____ GDP
7. _____ Invention
8. _____ Innovation
9. _____ Entrepreneur
10. _____ Research and development (R&D)
11. _____ High-Tech
12. _____ Ratchet
13. _____ Product innovation
14. _____ Process innovation
15. _____ Basic research
16. _____ Applied research
17. _____ Technology trading
18. _____ Cross licensing

a. Process of introducing new products or methods of production
b. Research on scientific knowledge and general principles
c. Total production divided by total hours of labor input
d. Individual who organizes a new firm
e. Research on specific products or processes
f. Agreements to share patents in return for money or access to other patents
g. Average income per person
h. Introduction of new products or major modification to existing products
i. Production processes controlled by private firms with minimal government control
j. Innovation that changes the way a commodity is produced
k. Growth in economic output
l. Organized efforts to invent new and improve existing products and processes
m. Shared use of technological innovations among firms
n. Total domestic production in a year
o. Permits increases but prevents decreases
p. New technologies that spurred economic growth in England toward the end of the 18th century
q. Firms and industries that use cutting edge technologies
r. Activity that creates uncompensated benefits or damages for third parties
s. Creation of new products and processes or the discovery of ideas that underlie them

BASIC EXERCISE

DOES IT REALLY MATTER?

Why all the fuss about innovation? Can a 1 percent difference in the rate of economic growth make all that much difference?

1. Complete **Table 16-1** to see if the rate of economic growth will make any difference for your great-grandchildren.

   Table 16-1

   The Impact of Differences in Economic Growth on GDP per Capita

Year	Growth Rate of GDP Per Capita 0%	0.5%	1.0%	1.5%	2.0%
2000	$31,000	$31,000	$31,000	$31,000	$31,000
2100	_____	_____	_____	_____	_____

2. According to the text, on average the standard of living in the United States increased by slightly more than sevenfold during the twentieth century. Which of the growth rates in Table 16-1 would produce a similar result during the twenty-first century?

SELF-TESTS FOR UNDERSTANDING

TEST A

Circle the most appropriate answer.

1. For the 1500 years before the Industrial Revolution, economic growth in Europe
   a. was actually negative.
   b. was close to zero.
   c. averaged 2.5 percent per year.
   d. resulted in labor that was twenty times more productive than in Roman times.

2. What type of economy has shown the strongest record of innovation and growth?
   a. socialist economies
   b. soviet-style central planning
   c. capitalist economies
   d. feudalism

205

3. According to the text, which two of the following have played especially crucial roles in the ability of capitalist economies to sustain high rates of innovation? (there may be more than one correct answer.)
   a. the encouragement of cartels in key sectors of the economy
   b. the use of innovation as a way of competing with rivals
   c. targeted investments by the government in key sectors of the economy
   d. markets that are free from tight regulation and limiting customs

4. Which of the following does not help to explain the record of innovation and growth in capitalist economies?
   a. enforceability of contracts
   b. development of the patent system
   c. competitive pressures for innovation
   d. royal prerogatives that give the king or emperor the rights to new innovations

5. Entrepreneurs are involved with which of the following? (there may be more than one correct answer.)
   a. The organization of new business.
   b. The exploitation of new production techniques
   c. The marketing of new products
   d. Risk taking

6. Breakthrough innovations
   a. are the focus of R&D efforts of large firms.
   b. come disproportionately from small, entrepreneurial firms.
   c. focus on user friendliness.
   d. involve small improvements to existing products.

7. Firms should expand spending on R&D as long as
   a. the marginal revenue from expected innovations exceeds marginal cost.
   b. the average revenue from all of a firm's innovations exceeds average cost.
   c. the results are patentable.
   d. it is on applied rather than basic research.

8. Consider a software company that spends $200 million to develop a new computer program that can be reproduced at $5 a copy. Setting price equal to the marginal cost of additional copies will
   a. guarantee positive profits.
   b. necessarily increase shareholder value.
   c. mean the company will never recover its R&D costs.
   d. be the same as setting marginal cost equal to marginal revenue.

9. Under conditions of free entry, one would expect that the returns to innovation as a whole would be
   a. very high.
   b. equal to market average rates of return.
   c. zero.
   d. negative.

10. Which of the following observations would you associate with the term ratchet?
    a. An arrangement that forces down technological spending.
    b. A serious shortcoming of free-enterprise economies.
    c. It explains why R&D spending is expected to reduce over a period of time.
    d. An arrangement that permits increases but prevents decreases.

11. Which is an example of a process innovation?
    a. A university researcher identifies the electrical properties of a new synthetic material.
    b. A chemist for DuPont discovers a new fabric.
    c. A partnership between a history and a computer science student results in a new computer-based action game set in sixteenth century Japan.
    d. An engineer for Ford finds an application, of existing technology, that when applied to rust proofing car bodies saves $150 per car.

12. Which is an example of a product innovation?
    a. Post-it notes
    b. a government grant to a researcher who is studying polymer chemistry
    c. Boeing reorganizes its production line to enhance worker productivity
    d. Einstein's theory of relativity

13. Which is an example of a basic research?
    a. new methods for making stronger sheets of glass for large windows
    b. new designs from Ralph Lauren
    c. the development of an artificial kidney
    d. the discovery of DNA

14. Which of the following is most likely to support basic research?
    a. the National Association of Manufacturers
    b. Microsoft
    c. the federal government
    d. Ford Motor Company

15. The term technology trading
    a. refers to the venture capitalists who specialize in funding high-tech startup companies.
    b. refers to the export and import of high-tech capital goods.
    c. was coined by the stockbroker who first sold shares of IBM.
    d. is a way that firms can try and manage the risk of research and development.

16. Which of the following is an example of technology trading?
    a. Eli Whitney left England for America with the plans for the cotton gin in his head.
    b. Two companies agree to share innovations.
    c. Jane is employed to reverse engineer the latest innovation from her firm's major competitors.
    d. The federal government supports basic research in university laboratories.

17. The kinked revenue model helps to explain
    a. the returns to innovation.
    b. product innovations rather than process innovations.
    c. why firms tend to match R&D spending of their competitors.
    d. why profit-maximizing firms are likely to favor applied research over basic research.

18. An innovation that improves an existing product would be an example of (there may be more than one correct answer)
    a. basic research.
    b. product innovation.
    c. process innovation.
    d. applied research.

19. In the United States, R&D spending is
    a. about 28 percent of GDP.
    b. about 2.8 percent of GDP.
    c. about 0.28 percent of GDP.
    d. only conducted by the federal government.

20. A process innovation that leads to a downward shift in a monopolist's marginal cost curve should
    a. lower price and lower output.
    b. lower price and increase output.
    c. increase price and increase output.
    d. increase price and lower output.

TEST B

Circle T or F for true or false.

T F 1. Labor today is not much more productive than it was 200 years ago.

T F 2. There is little reason to expect that capitalist economies will be more successful at innovation than centrally planned economies.

T F 3. Innovation is a major source of economic growth.

T F 4. The R&D efforts of large firms are often focused on improvements to existing products and process.

T F 5. The kinked revenue model of innovation works like a ratchet to sustain the level of R&D spending.

T F 6. Firms can reduce the risk associated with R&D efforts by engaging in technology trading.

T F 7. The development of a new or improved production process is an example of basic, not applied, research.

T F 8. Profit-maximizing firms are likely to devote more resources to applied research than basic research.

T F 9. The externality problem is likely more severe for basic rather than applied research.

T F 10. Process innovations should lower price and increase output, even for monopolists.

ECONOMICS IN ACTION

CREATIVE DESTRUCTION[1]

Was the boom-bust cycle of many dot-com companies at the turn of the century a unique event? Are the problems of large fixed costs and low variable costs unique to the Internet and software industry? Are the concepts of process and product innovation new?

Economist Hal Varian would answer all questions with a decisive no. Writing in *The New York Times,* Varian described the evolution of the automobile industry in the United States. During the first decade of the twentieth century, there were more than 240 startup companies in the automobile industry. Henry Ford developed a dominating position as he focused on process innovation. As Varian explains, "Ford experimented relentlessly with mass-production techniques. He built big and reaped the cost advantages from economies of scale and vertical integration . . . By 1923, Ford was producing nearly half the automobiles sold in America."

But Ford's dominant position was vulnerable to product innovation championed by Alfred Sloan of General Motors who introduced annual model changes. Ford, who is reported to have said that the American public could have a car in any color it wanted as long as it was black, found it difficult to compete against Sloan's innovation.

Varian argues that companies like Dell Computer have been able to emulate Ford's focus on lowering costs through process innovation, but he wonders if this makes them vulnerable to product innovation from future competitors.

Railroads showed a similar boom-bust cycle. Here the underlying dynamic was the importance of large-scale networks that entailed significant fixed costs but operated with low marginal costs. Railroad companies made significant fixed investments in track and rolling stock in the 1880s only to face fierce competition in the 1890s as the marginal cost of operating on tracks already laid with rolling stock that was already purchased was relative low. The result was that the investment boom of the 1880s was followed by widespread bankruptcies in the 1890s.

1. It is easy to identify the winners after the dust has settled, but how does one identify the winners in advance? One might argue that the experience of the railroads, the automobile industry and dot-com companies have involved a fair amount of overinvestment. Is this wasteful investment that should be controlled by the government or is this an essential element of the dynamic nature of capitalism?

Source: Hal R. Varian, "Economic Scene: The technology sector's rise and fall is a tale as American as the Model T," *The New York Times,* December 14, 2000.

---

[1] Economist Joseph Schumpeter first described the process of innovation and competition as "creative destruction." Schumpeter argued that it is an essential element of the vitality of capitalism.

STUDY QUESTIONS

1. Why do capitalist economies have a better record of innovation that planned economies?

2. What is the difference between basic and applied research? Which is more likely to be done by profit-maximizing firms? Why?

3. What is the difference between process and product innovation? Are these examples of basic or applied research?

4. Why don't software companies set prices equal to the marginal cost of reproducing their software programs?

5. What is meant by the kinked revenue model of spending on innovation?

6. How can firms control the risk associated with specific R&D projects?

7. What is meant by the public good aspect of innovations?

8. Does the American economy spend enough on research and development?

9. Should the government spend money on research and development? If so, should it favor basic or applied research? Why?

Externalities, the Environment, and Natural Resources

17

Important Terms and Concepts

Externality	Direct controls	Pollution charges (taxes on emissions)	Emissions permits

Learning Objectives

After completing this chapter, you should be able to:

- analyze environmental problems faced by planned and market economies.

- explain why, in most cases, it is impossible to reduce pollution to zero.

- explain why unrestricted competitive markets are likely to result in a socially unacceptable level of pollution.

- explain why it is unlikely that profit-maximizing private firms can be expected to clean up the environment.

- describe the three major approaches to limiting pollution.

- compare the advantages and disadvantages of using taxes and permits to control pollution.

- explain why the price of depletable resources should be expected to rise year by year.

- explain how and why actual prices of depletable resources have behaved differently.

- describe the three virtues of rising prices for scarce resources.

- explain why known reserves for many resources have not tended to fall over time.

CHAPTER REVIEW

This chapter explores the economics of environmental protection and resource conservation, with emphasis on the strengths and weaknesses of a market economy in dealing with both issues.

ENVIRONMENTAL PROTECTION

Pollution is one example where unregulated markets will fail to achieve an efficient allocation of resources. Typically, pollution imposes little or no cost on the polluter, yet it imposes costs on others. In the language of

(1) economists, pollution is an example of a detrimental _____. Pollution happens because individuals, firms, and government agencies use the air, land, and waterways as free dumping grounds for their waste. Economists believe that if there is a high cost to using these public resources, then the volume of pollution will (increase/decrease) because people will be more careful about producing wastes and/or they will choose less costly alternatives for waste disposal. One way to make the use of public resources costly is to impose (taxes/subsidies) in direct proportion to the volume of pollution emitted. This is an example of using the price system to clean up the environment.

(2)   Many government policies have relied on volunteerism and direct _____. Economists are skeptical of relying on voluntary cooperation as a long-range solution. Cleaning up the environment is costly, and firms that voluntarily incur these costs are likely to be undersold by less public-spirited competitors. A government ruling that mandates an equal percentage reduction in pollution activity by all polluters is an example of a direct control. Economists argue that since the costs of reducing pollution are apt to vary among polluters, an equal percentage reduction by all polluters is likely to be (efficient/inefficient) compared with other alternatives, such as emissions taxes. Differential reductions in pollution will be (less/more) efficient, as it is likely to cost less for some firms to reduce pollution.

(3)   Faced with an emissions tax, firms will reduce pollution until the (marginal/average) cost of further reductions exceeds the tax. Firms that continue to pollute pay the tax; other firms will pay for pollution-control devices. All firms will choose the least costly alternative. The sale or auction of emission permits also generates a market price that firms must pay if they pollute. One advantage of emission permits is that by controlling the number of permits, there may be greater control over the final volume of pollution.

While economists have a strong preference for market-based approaches to reducing pollution, there may be cases where one needs to rely on voluntarism or direct control. For example, when conditions have changed suddenly and action must be taken quickly, there may not be time to implement a program of pollution taxes or emission permits. If monitoring pollution is not possible or prohibitively expensive, direct controls may be a preferable alternative, and society may prefer to ban especially dangerous activities.

RESOURCE CONSERVATION

Some resources, such as trees and fish, are called renewable resources. As long as breeding stocks are not destroyed, these resources will replenish themselves. The rest of this chapter concentrates on nonrenewable or depletable resources such as minerals and oil. In this case there is no reproduction, although there may be recycling.

Many observers have voiced concern that the world is running out of natural resources. They allege that soon the quantity of resources supplied will not be able to keep up with the quantity of resources demanded and that the result will be massive shortages and chaos. Yet, in a free market we know that the quantity demanded (can/can never) exceed the quantity supplied, because demand and supply will always be brought into equi-   (4)
librium by adjustments in _____. This fundamental mechanism of free markets, first discussed in Chapter 4, is as applicable to the supply and demand of scarce resources as it is to any other commodity.

Over time one might expect the price of depletable resources to increase year by year as the most accessible and inexpensive sources of supply are used up first. That is, the prices of depletable resources should show a rising trend.[1] Economic analysis suggests that the trend in price is a better indicator of depletion than estimates of reserves, which are of necessity based on current extraction technology and exploration. The discovery of new resource reserves or new methods of manufacturing that economize on the use of resources, technological progress that reduces the cost of extraction, and government attempts at price controls can all affect the price of depletable resources.

Data on known reserves, rather than declining as implied in the literal interpretation of a nonrenewable resource, have typically shown increases during the past 50 years. These increases in reserves reflect the workings of the price system as the incentive from higher prices has induced new exploration and made the use of high-cost deposits profitable. It is important to remember that pressure for higher prices is what equates demand and supply, avoids chaos, and facilitates the adjustment to alternative technologies.

Many economists see increasing prices for depletable resources as an important virtue of free markets. Increasing prices help to deal with the problem of declining reserves in three important ways:

a. Increasing prices (encourage/discourage) consumption and waste and provide a(n)   (5)
(disincentive/incentive) for conservation on the part of consumers.

b. Increasing prices (encourage/discourage) more efficient use of scarce resources in the production of commodities.

c. Increasing prices provide a(n) (disincentive/incentive) for technological innovation and the use of substitutes as well as (encouraging/discouraging) additional exploration and the exploitation of high-cost sources of supply.

---

[1]Economist Harold Hotelling suggested that even if extraction costs are constant, the price of a depletable resource of known finite supply should increase at a rate equal to the rate of interest. This increase is necessary so that investments in the depletable resource offer a competitive rate of return.

IMPORTANT TERMS AND CONCEPTS QUIZ

Choose the most appropriate definition for each of the following terms.

1. _____ Externality

2. _____ Direct controls

3. _____ Pollution charges

4. _____ Emissions permit

a. Monetary penalties used to make polluting financially unattractive

b. Fees paid to polluting firms in exchange for reductions in pollution

c. Result of activities that affect other people, without corresponding compensation

d. Authorization to pollute up to a specified level

e. Legal limits on pollution emissions or performance specifications for polluting activities

BASIC EXERCISES

POLLUTION TAXES

This exercise examines the implications of alternative pollution taxes.

Assume that plastic trash bags are produced in a market that is best characterized as one of perfect competition. Manufacturers have long used local rivers as convenient dumping grounds for their industrial wastes. **Figure 17-1** plots the average cost of producing trash bags. These data are applicable for each firm.

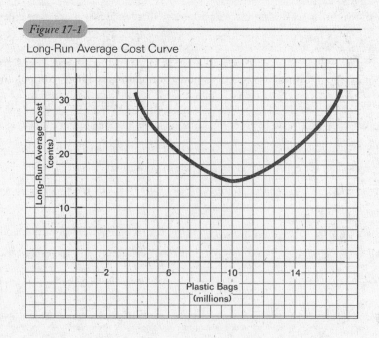

Figure 17-1

Long-Run Average Cost Curve

1. a. In the absence of pollution-control measures, what is the long-run equilibrium price of plastic bags?
   $_____. What is the long-run equilibrium level of output for each firm? $_____ million. (To answer
   this question you may want to review the material in Chapter 10 about long-run equilibrium under
   perfect competition.)

   b. The amount of pollution discharge is directly proportional to the number of bags produced. Assume
   that the government imposes a pollution charge of 5 cents per bag. Draw in the new average cost curve
   on Figure 17-1. In the long run, will there be an increase, a decrease, or no change in each of the following as a result of the pollution charge? (Assume for now that there is no pollution-control technology, that each firm must pay the tax, and that the demand for plastic bags declines as price rises.)

Industry output	_____
Price	_____
Number of firms in the industry	_____
Average cost curve for each firm	_____
Output level of each firm	_____
Total pollution	_____

   c. Assume that pollution-control equipment becomes available. This equipment will eliminate 75 percent
   of pollution at an average cost of 4 cents per bag. Explain why no firm will adopt the pollution-control
   equipment if the pollution charge is unchanged at 5 cents a bag. (Assume that the cost of the control
   equipment is all variable cost at 4 cents per bag and that there is no fixed-cost component.)

   d. Assume now that the tax is shifted to the volume of emissions, not to the number of bags produced,
   and that it is equivalent to 5 cents a bag if no pollution-control equipment is installed. Will any firm
   purchase the pollution-control equipment?

   e. With the emissions tax at a rate equivalent to 5 cents per bag, to what rate must the cost of pollution
   control decline before firms will use it? If the cost of pollution control is constant at 4 cents, to what
   rate must the tax increase to induce firms to install the pollution-control equipment?

   f. Assume now that the costs of reducing pollution are not identical for all firms. For simplicity, assume
   that there are two types of firms, low-cost pollution-control firms and high-cost pollution-control
   firms. The low-cost firms can eliminate pollution at costs lower than the emissions tax but the high-cost
   firms cannot. What is the result of imposing an emissions tax? What will happen to total industry output? Will any firms leave the industry? If so, which ones, the high-cost or the low-cost firms? Why?

Table 17-1

Year	Real GDP (Billions of $2000)	Energy Consumption (quadrillion BTUs)	Energy Consumption per $1,000 GDP (thousands of BTUs)	Year	Real GDP (Billions of $2000)	Energy Consumption (quadrillion BTUs)	Energy Consumption per $1,000 GDP (thousands of BTUs)
1970	3,771.9	67.8		1990	7,112.5	84.7	
1971	3,898.6	69.3		1991	7,100.5	84.6	
1972	4,105.0	72.7		1992	7,336.6	86.0	
1973	4,341.5	75.7		1993	7,532.7	87.6	
1974	4,319.6	74.0		1994	7,835.5	89.3	
1975	4,311.2	72.0		1995	8,031.7	91.2	
1976	4,540.9	76.0		1996	8,328.9	94.2	
1977	4,750.5	78.0		1997	8,703.5	94.7	
1978	5,015.0	80.0		1998	9,066.9	95.2	
1979	5,173.4	80.9		1999	9,470.3	96.8	
1980	5,161.7	78.3		2000	9,817.0	98.9	
1981	5,291.7	76.3		2001	9,890.7	96.4	
1982	5,189.3	73.3		2002	10,048.8	98.0	
1983	5,423.8	73.1		2003	10,301.3	98.8	
1984	5,813.6	76.7		2004	10,675.8	100.3	
1985	6,053.7	76.5		2005	11,003.4	100.6	
1986	6,263.6	76.8		2006	11,319.4	99.8	
1987	6,475.1	79.2					
1988	6,742.7	82.8					
1989	6,981.4	85.0					

Source: GDP: Bureau of Economic Analysis, U.S. Department of Commerce http://bea.gov/national/nipaweb/SelectTable.asp?Popular=Y , Table 1.1.6; Energy: Annual Energy Review, US Department of Energy, Table 1.5. http://www.eia.doe.gov/emeu/aer/txt/ptb0105.html and Monthly Energy Review http://www.eia.doe.gov/overview_hd.html; Prices: Economic Report of the President, 2005, Table B-60 http://www.gpoaccess.gov/eop/tables08.html Accessed: June 15, 2008.

2. a. **Table 17-1** contains data on real output and energy consumption for the U.S. economy. Use these data to compute the use of energy per thousand dollars of GDP.
   b. **Figure 17-2** shows real energy prices, i.e., energy prices divided by the consumer price index. Complete Figure 17-2 by plotting the data on energy consumption per thousand dollars of GDP. Use this graph to discuss the pattern of energy consumption during the last thirty years.

Figure 17-2

Energy Prices and Consumption

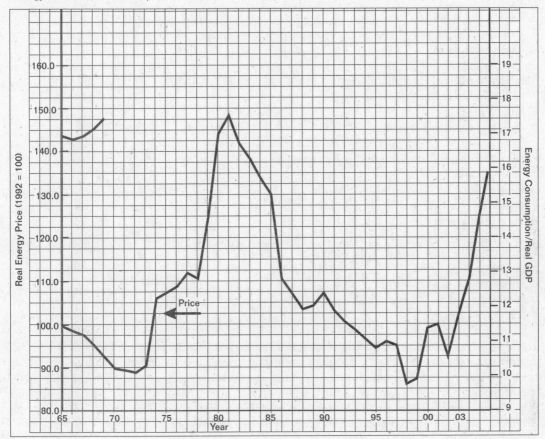

SELF-TESTS FOR UNDERSTANDING

TEST A

Circle the most appropriate answer.

1. Which of the following suggests that, except for recycling, all economic activity results in a disposal problem?
   a. OPEC
   b. the law of conservation of energy and matter
   c. emissions permits
   d. externalities

217

2. Which of the following countries has avoided significant pollution problems?
   a. China
   b. Russia
   c. The United States
   d. Poland
   e. none of the above

3. Measures of national air quality show _____ since 1975.
   a. marked deterioration
   b. little change
   c. some important improvements

4. Economists view pollution as a textbook example of
   a. public goods.
   b. externalities.
   c. increasing returns to scale.
   d. the evils of monopoly.

5. Significant pollution is caused by the actions of
   a. business.
   b. government.
   c. consumers.
   d. all of the above.

6. The fact that pollution is often a detrimental externality suggests that
   a. cleaning up the environment must be done by direct government expenditures.
   b. without government intervention, profit-maximizing private firms cannot be expected to clean up the environment.
   c. public agencies have been responsible for most pollution.
   d. direct controls are superior to other forms of government intervention.

7. Which of the following is not an example of using financial incentives to clean up the environment?
   a. mandated pollution-control equipment so all producers will reduce the emission of industrial pollutants by 50 percent
   b. a graduated tax that increases with the polluting characteristics of each automobile engine
   c. the sale of a limited number of permits to control emissions into Lake Erie
   d. allowing firms to buy and sell emission rights originally assigned under a program of direct controls

8. The use of pollution charges as a means of cleaning up the environment
   a. is the predominant form of pollution control in the United States.
   b. is likely to be more efficient than a system of direct controls.
   c. would be most appropriate in situations calling for sudden action, such as a serious smog condition.
   d. would have exactly the same effects on the volume of pollution as do subsidies for pollution-control equipment.

9. As a strategy to control pollution, voluntarism
   a. is the best long-run strategy.
   b. may be the only practical alternative in cases where surveillance is impractical.
   c. should be the most effective alternative.
   d. has significant efficiency advantages as compared with pollution taxes.

10. Economists typically argue that _____ are likely to be most effective in reducing pollution over the long run.
    a. direct controls
    b. taxes on emissions
    c. voluntary programs
    d. specifications as to allowable equipment and/or procedures

11. Pollution charges are likely to be more efficient than direct controls because
    a. most of the reduction in pollution will be done by those who can implement reductions at low cost.
    b. everyone will be forced to show the same percentage reduction in pollution.
    c. no one likes paying taxes.
    d. pollution is a detrimental externality.

12. Compared with a system of direct controls, pollution charges
    a. are basically a "carrot" approach, relying on everyone's voluntary cooperation.
    b. are likely to lead to an equal percentage reduction in emissions from all pollution sources.
    c. will not reduce pollution, as firms will simply pass on these costs to their consumers with no impact on output levels.
    d. offer an incentive for continually reducing emissions, rather than reducing them just to some mandated level.

13. On free markets, the depletion of a scarce natural resource should lead to
    a. declining prices.
    b. no change in prices.
    c. rising prices.

14. Which one of the following would be expected to reduce the price of a depletable natural resource?
    a. the establishment of an effective producer cartel
    b. the discovery of previously unknown reserves
    c. an increase in the rate of inflation
    d. an increase in GDP

15. The quantity demanded of a scarce resource can exceed the quantity supplied
    a. if there is a sudden surge in demand.
    b. as economic growth increases demand.
    c. if monopolistic suppliers withhold supply.
    d. only if something prevents prices from adjusting.

16. The record of resource prices in the twentieth century shows
    a. a steady trend toward lower real prices for all resources.
    b. little trend in the real price of many resources.
    c. that most have increased year by year.

17. Rising resource prices can be a virtue as they provide an incentive for all but which one of the following?
    a. increased waste
    b. increased use of substitutes
    c. increased conservation
    d. increased innovation

18. Known reserves of a number of natural resources have
    a. declined.
    b. remained roughly constant.
    c. actually increased.

19. Measured relative to total output, i.e., GDP, the use of energy in the United States is now
    a. about as high as it has ever been.
    b. about the same as it has been for the last 20 years.
    c. significantly lower than it was 20 years ago.

20. Effective price ceilings for natural resources would likely
    a. provide an increased incentive for further exploration.
    b. shift the demand curve to the left.
    c. induce consumers to conserve.
    d. lead to resource shortages.

TEST B

Circle T or F for true or false.

T F 1. Pollution has been a serious problem only since World War II.

T F 2. Only capitalist economies suffer from extensive pollution.

T F 3. When considering public policies to limit discharges of wastes into a river basin, an equal percentage reduction by all polluters is likely to be the most economically efficient policy.

T F 4. Pollution charges imposed on monopolist firms will have no effect on the volume of their polluting activity because they will simply pass on the higher costs in the form of higher prices.

T F 5. Efficiency considerations strongly suggest that society should spend enough to reduce all pollution to zero.

T F 6. If left unchecked, the free-market mechanism will cause the demand for natural resources to exceed supply.

T F 7. During the past 100 years, the relative prices of virtually all natural resources have shown dramatic increases.

T F 8. Since 1950 known reserves of most minerals have dropped dramatically.

T F 9. Rising prices for natural resources provide an incentive for increased exploration and the development of new extraction technology.

T F 10. Rising prices can help control resource depletion as they induce firms and households to conserve.

SUPPLEMENTARY EXERCISES

POLLUTION AND PRICES

Can a producer simply pass on to its customers any pollution charges it must pay? This numerical example expands upon the problem in the Basic Exercise.

Consider the production of plastic bags, which cause pollution in direct proportion to the volume of production. The demand for bags is given by

$$Q = 2,600 - 40P$$

where Q is measured in millions of bags and P is measured in cents.

1. Assume that plastic bags are produced by a monopolist at a cost of 15 cents a bag; that is,

$$TC = 15 \times Q.$$

   Plot the demand, marginal revenue, average cost, and marginal cost curves on a piece of graph paper. What is the monopolist's profit-maximizing level of output, the associated price, and its profits?

2. The government now imposes a pollution tax equivalent to 5 cents a bag, that is, $TC = 0.20 \times Q$. What happens to output, prices, and profits if the monopolist simply raises the price by 5 cents? Can he do better by charging a different price? If so, what is that price, the associated quantity, and the new level of profits?

3. Assume now that bags are produced by identical small firms under conditions of perfect competition. Each firm produces bags with average cost given by

$$AC = 0.4(Q - 10)^2 + 15.$$

   What is the long-run market equilibrium price and quantity? How many firms are in the industry? How many bags does each firm produce?

4. Again the government imposes a pollution tax equivalent to 5 cents a bag on each producer. What happens in the short run when there are still the same number of bag producers? What about the long run? How many firms will produce how many bags at what price?

ECONOMICS IN ACTION

HEAVY METAL

It seems like we cannot pick up a newspaper without reading about some impending ecological disaster or some resource that is about to disappear. The late economist Julian Simon was an outspoken critic of such doomsday forecasts. He argued that our ancestors faced similar apparent disasters and, with some effort, overcame them. In many cases this involved learning how to use new metals or new sources of energy. According to Simon, the ultimate resource is human ingenuity. He was fond of quoting Henry George: "Both the jayhawk and the man eat chickens, but the more jayhawks, the fewer the chickens, while the more men, the more chickens."

In 1980 Simon issued a challenge to those predicting disaster. He argued that if resources were becoming increasingly scarce, their real price should increase. Simon offered the following $1,000 bet: Pick any resources and any future date. On that date, look to see if resource prices have risen by more or less than inflation. If prices were to rise by more than inflation, Simon would pay. If prices had not risen as fast as inflation, Simon would collect.

Simon's challenge was accepted in October 1980 by Paul Ehrlich, author of *Population Bomb*, along with John Harte and John Holdren. They chose five metals: chrome, copper, nickel, tin, and tungsten. On paper, they spent $200 on each metal, buying 51.28 pounds of chrome, 196.56 pounds of copper, 65.32 pounds of nickel, 229.16 pounds of tin, and 13.64 pounds of tungsten. The bet was to look at the inflation-adjusted price of this market basket of metal in October 1990. If, after adjusting for inflation, the market basket of metal cost more than $1,000, Simon would pay Ehrlich, Harte, and Holdren the difference from $1,000. On the other hand, if the total cost were less than $1,000, Ehrlich, Harte and Holdren owed Simon the difference.

The controversy was renewed in the spring of 1995 when, writing in the *San Francisco Chronicle*, Simon again offered to accept a bet, this time on "any trend pertaining to human welfare." Paul Ehrlich and Stephen Schneider responded by offering a package bet on 15 measures including average global temperature, the concentration of tropospheric ozone, emissions of sulfur dioxide in Asia, and biodiversity. Simon rejected their offer arguing that their measures would have only indirect effects on people. Simon preferred more direct measures such as life expectancy or the trend in deaths from skin cancer.

1. Who do you think won the original bet? What was the magnitude of the payoff?

2. What has happened to the prices of the five metals since 1990? (Remember you will need to correct for inflation as the bet concerned relative prices.)

3. If, today, you could choose either side of the original bet, with the outcome to be determined ten years from now, which would you take and why?

4. What about the most recent set of proposed wagers? What has happened to Ehrlich's and Schneider's preferred measures? What has happened to Simon's preferred measures? Which do you think is a more reasonable measure of trends in human welfare? Which side would you take? (Remember to check your wager against actual results in ten years.)

STUDY QUESTIONS

1. What do economists mean when they say pollution is an externality?

2. Why do unregulated competitive markets tend to produce more pollution than is socially desirable?

3. Would it be a good idea to reduce all pollution to zero? Why?

4. Why do economists argue that emission taxes are a more efficient means of reducing pollution than direct controls?

5. Why do economists argue that price is a better indicator of the scarcity of resources than estimates of reserves?

6. If we are running out of a particular resource, why would economists expect its price to rise?

7. What is the history of resource prices over the twentieth century?

8. Under what circumstances can the quantity demanded of a depletable resource exceed the quantity supplied?

9. What are the three virtues of rising prices for natural resources?

10. Why haven't reserves for many resources been falling over time as use of these resources continues to grow every year?

ECONOMICS ONLINE

Lots of information on energy production, consumption, and prices is available from the U.S. Department of Energy

http://www.eia.doe.gov/emeu

Taxation and Resource Allocation

18

Important Terms and Concepts

Ability-to-pay principle

Average tax rate

Benefits principle of taxation

Burden of a tax

Corporate income tax

Direct taxes

Economic efficiency

Excess burden

Excise tax

Fiscal federalism

Horizontal equity

Incidence of a tax

Indirect taxes

Marginal tax rate

Payroll tax

Personal income tax

Progressive taxes

Property tax

Proportional taxes

Regressive taxes

Social Security system

Tax deductions

Tax exempt

Tax loopholes

Tax shifting

Vertical equity

Learning Objectives

After completing this chapter, you should be able to:

- distinguish between progressive, proportional, and regressive tax systems.

- describe the major taxes levied by the federal government and identify which are direct taxes and which are indirect taxes.

- explain why the payroll tax is regressive.

- explain what issues make the financing of Social Security controversial.

- describe the major taxes levied by state, and local governments.

- explain the concept of fiscal federalism.

- contrast various concepts of fair or equitable taxation.

- explain the concept of efficiency in taxation and the difference between the burden and the excess burden of a tax.

- explain how changes in economic behavior can enable individuals to shift the burden of a tax, that is, explain what is wrong with the flypaper theory of tax incidence.

- explain what factors influence how the burden of a tax will be shared by consumers and suppliers.

- explain how some taxes can lead to efficiency gains, not losses.

CHAPTER REVIEW

This chapter concentrates on taxes: What taxes are collected in America and what economic effects they have. Few people like paying taxes. In fact, many people make adjustments in their behavior to reduce the taxes they must pay. These adjustments are an important part of the economic impact of taxes, an aspect often overlooked in popular discussions.

(1) Taxes are levied by federal, state, and local governments. For the most part, federal taxes tend to be (direct/indirect) taxes, while state and local governments rely more on _____ taxes. The largest revenue raiser for the federal government is the _____ _____ tax. Next in line in terms of revenue raised is the _____ tax. Other important federal taxes include the _____ income tax and excise taxes.

(2) When talking about income tax systems it is important to distinguish between average and marginal tax rates. The fraction of total income paid as income taxes is the (average/marginal) tax rate, while the fraction of each additional dollar of income paid as taxes is the _____ tax rate. If the average tax rate increases with income, the tax system is called _____. If the average tax rate stays constant for all levels of income, the tax system is said to be _____, while if the average tax rate falls as income increases, the result is a(n) _____ tax system. Tax exemptions have been used to influence favored activities, sometimes for broad social purposes and other times in response to effective political lobbying of special interests. Regardless of why they were enacted, tax exemptions typically (do not affect/increase/reduce) the progressivity of the personal income tax.

(3) The Social Security system is financed by (income/payroll) taxes. These taxes are considered (regressive/progressive) because they (do/do not) apply to all sources of income and because, except for taxes to support Medicare, after a certain level of income the marginal tax rate becomes _____. Social Security benefits do not work like private pension funds because benefits are not limited by individual contributions. The Social Security system was able to offer retired people good benefits for two reasons: (a) Real wages and incomes of those currently employed showed substantial growth; and (b) the number of working people was large relative to the number of retired individuals. The slowdown in the growth of real wages, changes in the age structure of the population, and the increasing lifespan of retirees required changes in the earlier approach to Social Security. Adjustments in both taxes and benefits have attempted to solve the problem by accumulating a surplus in the Social Security trust fund to pay future benefits. However, these adjustments (are/are not) sufficient for a permanent solution.

(4) The major state and local taxes, _____ taxes, and _____ taxes, are indirect taxes. State income taxes are also an important source of revenue for many states. In addition to the taxes raised by state governments, there is a system of transfers from the federal to state governments called fiscal _____.

Economists use the dual criteria of equity and efficiency to judge taxes. When talking about the fairness

of a tax, we are talking about _____. Various criteria have been advanced to judge the fair-   (5)

ness of a particular tax. The principle that equally situated individuals should pay equal taxes is referred to as

_____ equity. The principle that differentially situated individuals should be taxed in ways that

society deems fair is referred to as _____ equity. The ability-to-pay principle is an example of

_____ equity. Rather than looking at the income and wealth of families, there is an alterna-

tive approach to taxation that says people should pay in proportion to what they get from public services. This

principle for taxation is called the _____ principle. User fees, for example using gas taxes for high-

ways or entrance fees for parks, are examples of the _____ principle.

Efficiency is the other criterion that economists use to judge taxes. Almost all taxes cause some inefficiency.

The amount of money that would make an individual as well off with a tax as she was without the tax is called

the _____ of the tax. Sometimes it just equals the tax payment an individual makes, but more   (6)

generally it is (greater/less) than an individual's tax payment. The difference between the total burden and tax

payments is called the _____ _____. The reason that tax payments typically understate

the total burden of a tax is that the existence of the tax will often induce a change in behavior. Measuring only

the taxes paid (does/does not) take account of the loss of satisfaction resulting from the induced change in

behavior. The excess burden is the measure of the inefficiency of a particular tax. The principle of efficiency in

taxation calls for using taxes that raise the same revenue but with the (largest/smallest) excess burden. That is,

the principle of efficiency calls for using taxes that induce the smallest changes in behavior.

Often taxes will affect even those people who do not
pay them. Imagine that the government imposes a $50
excise tax on bicycles, paid by consumers at the time of
purchase. The tax will shift in the supply curve, as illustrated in **Figure 18-1**. Consumers do not care why the
price of bicycles has increased; there is no reason for
their demand curve to shift. The change in price from
the new tax will lead to a movement along the demand
curve. Suppliers collect the tax for the government and
are concerned with what is left over after taxes in order
to pay their suppliers and cover their labor cost and the
opportunity cost of their capital. How suppliers will
respond to the after-tax price is given by the original
supply curve. The price that consumers must pay comes
from adding the excise tax onto the original supply
curve and is given by the dashed line in Figure 18-1.

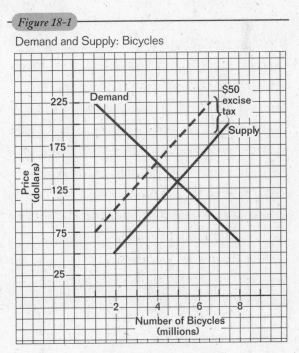

Figure 18-1

Demand and Supply: Bicycles

227

Looking at **Figure 18-1,** we see that compared with the original equilibrium, the new equilibrium involves a
(7) (higher/lower) price to consumers, a (higher/lower) price to suppliers, and a (larger/smaller) quantity of bicycles
produced. It would not be surprising if the change in supply resulted in unemployed bicycle workers, lower
wages for employed bicycle workers, and fewer bicycle firms. None of these workers or firms paid the tax, yet all
were affected by it.

As seen in the bicycle example, when consumers adjust to the new tax, they shift part of the burden onto
others. The question of how the burden of taxes is divided among different groups is the question of tax
(8) _____. At first glance it might appear that the burden of the tax is borne entirely by consumers who pay it at the time of sale. As the bicycle example makes clear, if consumers change their behavior as
a result of the tax, they may succeed in _____ part of the burden of the tax.

The study of tax incidence shows that the incidence of excise or sales taxes depends on the slopes of both
(9) the _____ and _____ curves. Payroll taxes, such as Social Security taxes, are like an
excise tax on labor services. Statistical work suggests that for most workers the supply of labor services is relatively (elastic/inelastic) with respect to wage rates, which in turn suggests that (workers/firms) rather than
_____ bear most of the burden of the payroll tax.

© 2012 Cengage Learning. All Rights Reserved. May not be scanned, copied or duplicated, or posted to a publicly accessible website, in whole or in part.

IMPORTANT TERMS AND CONCEPTS QUIZ

Choose the most appropriate definition for each of the following terms.

1. _____ Progressive tax
2. _____ Proportional tax
3. _____ Regressive tax
4. _____ Average tax rate
5. _____ Marginal tax rate
6. _____ Direct taxes
7. _____ Indirect taxes
8. _____ Personal income tax
9. _____ Tax loopholes
10. _____ Tax exempt
11. _____ Tax deductions
12. _____ Payroll tax
13. _____ Corporate income tax
14. _____ Excise tax
15. _____ Social Security system
16. _____ Property tax
17. _____ Fiscal federalism
18. _____ Horizontal equity
19. _____ Vertical equity
20. _____ Ability-to-pay principle
21. _____ Benefits principle of taxation
22. _____ Economic efficiency
23. _____ Burden of a tax
24. _____ Excess burden
25. _____ Incidence of a tax
26. _____ Tax shifting

a. Provision in the tax code that reduces taxes below statutory rates if certain conditions are met
b. Average tax rate increases with income
c. People who derive benefits from a government-provided service should pay the taxes to support it
d. Amount an individual would have to receive to make her as well off with the tax as she was without it
e. Allocation of the burden of a tax to specific groups
f. Tax levied on the assessed values of houses, office buildings, etc.
g. Taxes levied on people
h. Equally situated individuals should be taxed equally
i. Average tax rate falls as income rises
j. Income that is not included in taxable income
k. Sales tax on a specific commodity
l. Situation where economic reactions to a tax mean others bear part of the burden of the tax
m. System of grants from one level of government to the next
n. Ratio of taxes to income
o. Wealthier people should pay higher taxes
p. Average tax rate is the same at all income levels
q. Amount by which the burden of a tax exceeds the tax paid
r. Fraction of each additional dollar of income that is paid in taxes
s. Taxes levied on specific economic activities
t. Differently situated individuals should be taxed differently in a way society deems fair
u. Items that are subtracted before computing taxable income
v. Tax levied on the income of an individual or a family
w. A highly regressive tax levied on the earnings from work
x. Tax levied on the profits of corporations
y. Raises funds from the payroll tax and pays benefits to retirees
z. An economy uses every available opportunity to make someone better off without making anyone else worse off

229

BASIC EXERCISES

This exercise is designed to illustrate how the incidence of an excise tax depends on the elasticity (slope) of the demand and supply curves.

1. **Table 18-1** has data on the demand and supply of running shoes. In **Figure 18-2,** plot the demand curve from column 1 and the supply curve from column 3.

2. Determine the initial equilibrium price and quantity of running shoes.

   Price $ _____

   Quantity _____

3. Now assume that in a fit of pique, non-running legislators impose a fitness tax of $10 on each pair of shoes. Draw the new supply curve by shifting the original supply curve by the magnitude of the excise tax. The new equilibrium price is $ _____ and the new equilibrium quantity is _____.

4. How much more do consumers, who continue to buy running shoes, pay? $ _____. How does this increase in price compare with the excise tax of $10?

5. What is likely to happen to employment, wages, and profits in the running shoe industry?

Table 18-1

Demand for and Supply of Running Shoes

Demand (millions of pairs)		Price (dollars)	Supply (millions of pairs)	
(1)	(2)		(3)	(4)
68	53.0	30	38	48.00
65	52.5	32	40	48.33
62	52.0	34	42	48.67
59	51.5	36	44	49.00
56	51.0	38	46	49.33
53	50.5	40	48	49.67
50	50.0	42	50	50.00
47	49.5	44	52	50.33
44	49.0	46	54	50.67
41	48.5	48	56	51.00
38	48.0	50	58	51.33
35	47.5	52	60	51.67
32	47.0	54	62	52.00

Figure 18-2

Demand for and Supply: Running Shoes

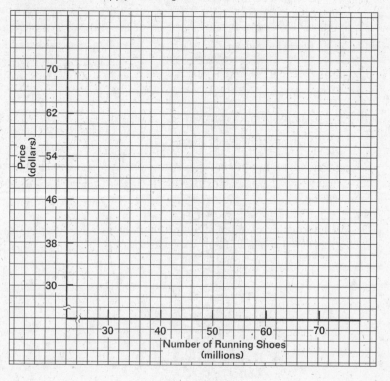

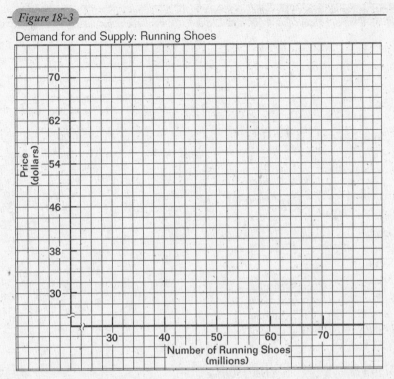

Figure 18-3

Demand for and Supply: Running Shoes

6. On **Figure 18-3,** plot the demand curve from column 2 and supply curve from column 3 of Table 18-1. Comparing Figures 18-2 and 18-3, we have the same supply curve but different demand curves. Both figures should show the same initial equilibrium price and quantity.

7. At the initial equilibrium price and quantity, which demand curve is more elastic? _____. (Review the appropriate material in Chapter 8 if you do not remember how to compute the price elasticity of a demand curve. Remember this distinction when it comes to comparing results.)

8. Now analyze the impact of the imposition of the same excise tax of $10 per pair of running shoes using Figure 18-3. The new equilibrium price is $ _____ and the new equilibrium quantity _____. In which case, Figure 18-2 or Figure 18-3, does the equilibrium price of running shoes rise the most? In which case are the volume of employment and the level of wages likely to fall the least? From this comparison we can conclude that the more inelastic the demand curve, the more the burden of an excise tax will be borne by _____.

9. Use information on demand from either column 1 or 2 and the two supply curves in columns 3 and 4 in Table 18-1 to analyze how the incidence of the tax is affected as the elasticity of supply changes.

SELF-TESTS FOR UNDERSTANDING

TEST A

Circle the most appropriate answer.

1. In the United States during the past 30 years, federal, state, and local taxes as a proportion of GDP have
   a. declined continuously.
   b. fluctuated with little trend.
   c. increased dramatically.

2. For the most part the federal government relies on _____ taxes while state and local governments rely on _____ taxes.
   a. excise; property
   b. sales; income
   c. property; sales
   d. direct; indirect

3. Direct taxes are levied on
   a. specific economic activities.
   b. reproducible property.
   c. people.
   d. the value added at each stage of production.

4. Which of the following are examples of direct taxes? (There may be more than one correct answer.)
   a. excise taxes
   b. income taxes
   c. estate taxes
   d. property taxes

5. Which of the following is an indirect tax?
   a. income taxes
   b. inheritance taxes
   c. head taxes
   d. sales taxes

6. Fiscal federalism refers to
   a. Alexander Hamilton's plan for assuming the debts of the individual states.
   b. federal government control of state and local spending.
   c. grants from one level of government to another.
   d. the balance between taxes paid to the federal government and the value of federal contracts received, measured on a state-by-state basis.

7. If income taxes are progressive, then the average tax rate
   a. decreases as income increases.
   b. is unchanged as income increases.
   c. increases as income increases.

8. If income taxes are progressive, then the marginal tax rate will _____ as income increases.
   a. decrease
   b. remain constant
   c. increase
   d. Any of the above are correct.

9. Christopher earned $20,000 last year and paid 10 percent or $2,000 in income taxes. His marginal income tax rate is 15 percent. If his income rises by $10,000 this year to $30,000, his income taxes will go up by
   a. $1,000.
   b. $1,500.
   c. $2,500.
   d. $10,000.

Use the following income tax schedule to answer questions 10 through 12.

Income	Taxes
$20,000	$4,000
$50,000	$10,000
$100,000	$20,000

10. The marginal tax rate
    a. decreases.
    b. is constant.
    c. increases.

11. The average tax rate
    a. decreases.
    b. is constant.
    c. increases.

12. This income tax system is
    a. regressive.
    b. proportional.
    c. progressive.

13. The ability-to-pay principle of taxation is an example of
    a. horizontal equity.
    b. vertical equity.
    c. the benefits principle.
    d. fiscal federalism.

14. If two families are identical in all respects, the principle of horizontal equity says that
    a. both families should pay more income taxes than other families with less income.
    b. both families should pay the same income tax.
    c. both families should have a lower average tax rate than a richer family.
    d. income taxes are, from a social viewpoint, a more appropriate form of taxation than are payroll taxes.

233

15. Which of the following is an example of the benefits principle of taxation?
    a. excise taxes on expensive jewelry
    b. higher property taxes as a percent of market value for more expensive homes
    c. public support for a new baseball stadium that is financed by a tax on baseball tickets
    d. Social Security taxes

16. The burden of a tax is defined as
    a. revenue raised minus the cost of collection.
    b. the proportion of taxes paid by individuals rather than corporations.
    c. the amount of money that would make a taxpayer as well off as he was before the tax was introduced.
    d. revenue raised plus the cost of collection.

17. The burden of most taxes is _____ the revenue raised.
    a. less than
    b. equal to
    c. greater than

18. The excess burden of a tax is
    a. the cost of collecting the tax.
    b. a measure of the inefficiency of the tax.
    c. best measured by the amount of complaining done by taxpayers.
    d. highest when the tax induces the least change in behavior.

19. A sales tax on which of the following will involve a small excess burden?
    a. a tax on a commodity with a zero price elasticity of demand
    b. a tax on a commodity with a very high elasticity of demand
    c. a tax on a commodity consumed primarily by poor families
    d. a tax on a commodity consumed primarily by rich families

20. The flypaper theory of tax incidence, which says that the burden of a tax is borne by those who pay the tax, is
    a. usually right.
    b. an example of the benefits approach to taxation.
    c. usually wrong.
    d. a measure of the vertical inequity of taxes.

21. Tax loopholes typically introduce new inefficiencies and _____ the progressivity of the income tax.
    a. reduce
    b. have little effect on
    c. increase

TEST B

Circle T or F for true or false.

T F   1. During the past 30 years federal, state, and local taxes have taken an ever-increasing share of the GDP.

T F   2. Federal payroll taxes are a more important source of revenue than the federal corporate income tax.

T F 3. State personal income taxes are an example of a direct, as opposed to indirect, tax.

T F 4. State taxes are primarily indirect taxes.

T F 5. The principle of horizontal equity says that equally situated individuals should be taxed equally.

T F 6. The ability-to-pay principle says that people who derive benefits from a particular public service should pay the taxes to finance it.

T F 7. The burden of a tax is normally less than the revenue raised by the tax.

T F 8. If a tax does not induce a change in economic behavior, then there is no excess burden.

T F 9. The flypaper theory of incidence is correct in regard to Social Security taxes.

T F 10. The concept of excess burden proves that taxes can never improve efficiency.

SUPPLEMENTARY EXERCISES

1. How Flat Is the Flat Tax?

The proposition that a comprehensive income tax with no loopholes would increase efficiency has led some to advocate what is called a flat tax. Most flat tax proposals have a basic exemption after which all income is taxed at the same rate. Proposals differ in the magnitude of the basic exemption, the tax rate to be used after that, whether some forms of income might be excluded from taxation, or whether some deductions would be allowed. (See Economics in Action below for a discussion of this last point.)

Consider a flat tax that uses a rate of 20 percent but allows a personal exemption of $5,000 for every individual— man, woman, or child. Taxable income for a family of four would be $20,000 less than their before-tax income. Complete **Table 18-2** to compute the marginal and average tax rates that a

Table 18-2

Marginal and Average Tax Rates for a Family of Four

Before Tax Income	Total Taxes	Average Tax Rate[a]	Marginal Tax Rate[b]
$20,000	_____	_____	
$30,000	_____	_____	_____
$40,000	_____	_____	_____
$50,000	_____	_____	_____
$100,000	_____	_____	_____
$250,000	_____	_____	_____

[a]Average tax rate = (Total taxes) ÷ (Before tax Income)
[b]Marginal tax rate = (Change in taxes) ÷ (Change in income)

family of four would face at different levels of income.

2. Revenue-Maximizing Cigarette Taxes

In the early 1990s there was considerable discussion of a possible increase in the federal tax on cigarettes. Some saw an increase as a cash cow to finance medical care reform or to help reduce the federal deficit. If interested in maximizing the amount of revenue, one would need to be careful not to raise the tax so high that demand fell so much and tax revenues actually declined.

Writing separately in *The New York Times* in June of 1993, economists Jeffrey Harris and Michael Grossman offered dramatically different estimates of the demand elasticity. Drawing on Canadian experience, Harris suggested that the price elasticity of demand for cigarettes was around 0.25. He estimated that a $2 increase in cigarette taxes would raise an additional $28 billion in revenue each year. Grossman argued that because of the addictive properties of smoking, the response to a change in price would be small in the short run but much larger in the long run.

The following straight-line demand curves are approximations of the Harris estimate and Grossman's long-run demand curve. Both of these demand curves have been constructed to mimic actual price and quantity data for 1992 when 24.9 billion packs of cigarettes were sold in the United States at an average price of $2 a pack that included a tax of $0.24.

Harris: $Q = 30.80 - 2.95 (P + T)$

Grossman: $Q = 46.72 - 10.91 (P + T)$

a. Verify that when $P + T = 2$ each demand curve is consistent with the 1992 quantity and price combination.
b. For each estimate of the demand curve and on the assumption that the supply curve for cigarettes is horizontal at a net-of-tax price of $1.76 a pack, i.e., $P = 1.76$, what tax maximizes tax revenues? (If you have access to a spreadsheet program on a computer, you might set up a small example that calculates the quantity demanded and tax revenues at different taxes. Alternatively, after writing down the expression for total tax revenues, you could differentiate the expression to find the value of T that maximizes revenue.)
c. What is the price elasticity of demand for each demand curve? For which estimate of demand, the estimate with the high or low elasticity, is the revenue-maximizing tax highest? Why?
d. Actual tax revenues will depend upon the price elasticity of supply as well as the price elasticity of demand. Question b assumed that the price elasticity of supply was infinite. What would happen to the incidence of any increase in taxes if the price elasticity of supply were zero or somewhere in between?

ECONOMICS IN ACTION

A PERSON'S MORTGAGE IS HER TAX DEDUCTION

While a person's home may or may not be a castle, her mortgage is likely to yield a handsome tax deduction. Under current law, taxpayers may deduct from taxable income mortgage interest on up to $1 million of mortgage debt they have used to acquire and improve first or second homes and interest on up to $100,000 of home-equity loans regardless of the purpose of the loan. No other consumer interest is deductible. Whether it is in an individual's best interest to take the mortgage interest deduction depends upon the magnitude of her mortgage interest and other deductions vis-à-vis the standard deduction. For example, in 2004, a family could itemize deductions or take a standard deduction of $9,500. If a family's deductions, including mortgage interest, totaled less than $9,500, then it made more sense to use the standard deduction. In the mid-1990s, at a time when about 64 percent of households were homeowners and, of these, a bit less than 60 percent had a mortgage, only 28 percent of taxpayers used the mortgage interest deduction. For the others, using the standard deduction rather than itemizing was preferable.

Not surprisingly, higher income taxpayers with larger homes and larger mortgages derive the largest benefit from the mortgage interest deduction. Peter Dreier, a professor of public policy at Occidental College in Los Angeles, estimated that in the mid-1990s, 44 percent of the tax benefits associated with the mortgage interest deduction went to the richest 5 percent of taxpayers. Professor Dreier estimated that the tax savings for these rich taxpayers was about $22 billion annually, an amount that was roughly the same as government spending on subsidized housing for the poor.

The popularity of the mortgage interest deduction is such that a number of prominent flat tax proposals would retain the deduction while attempting to eliminate other deductions and loopholes. For example, in early 1996 Republican candidates for president were divided on this issue. According to a story in *The New York Times* subtitled "Republicans tiptoe around the mortgage deduction," only Malcolm Forbes, Jr. stated publicly that he favored elimination of the mortgage interest deduction as part of implementation of a flat tax. Pat Buchanan wanted to retain it, while Senators Bob Dole and Phil Gramm managed to avoid taking a hard position one way or the other.

What explains the popularity of a mortgage interest deduction when only a minority of taxpayers use the deduction each year and the benefits go disproportionately to rich taxpayers? Counting only those who use the deduction in a single year understates the constituency who supports the deduction. Many homeowners took advantage of the mortgage interest deduction when they first bought their home. Sellers and potential homeowners see the deduction as an important part of a buyer's financial planning. Some argue that public policy should support home ownership and that the mortgage interest deduction does just that. Others argue that one could achieve the same objective with a tax credit rather than a tax deduction and that a tax credit would be fairer.[1] Stricter limits on the magnitude of mortgage interest that could be deducted have also been proposed. States with the highest house prices, for example, California, New York, Connecticut, and New Jersey, would be most affected by such a change.

There is concern that elimination of the mortgage interest deduction would disrupt housing markets causing the price of many homes to decline. Estimates of such effects vary, but most analysts agree that the largest adjustments would occur for the most expensive homes. Should the deduction be eliminated suddenly, the Mortgage Bankers Association projects an increase in mortgage defaults. Economists who argue in favor of elimination of the mortgage interest deduction see it as part of a broader strategy of tax reform. They are concerned that the favorable tax treatment of mortgage interest has distorted investment away from business

---

[1]Assume that two families each pay $1,000 mortgage interest. A tax credit of 20 percent would reduce the taxes of both families by $200. In contrast the value of a deduction depends upon a family's marginal tax rate, which in turn depends upon its income. For example, in 2004 the value of a $1,000 deduction to a family of four earning $35,000 was $100 while the same $1,000 deduction would save $350 for a rich family paying the highest marginal tax rate.

237

capital toward houses, in particular, housing for the rich. One might also note that not all countries allow homeowners to deduct mortgage interest. For example, levels of home ownership are high in Canada and Australia, two countries without mortgage interest deduction.

1. Should anything be done about the mortgage interest deduction? Should it be eliminated? Should stricter limits be adopted? Should it be turned into a tax credit?

2. If a decision were made to eliminate or change the mortgage interest deduction, what would you expect to happen to house prices and the affordability of housing? What provisions, if any, should be made for homeowners who purchased homes believing that the mortgage interest deduction would not be changed?

SOURCE: "The Pitfall in the Flat Tax, Republicans Tiptoe Around the Mortgage Deduction," *The New York Times*, January 12, 1996.

STUDY QUESTIONS

1. Should income taxes be progressive or proportional? Explain your reasoning.

2. Without changing the level of spending, should your state increase income taxes in order to reduce sales taxes or increase sales taxes to reduce income taxes? Why?

3. Why do economists consider the Social Security tax to be regressive?

4. In the final analysis, who pays the Social Security tax, workers or firms?

5. What is fiscal federalism?

6. What is the difference between horizontal and vertical equity?

7. If a progressive income tax meets social concerns about vertical equity, can it also satisfy concerns about horizontal equity? Explain.

8. What is the difference between the benefits principle of taxation and the concept of ability to pay?

9. Why do economists say that the burden of a tax is usually greater than the revenue raised by the tax?

10. Is it true that the more elastic the demand curve, the smaller the amount of any sales tax that consumers will pay? Explain.

11. Should the United States move to a flat tax system?

12. What would you do about Social Security?

ECONOMICS ONLINE

Get your tax forms and find data about the federal tax system from the IRS homepage.

http://www.irs.gov/

Should states use tax incentives as a way to attract businesses? Does the country as a whole benefit from this sort of activity or is this just a way for companies to minimize their taxes by playing off states against each other? Examine these questions at a web site maintained by the Federal Reserve Bank of Minneapolis:

http://minneapolisfed.org/research/studies/econwar

The Congressional Budget Office releases studies on a variety of tax topics on a regular basis. The CBO can be found on the web at http://www.cbo.gov. Studies that might be of special interest include the following:

• Effective Federal Tax Rates: 1979-2001, April 2004

http://www.cbo.gov/showdoc.cfm?index=5324

• Effective Federal Tax Rates Under Current Law, 2001 to 2014, August 2004

http://www.cbo.gov/showdoc.cfm?index=5746

• Recent CBO studies on Social Security are listed at

http://www.cbo.gov/publications/collections/collections.cfm?collect=5

The Tax Policy Center is a joint venture of the Urban Institute and Brookings Institution "to provide independent analyses of current and longer-term tax issues and to communicate its analyses to the public and to policymakers in a timely and accessible manner."

http://www.taxpolicycenter.org

Pricing the Factors
of Production

Important Terms and Concepts

Factors of production

Entrepreneurship

Marginal physical product
(MPP)

Marginal revenue product
(MRP)

Derived demand

Capital

Investment

Interest

Economic rent

Marginal land

Economic profit

Invention

Innovation

Learning Objectives

After completing this chapter, you should be able to:

- explain why the demand curve for a factor of production is the downward-sloping portion of its marginal revenue product curve.

- explain why the demand for inputs is a derived demand.

- distinguish between investment and capital.

- explain how changes in interest rates may affect the profitability of specific investment decisions and hence the demand for funds.

- explain why the supply of funds from savers with fixed savings objectives may not increase when interest rates rise.

- explain who gains, who loses, and why, under an effective usury ceiling.

- distinguish between land rents and economic rents.

- identify inputs that receive economic rent, given supply curves of various slopes.

- explain why the fact that apartment buildings need to be maintained and that they can be reproduced at close to constant cost implies that, in the long run, rent control measures are likely to be self-defeating.

- explain why, in the real world, profits are likely to offer returns in excess of the interest rate.

- explain how the concept of economic rent is relevant to issues concerning the taxation of profits.

CHAPTER REVIEW

This chapter initiates the discussion of input prices by considering what determines the rental price of money, the rental price of land, and the income of entrepreneurs. If this material is combined with the material in the next chapter on wages—the rental price for labor services—and the material in Chapter 17 on the price of natural resources, we have a complete theory of income distribution based on marginal

(1) _____. This chapter and the next build upon our earlier discussion of optimal input use by firms. We saw earlier that the demand for factors of production can be derived from profit-maximizing considerations. A firm should be willing to pay for labor, land, natural resources, and so forth because it can use these factors to produce and sell output. As we have learned, the demand curve for a particular factor of production is derived from the downward-sloping portion of the marginal _____ product curve.

INTEREST

Interest rates adjust to balance the demand for funds by borrowers and the supply of funds from lenders. The
(2) demand curve for funds has a (negative/positive) slope, indicating that at lower interest rates people will want to borrow (less/more). The supply curve of funds is most likely to have a (negative/positive) slope, indicating that a (higher/lower) interest rate is necessary to induce lenders to increase the supply of loans.[1] An effective usury ceiling would impose an interest rate (above/below) the market clearing rate as determined by the intersection of the demand and supply curves.

The demand for funds for business borrowing derives from a consideration of the profitability of investment projects. In earlier chapters we talked about capital and labor as factors of production. Investment projects add to the stock of capital. The profitability of investment projects is another way of referring to the marginal revenue product of more capital. The profitability of investment projects is complicated because most projects require dollar outlays immediately while offering returns in the future. To evaluate the profitability of an investment we need some way of comparing current and future dollars. Economists and business people compare future and present dollars through a process called _____. As explained in the appendix to this chapter, this process relies on interest rate calculations. Higher interest rates will mean that (fewer/more) investment projects will be profitable. Thus higher interest rates will be associated with a (higher/lower) quantity of funds demanded and imply a negatively sloped demand curve for business borrowing.

RENT

When considering the notion of rent, remember that economists use the term in a special way different from
(3) everyday usage. Most of the rent that you may pay for an apartment (is/is not) economic rent. Economic rent refers to the earnings of a factor of production that (equal/exceed) the minimum amount necessary to keep that factor in its current employment.

---

[1]Savers with fixed goals, e.g., saving for a specific purpose, may be able to reduce the amount of money they need to lend if interest rates increase.

If the supply curve of some factor, such as land, is really vertical, it means that the factor would be willing to work for as little as nothing. It also means that it is impossible to duplicate this factor at any cost; otherwise, a high enough price would induce an increase in supply, and the supply curve would not be vertical. In the case of a vertical supply curve, (some/all) of the market price would be economic rent. If the supply curve of some fac- (4) tor is a horizontal line, the market price will reflect exactly what is necessary to induce any supply. In this case an economist would say that the factor receives _____ economic rent.

An upward-sloping supply curve means that higher prices will induce an increase in supply, but there will be some units of supply that would have been present at lower prices. In this case (most/all) units of the factor (5) will receive some economic rent. In fact, it is only the marginal unit, the unit on the supply curve at the market equilibrium price, that earns no economic rent. The market price is as high as it is to induce this last unit to supply itself. All other units would have been available at a lower price, and thus (part/all) of their earnings are economic rent. Land is a traditional input to use when talking about rent, but remember that land is not the only factor to earn economic rent. Anyone who would stay in a particular job for less pay, because he or she likes the work or the location, or for any other reason, (is/is not) earning some economic rent.

When considering land rentals it is clear that not all land is the same: Some parcels are more productive or better located than others. Economists would expect that land rents, the price for using a piece of land for a period of time, will adjust to reflect these differences. More productive land that produces the same output at lower cost will receive a (higher/lower) land rent. In equilibrium, rents should adjust so that the cost of produc- (6) ing the same quantity of output, including land rents, will be _____ on all parcels of land. If not, there is a clear incentive to use the land with lower total cost. This incentive to switch parcels increases the rent on the originally low-cost piece of land and decreases rent on the other pieces of land. The process stops only when land rentals have adjusted to again equate total cost.

As with any other productive factor, an increase in the demand for goods produced with land will (decrease/increase) the demand for land. Poor quality land, whose use was unprofitable at lower output prices, (7) will now become profitable to use. Thus, more land will be used, and land rents will again adjust to equal- ize the costs of production on all parcels. As a result, the rent on previously used, higher quality land will (increase/decrease). An additional part of the response to increased land demand is likely to be (more/less) in- tensive use of existing land.

PROFIT

Profits are a residual item after revenues have been used to pay other costs—labor, material inputs, interest on borrowed funds, rent, and taxes. Profits also represent the return on equity investments in a firm.[2] In a world of perfect certainty, capitalists should expect the profits on their investments to offer a return just equal to the in- terest rate. The rate of interest would be the opportunity cost of their equity investment in the firm. Any higher

---

[2]Equity refers here to the amount of their own money the owners have invested in their company. Specifically, if they dissolved the company and paid off its creditors, the amount left over is their equity.

return would be competed away. Any lower return would lead some funds to be invested elsewhere in the pursuit of returns at least equal to the interest rate. (Remember that in simple competitive markets, economic profits equal zero in long-run equilibrium.)

In the real world, investments are not certain. Many business investments look like uncertain gambles. If entrepreneurs dislike taking risks, then profits will have to offer them the expectation of returns that are (greater/less) than the rate of interest. Profits that are the result of monopoly power would be (greater/less) than the interest rate. Finally, successful innovation will often give an entrepreneur temporary monopoly profits and lead to a rate of profit that is (greater/less) than the interest rate. The effects of taxing profits will depend upon whether profits are mostly economic rents or mostly a necessary return to attract entrepreneurial talent.

IMPORTANT TERMS AND CONCEPTS QUIZ

Choose the best definition for the following terms.

1. _____ Factors of production
2. _____ Entrepreneurship
3. _____ Marginal physical product
4. _____ Marginal revenue product
5. _____ Derived demand
6. _____ Capital
7. _____ Investment
8. _____ Interest
9. _____ Economic rent
10. _____ Marginal land
11. _____ Economic profit
12. _____ Invention
13. _____ Innovation

a. Payment to a factor of production in excess of the minimum amount necessary to keep the factor in its present employment

b. Additional units of a given input add diminishing amounts to total output

c. Starting firms, introducing innovations, and taking the necessary risks in seeking business opportunities

d. Change in sales revenue from selling the marginal physical product of an additional unit of input

e. Flow of resources into the production of new capital

f. Act of generating a new idea

g. Inputs used in the production process

h. Payment for the use of funds

i. Land on the borderline of being used

j. Producer's demand for inputs

k. Act of putting a new idea into practical use

l. Increase in output from a one-unit increase in a given input

m. Stock of plant and equipment from past investment

n. Total revenue minus total cost including the opportunity cost of owner-supplied inputs

244

BASIC EXERCISES

This exercise is designed to illustrate how differences in land rents reflect differences in productivity.

This summer Darlene can work as a checker at the local grocery store for as many hours as she wants, earning $10 an hour. She also is considering raising flowers for sale on one of two plots of land. The sunny plot has good soil, and Darlene estimates that if she worked 40 hours a week she could earn $500 a week raising flowers on this land. The second plot is marginal land available for free. It would require the use of fertilizer and special mulches to raise the same quantity of flowers. Darlene estimates these extra costs would total $60 a week.

1. Calculate Darlene's economic profit from using the marginal plot of land on the assumption that it is available at zero rent. Do not forget to include the opportunity cost of Darlene's own work as an element of cost.

2. If Darlene's estimate of the increased cost of using the marginal land is typical of other uses, what market rent would you expect to be charged for the use of the sunny plot and why?

3. Explain why the profit that Darlene could earn from using the marginal plot of land limits the rent the owner of the sunny plot will be able to charge.

SELF-TESTS FOR UNDERSTANDING

TEST A

Circle the most appropriate answer.

1. The demand for factors of production is
   a. an applied demand.
   b. insensitive to changes in the price of factors.
   c. best represented as an upward-sloping curve.
   d. a derived demand.

2. Profit-maximizing firms will use more of a productive factor as long as the price of the factor is less than its
   a. marginal revenue product.
   b. marginal cost.
   c. marginal physical product.
   d. average product.

3. The demand curve for productive factors is the downward-sloping portion of the relevant
   a. marginal physical product curve.
   b. marginal cost curve.
   c. marginal revenue product curve.
   d. average cost curve.

4. If the price of widgets increases,
   a. we should see a movement along the demand curves for factors producing widgets.
   b. the demand curves for factors producing widgets should shift to the right.
   c. the best guess is that there will be little change in the demand for factors producing widgets.
   d. the demand curves for factors producing widgets should shift to the left.

5. The concept of discounting suggests that when compared with a dollar next year, a dollar today is worth
   a. less.
   b. the same.
   c. more.

6. If interest rates increase, the difference in the value of $100 today compared with $100 next year will
   a. decrease.
   b. be unchanged.
   c. increase.
   d. be impossible to determine.

7. Firms produce output using land, labor, natural resources, entrepreneurship, and
   a. capital.
   b. investment.
   c. interest.
   d. economic rent.

8. Firms undertake _____ to add to the stock of _____.
   a. innovation; invention
   b. discounting; investment
   c. investment; capital
   d. capital; investment

9. Which of the following is an example of investment as opposed to capital?
   a. the fleet of 747s owned by American Airlines
   b. Julia's purchase of 100 shares of Xerox stock
   c. the five apartment buildings owned by Julio
   d. the new warehouse that Kimberly will have built this year

10. Economists expect that land rents will
    a. adjust to equalize total costs of production across different parcels of land.
    b. mean that more productive parcels of land receive higher rents.
    c. result in more intensive use of more productive parcels of land.
    d. all of the above.

11. Parcel of land G can be used to raise corn at a cost of $50,000. The same amount of corn can be raised on parcel P for $75,000. An economist would expect the rent on parcel G to exceed that on parcel P by
    a. $25,000.
    b. $50,000.
    c. $75,000.
    d. $125,000.

12. Marginal land refers to land that
    a. is most productive for growing any given crop.
    b. is on the borderline of being used in productive activity.
    c. earns economic rent.
    d. borders interstate highways in rural areas.

13. The term economic rent refers to
    a. the sales tax portion of consumer purchases.
    b. rent paid by economists for their apartments.
    c. earnings by factors of production greater than necessary to induce supply.
    d. land rents.

14. If the supply curve for some factor of production can be represented as a horizontal line, an economist would say that _____ of the income earned by this factor is economic rent.
    a. none
    b. some
    c. all

15. An input will earn pure economic rent if the supply curve for the input is
    a. horizontal.
    b. upward sloping.
    c. vertical.

16. Which of the following individuals are earning economic rent?
    a. Ruth, who says, "If this job paid any less I'd quit; it wouldn't be worth the hassle."
    b. Sergio, who says, "This job is so interesting I'd work here even for a lot less."
    c. Nick, whose purchase of an apartment building should bring him a return equal to the interest rate.
    d. Sophia, who is expecting a substantial profit from her investment in the manufacture of solar energy panels to compensate her for the risks she is taking.

17. Rent seeking refers to
    a. efforts of college students to find apartments each fall.
    b. the use of productive resources in the pursuit of political opportunities for profits.
    c. attempts to get departments within a company to pay for space they occupy.
    d. a landlord's efforts to collect from deadbeat tenants.

18. In a world of competitive firms with no uncertainty or risk, economists expect that the profit rate will be
    a. less than the rate of interest.
    b. equal to the rate of interest.
    c. higher than the rate of interest.

19. Monopoly power, whether permanent or temporary, means that profits will be
    a. less than the rate of interest.
    b. equal to the rate of interest.
    c. higher than the rate of interest.

247

20. Higher taxes on profits will have little impact if
    a. profits are mostly economic rent.
    b. profits are equal to nominal interest rates.
    c. profits are growing.
    d. the supply curve for entrepreneurial talent is horizontal.

TEST B

Circle T or F for true or false.

T F 1. The demand curve for a factor of production is identical to its curve of marginal physical productivity.

T F 2. Interest rates represent the market price for the use of funds.

T F 3. Discounting means using the rate of interest to compare future and present dollars.

T F 4. The factories that the Ford Motor Company uses to produce cars are an example of capital rather than investment.

T F 5. According to economists, only land earns economic rent.

T F 6. Inputs available in perfectly elastic supply will earn no economic rent.

T F 7. The rent on any piece of land should equal the difference between production costs on that piece of land and production costs on the next-best available piece of land.

T F 8. The law of diminishing returns implies that an increase in the demand for land will actually reduce the rent paid on most parcels of land.

T F 9. The reason that most rent-control laws have adverse effects in the long run is that the long-run supply of structures, as opposed to land, is likely to be quite elastic.

T F 10. Economic theory proves that the rate of profits must equal the rate of interest.

| Appendix | *Discounting and Present Value*

Important Terms and Concepts

Discounting

Present value

Learning Objective

After completing the exercises below, you should be able to

* appreciate how discounting or present value calculations can help when considering investment decisions.

IMPORTANT TERMS AND CONCEPTS QUIZ

Choose the best definition for the following term.

1. _____ Present value

   a. The current value of dollars to be received or paid at various dates in the future

   b. Future worth of a sum of money receivable or payable at the present date

BASIC EXERCISES

1. **Discounting and Investment Decision**

   Eric has an opportunity to purchase a machine to make gyros. The machine cost $4,000 and is expected to last two years. After other expenses, Eric expects this investment to return $2,000 next year and $2,500 in two years. Is buying the machine a good investment?

   a. Fill in the column of **Table 19-1** to compute the present value of costs and returns on the assumption that Eric uses his own $4,000 and the interest rate is 10 percent.

   Table 19-1

   Cash Flows from Investing in Eric's Gyro Machine

Time	Item	Amount	Present Value* 5 percent	Present Value* 10 percent
Now	Cost	$4,000	$4,000	$4,000
One year	Return	2,000	_____	_____
Two years	Return	2,500	_____	_____
		Present value of all returns	_____	_____
		Net present value of project	_____	_____

   *Present value = dollars in n years $\div (1 + i)^n$ = (dollars in the nth year) divided by (1 plus the rate of interest multiplied by itself n times)

   b. Add up the present value of the returns and compare this sum with the cost of the machine. Which is greater? _____. If the interest rate is 10 percent, should Eric purchase the machine? _____.

c. Assume now that the interest rate is 5 percent. Fill in the relevant column of the table to compute the present value of the returns at an interest rate of 5 percent.

d. Sum the present value of the returns and compare this sum with the cost of the machine. Which is greater? _____. If the interest rate is 5 percent, should Eric purchase the machine? _____.

e. The decision rule discussed in the text, and the one you should have used when answering questions b and d, compares the present value of future returns to the cost of an investment project.[3] If the present value of the returns exceeds the cost, it means that Eric can do better by undertaking the investment than by investing in financial assets that yield the rate of interest we used to discount the future returns. If the present value of the returns is less than the cost, it means that Eric would do better with a financial investment. You can verify that this is the case by filling in the missing parts of **Table 19-2** for interest rates of 5 and 10 percent.

Table 19-2

Can Eric Do as Well by Investing $4,000 at the Rate of Interest?

	Interest Rate	
	5 percent	10 percent
1. Initial deposit	$4,000	$4,000
2. Interest after one year (5 percent and 10 percent of line 1)	_____	_____
3. Balance after one year (line 1 plus line 2)	_____	_____
4. Withdrawal after one year*	$2,000	$2,000
5. New balance (line 3 minus line 4)	_____	_____
6. Interest during second year (5 percent and 10 percent of line 5)	_____	_____
7. Balance after second year (line 5 plus line 6)	_____	_____

Compare line 7 with the $2,500 Eric would have received in the second year if he had bought the gyro machine. Line 7 should be greater (less) if the net present value of the project in Table 17-1 is negative (positive). That is, if the net present value of the project is negative (positive), Eric will do better (worse) by making a financial investment at the given rate of interest.

*This $2,000 matches the return after one year from the gyro investment.

---

f. What if Eric had to borrow the money? Would the same sorts of calculations be sufficient to help you decide whether he should borrow the money? The answer is yes. The reason is that while figuring the present value of the returns, you are accounting for interest payments whether Eric has the money or not. If he does not have the money, he will need to pay a lender. Even if he does have the money he will need to "pay" himself as much as he might have earned in some other investment. That is, he will need to meet the opportunity cost of his own money. Fill in the missing parts of **Table 19-3**, which has been constructed to illustrate just this point.

To summarize:

a. Present value calculations use interest rates to transform dollars in the future into their equivalent today.

b. Comparing the present value of returns and costs is a good way to evaluate investment opportunities.

c. Comparing the present value of returns and costs is a good procedure whether you have to borrow the money or not, assuming that you can borrow or lend at the same rate of interest you are using in your present value calculations.

---

[3]In this example all costs occur "today" and all returns come in the future. Thus one needs to discount the returns and compare them to the cost. If a project will incur costs in future years, then one should compare the present value of all current and future costs with the present value of all future returns.

Table 19-3

What if Eric Had to Borrow the $4,000?

		Interest Rate	
		5 percent	10 percent
1.	Amount borrowed	$4,000	$4,000
2.	Interest due at end of first year	$ 200	$ 400
3.	Cash flow from investment	$2,000	$2,000
4.	Net cash flow after interest payment (line 3 minus line 2)	_____	_____
5.	Interest earned during second year by investing net cash flow (5 percent and 10 percent of line 4)	_____	_____
6.	Cash flow from investment	$2,500	$2,500
7.	Total at end of second year (line 4 plus line 5 plus line 6)	_____	_____
8.	Interest due at end of second year	$ 200	$ 400
9.	Loan repayment	$4,000	$4,000
10.	Net (line 7 minus line 8 and line 9)	_____	_____

The crucial question is whether the gyro investment offers any return after paying back the loan with interest. Any dollars left over are pure profit for Eric since he did not invest any of his own money. It should be true that Eric will have a positive (negative) net if the present value of returns is greater (less) than the present value of costs. Is it?

(The entries on line 10 are dollars in the second year. What is the present value of these dollars? How do these present values compare with the net present values calculated in Table 17-1 above?)

d. If the present value of returns equals the present value of costs, an investment opportunity offers the same return as investing at the rate of interest.

e. If the present value of returns exceeds the present value of costs, an investment opportunity offers a greater return than investing at the rate of interest.

f. If the present value of returns is less than the present value of costs, an investment opportunity offers a worse return than investing at the rate of interest.

2. **When Is $1,000,000 Not $1,000,000?**

On Wednesday, April 14, 1993, Don Calhoun earned $1,000,000 for about five seconds of work. Or did he? After reluctantly accompanying a friend to a basketball game between the Chicago Bulls and Miami Heat, Mr. Calhoun was chosen at random from the audience. Standing at one free-throw line, he was given one shot at the basket at the other end of the court. His baseball-like hurl was all net.

Like most state lotteries, the million dollars that Mr. Calhoun received was not $1,000,000 immediately, rather it was a commitment to pay $50,000 a year for 20 years. What is the cost of Mr. Calhoun's $1,000,000 to the restaurant and soft-drink sponsors of the long free-throw contest (or their insurance company)? Why is it less than $1,000,000?

SUPPLEMENTARY EXERCISES

CAN YOU SHARE IN MONOPOLY PROFITS?

Assume that the major oil companies are able to exercise considerable monopoly power and, as a result, earn substantial monopoly profits on their investments, far in excess of the interest rate. Can you share these profits and earn the same high rate of return by buying oil company stocks?

What determines the price of oil company stocks? An economist would expect the market price to be close to the present value of the future returns from owning the stock, that is, close to the present value of expected future dividends and capital gains. Thus if dividends are high because of huge monopoly profits, the price of the stock will be _____. If huge monopoly profits and the resulting future dividends were known for sure, what rate of return do you think you could earn by buying oil company stocks? Just who does earn those monopoly profits?

ECONOMICS IN ACTION

NICE WORK IF YOU CAN GET IT

A number of observers have charged that compensation for executives of American corporations is excessive. Certainly the compensation received by some individuals has been eye-catching, notably the $650 million that Charles Wang, CEO of Computer Associates, realized in 1999 and the $706 million that Lawrence Ellison, CEO of Oracle, received in 2002. The $236 million that Michael Dell, CEO of Dell Computer, received in 2000 seem puny only by comparison. In the 1980s, direct salary payments were a major part of executive compensation. Since then stock options have become increasingly important and by the late 1990s accounted for over half of executive compensation at large companies.[4] Stock options give an individual the right to purchase stock at a specified price. This price is called the exercise price of the option. If a company does well and its stock price increases, there may be a substantial difference between the stock price and the exercise price. The increasing importance of stock options in executive compensation reflects several factors: legislation authored by U.S. Representative Martin Sabo (D-Minnesota) to limit the ability of corporations to deduct large salary payments from taxable income; criticism that compensation bore little relation to performance; the 1990s stock market boom; and changes in tax laws that tax capital gains at lower rates than salary.

While stock options would seem to link compensation to performance, critics say that in practice compensation and the awarding of options often bear little relation to stock performance. Since executives sit on each other's boards of directors they are hardly the ones to be trusted when it comes to setting each other's compensation. There was much criticism of rising executive compensation in 2001 and 2002, a period when stock prices dropped by an average of 40 percent. *Forbes* magazine reports annually on CEO compensation and grades pay

---

[4]Stock options are not restricted just to top executives. Startup companies often offer stock options to attract employees.

against performance. In 2004 Forbes gave the Disney Corporation an F for awarding its CEO, Michael Eisner, compensation that averaged $121 million a year over the previous six years when investors in Disney stock were losing 5 percent a year.

Writing in *The Wall Street Journal* in 1999, Alfred Rappaport, professor emeritus at Northwestern University, Kellogg Graduate School of Management, argued that the structure of stock options is not efficient. Just as a rising tide raises all boats, a rising stock market is likely to result in stock price increases that have nothing to do with the performance or leadership of individual CEOs. Rappaport argues that much of the rise in stock values in the late 1990s was related to declines in interest rates and inflation, factors that bore no relation to the contributions of an individual CEO. Citing a survey by LEK Consulting, Rappaport notes that more than 60 percent of stock options granted from 1993 to 1999 were for below average performance; that is, the increase in the price of stock of these companies was less than the increase in broad market averages. Rappaport argues that the exercise price of stock options should be linked to an index of the stock of a company's competition as is the case for a number of European companies. In this way, options would have value only if the company's stock outperformed its competitors.

SOURCE: Alfred Rappaport, "Stock Options that Don't Reward Laggards," *The Wall Street Journal,* March 30, 1999; "Executive Pay," *The Wall Street Journal,* April 8, 1999; "CEOs and Their Indian Rope Trick," *The Economist,* December 11, 2004.

1. What sorts of incentives and rewards for executive performance are in the best interests of stockholders? of the economy?

2. Should there be limits on executive compensation? If so, what and why? What would be the effect on incentives of different limits?

3. What do you think of Rappaport's idea to link the exercise price of stock options to a relevant stock price index?

STUDY QUESTIONS

1. What does it mean to say that the demand for a factor of production is a derived demand?

2. Why is the demand curve for a factor of production the downward-sloping portion of the factor's curve of marginal revenue product?

3. What is the difference between investment and capital?

4. How does discounting help a firm determine the profitability of investment projects?

5. How is the profitability of investment projects affected when interest rates change?

6. What is the definition of economic rent?

7. Why isn't the rent you pay for an apartment economic rent?

8. What is meant by the statement in the text that almost all employees earn some economic rent?

9. What explains differences in rent for different parcels of land?

10. Why doesn't competition work to limit profits to the rate of interest?

11. What is the difference between invention and innovation?

ECONOMICS ONLINE

You can get information on executive compensation online from *Forbes* magazine.

http://www.forbes.com/ceos

The AFL-CIO maintains a web page that tracks executive compensation.

http://www.aflcio.org/corporateamerica/paywatch/

Labor and Entrepreneurship: The Human Inputs

20

Important Terms and Concepts

Investments in human capital

Substitution effect

Income effect

Backward-bending

Human capital theory

Labor union

Monopsony

Bilateral monopoly

Collective bargaining

Innovative entrepreneurship

Marginal revenue product of labor (MRP_l)

Learning Objectives

After completing this chapter, you should be able to:

- explain how the demand for labor is derived from a firm's profit-maximizing decisions about the use of factors of production.

- discuss recent trends in American labor markets.

- describe the impact of labor saving innovations on wages.

- explain how income and substitution effects influence the slope of the supply curve of labor.

- explain how income and substitution effects influence the slope of the supply curve of labor.

- use demand and supply curves to determine the equilibrium wage and employment in a competitive labor market.

- discuss the factors that help explain why wages differ among individuals.

- discuss how human capital theory explains the observed correlation between more education and higher wages.

- distinguish between a monopsonist and a monopolist.

- explain the role of entrepreneurs in guiding critical market activities.

CHAPTER REVIEW

In a competitive market without minimum wages or unions, wages and employment—the price and quantity of labor services—will be determined by the interaction of the demand for and the supply of labor services and can be analyzed with tools that should now be familiar—demand and supply curves.

The supply of labor comes from individual decisions to work. Individual decisions to supply work are simultaneously decisions to forgo leisure. Thus, a decision to supply less labor is simultaneously a decision to demand (1) _____. At higher wages, the same number of working hours will mean a larger income. If leisure is not an inferior good, people are apt to demand (more/less) leisure as their income increases. This suggests that the supply of labor might (increase/decrease) as wages increase. This is called the (income/substitution) effect of higher wages, but it is only part of the story.

Higher wages also increase the opportunity cost of an hour of leisure. As a result we expect that as wages (2) increase the substitution effect will lead people to work (more/less). The ultimate effect of increased wages comes from the sum of the income and substitution effects. Statistical evidence suggests that at low wages the _____ effect predominates and labor supply (increases/decreases) with an increase in wages, while at high wages the two effects tend to (enhance/offset) each other. The response of individuals to a change in wages, the income and substitution effects, helps determine the slope of the labor supply curve. Other factors, such as the size of the available working population and nonmonetary aspects of many jobs, help determine the position of the labor supply curve. The strength of the income and substitution effects is important for an understanding of the historical evidence on real wages and average weekly hours in the United States.

The demand for labor comes from the decisions of firms to use labor as one of many factors of production. Labor services are valuable because they add to output and, businesses hope, to profits. Thus the demand for labor is a derived demand. The discussion in earlier chapters of how a profit-maximizing firm makes optimal decisions about the use of factors of production showed that a firm should use more of any factor as long as the addition to revenue exceeds the addition to cost or, in technical terms, as long as the marginal revenue product (3) of the factor is (greater/less) than the marginal cost of the factor. A firm's demand curve for labor is determined by its curve of marginal (physical/revenue) product. The curve has a (negative/positive) slope because of the law of diminishing marginal returns.

In competitive markets, equilibrium wages and employment are determined by the intersection of the market demand and supply curves, which come from the horizontal summation of firms' demand curves and individuals' supply curves. Any factor that shifts either curve will change equilibrium wages and employment. For example, an increase in the demand for a firm's output or a technological innovation that increases the productivity of (4) labor should shift the (demand/supply) curve and lead to (higher/lower) wages, employment, or both. It is often argued that labor-saving innovations eliminate jobs as the same output can be produced with fewer workers. Yet these innovations also increase the productivity of workers and shift a country's production possibilities frontier.

As long as macroeconomic policy works to match aggregate demand with a country's aggregate supply potential, innovations should, over time, work to increase real wages.

Wages will differ for a number of reasons. Differences in abilities and work effort will affect individual wages. Differing amounts of other factors of production would also be expected to affect the marginal physical product of labor and hence wages. If individual skills are not easily duplicated, as may be the case for star athletes or performers, wages will be high as they contain significant economic rents. If skills are easily duplicated, one would expect that competition in the form of entry would work to keep wages in line with the costs of acquiring skills.

Education and wages are positively correlated—people with more education typically earn higher wages. Human capital theory views these higher wages as the return from investments in human capital—that is, the time, money, and effort spent on schooling and training.

Currently, about 13 percent of American workers belong to unions. Union membership as a proportion of the labor force has been declining since the 1950s. The shift from manufacturing to service industries, deregulation, changing preferences of American workers, and the threat of foreign competition have all been suggested as possible explanations for this decline.

In some labor markets, unions are the only supplier of labor services; that is, they are a (monopolist/monopsonist). As such, they face a trade-off between wages and employment just as a monopoly supplier of widgets faces a trade-off between price and output. Sometimes a union, as a monopolistic supplier of labor, faces a single buyer of labor services. When one buyer constitutes the entire market demand, the buyer is called a(n) _____. Both monopolists and monopsonists realize that their decisions about quantity must at the same time affect price. Monopolists who want to sell more must accept a (higher/lower) price (wage), and monopsonists who want to buy more must pay a(n) _____ price (wage). If a monopsonist faces a monopolist, then the whole market has only _____ participants. The technical term for this situation is _____ monopoly. Each will consider the actions of the other, and, as for oligopoly, the outcome is difficult to predict.

_____ provide guidance to some critical market activities. It is they who organize and establish new firms. They design new enterprises and often use new firms to introduce innovations that play such a critical part in the economic growth. Innovations allow them to earn _____ profit for a short period of time. Generous profit will attract other individuals with entrepreneurial ambitions, who seek to enter the market with competitive and imitative products. This competitive entry first (reduces/increases) and finally brings to an end the temporary excess of price over the competitive level that was initially enjoyed by the entrepreneur.

There are two special features of invention: first, the (fixed/variable) cost characteristic of the required R&D expenditures and many of the other costs entailed in bringing an invention to market successfully and, second, the (public/private) good attribute of invention. Both of these attributes mean that there is a significant portion

(5)

(6)

(7)

of the cost of an invention that is totally absent from marginal cost. This has several implications. First, invention cannot be successful financially if the price is set equal to_____ cost. Such a price would not cover any of the R&D cost and the related outlays are entirely absent from the marginal cost of an innovation. So for innovative products, $P = MC$ is a recipe for financial loss and disaster in an innovative firm. Second, this means that, initial monopoly profits may only be the amount of revenue needed to cover those fixed R&D costs and any similar outlays.

IMPORTANT TERMS AND CONCEPTS QUIZ

Choose the most appropriate definition for each of the following terms.

1. _____ Marginal Revenue Product of Labor (MRP_L)
2. _____ Income effect (of higher wages)
3. _____ Substitution effect (of higher wages)
4. _____ Backward-bending supply curve of labor
5. _____ Human capital theory
6. _____ Union
7. _____ Monopsony
8. _____ Bilateral monopoly
9. _____ Collective bargaining
10. _____ Innovative entrepreneurship

a. Reduction in supply of labor as wages increase
b. Market situation in which there is only one producer
c. Viewing education as an investment in a person's earning potential
d. Market composed of a single seller and a single buyer
e. Organization of workers to negotiate with employers over wages and other terms and conditions of employment
f. Impact on demand for increased leisure from higher income when wages increase
g. Market situation in which there is only one buyer
h. Increased opportunity cost of leisure as wages increase
i. Addition to revenue from hiring one more worker to increase output
j. Discussions between labor and management to determine wages and other conditions of employment
k. Someone who introduces a new product, new production process or finds a new market for his products

BASIC EXERCISES

This problem illustrates the determination of wages and employment in both a competitive market and a market monopolized by a labor union.

Tony runs a small company, Bearpaw Boots that manufactures hiking boots. **Table 20-1** shows output per month for different quantities of labor.

1. Fill in the third column by using the data in the second column to compute the marginal physical product of each additional worker.

2. Tony can sell boots for $120 a pair. Each boot contains $40 worth of leather, leaving $80 for wages or profits. As Tony has a small firm, the price of boots is unaffected by the quantity that he sells. Fill in the fourth column by computing the marginal revenue products of each worker. Be sure to use the $80 net figure rather than the $120 gross.

3. Tony wants to maximize profits. How many workers should he employ if monthly wages are $2,200?

_____ (You can check to be sure your answer maximizes profits by checking profits when Tony hires one more or one less worker.)

4. **Figure 20-1** shows the supply of bootmakers for the entire industry.

Assume there are 100 competitive firms just like Tony's. Using your data on the marginal revenue product for a typical firm, plot the market demand for bootmakers. What is the equilibrium market wage and employment? $_____ and _____. At the equilibrium market wage, how many workers should Tony employ? _____ What are Tony's profits? _____.

Table 20-1

Employment and Output for Bearpaw Boots

Number of Bootmakers	Total Number of Pairs of Boots per Month	Marginal Physical Product (boots)	Marginal Revenue Product (dollars)
1	60	_____	_____
2	115	_____	_____
3	165	_____	_____
4	210	_____	_____
5	250	_____	_____
6	285	_____	_____
7	315	_____	_____
8	340	_____	_____
9	360	_____	_____
10	375	_____	_____

Figure 20-1

Demand and Supply: Bootmakers

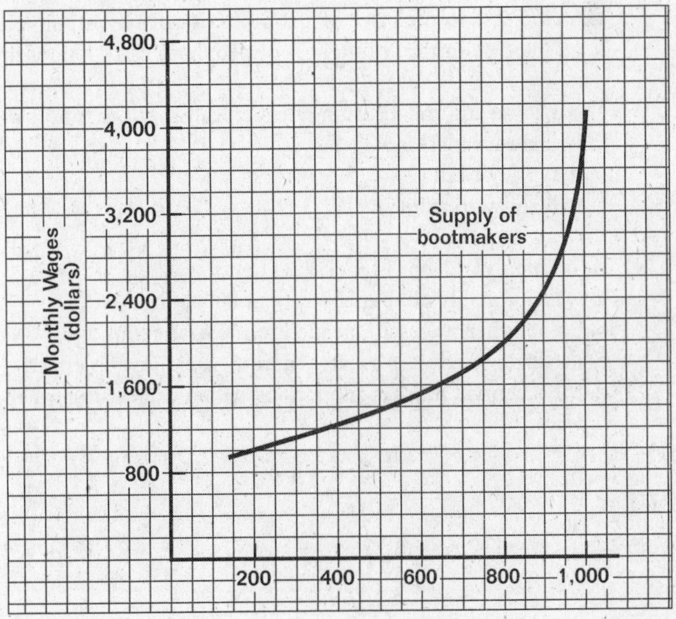

5. Assume now that the IAB, the International Association of Bootmakers, has been successful in unionizing bootmakers. In order to evaluate possible alternative goals, the union has asked you to use your knowledge of the industry demand curve to answer the following questions:

a. If union membership is limited to 400 persons, what is the maximum monthly wage the union can get from employers? $_____

b. If the union wage is set at $1,400 a month, what is the maximum amount of employment? $_____

c. What wage and employment combination will maximize total wage payments? $_____

SELF-TESTS FOR UNDERSTANDING

TEST A

Circle the most appropriate answer.

1. A change in which of the following will affect the slope of the labor supply curve?
   a. an increase in the working age population
   b. a technological innovation that increases labor productivity
   c. an increase in the price of a competitive firm's output
   d. an increase in the willingness of people to trade higher money incomes for more leisure

2. A change in which of the following will affect the position of the labor supply curve?
   a. an increase in the working age population
   b. a technological innovation that increases labor productivity
   c. an increase in the price of a competitive firm's output
   d. an increase in the willingness of people to work longer hours in return for higher wages

3. The income and substitution effects mean that the supply of labor _____ when wages increase.
   a. will always increase
   b. may rise or fall
   c. will always decline

4. If the supply of labor is backward bending, then
   a. we're probably talking about manual labor.
   b. even higher wages are needed to increase supply.
   c. the income effect is greater than the substitution effect.
   d. the incentive to work more hours when wages are higher is outweighing the income effect of higher wages.

5. Historical data that show a declining workweek along with rising real wages are probably reflecting
   a. minimum wage laws.
   b. the income effect of higher wages.
   c. the substitution effect of higher wages.
   d. the Taft-Hartley Act.

6. The demand for labor is the downward-sloping portion of the _____ curve for labor.
   a. marginal physical product
   b. marginal cost
   c. marginal revenue product
   d. average revenue

7. A change in which of the following will affect the demand for labor by shifting the marginal physical product of labor schedule?
   a. the demand for a firm's output
   b. the amount of other factors of production per worker
   c. the supply of labor
   d. the minimum wage

8. A change in which of the following will affect the demand for labor by shifting the marginal revenue product of labor schedule?
   a. the demand for a firm's output
   b. union militancy
   c. the supply of labor
   d. the minimum wage

9. The dramatic reduction in the proportion of the labor force in agriculture in the past 200 years reflects
   a. a decline in the demand for food.
   b. increased foreign competition.
   c. government policies that have discriminated against agriculture.
   d. the increased productivity of farm workers.

10. The supply curve for schmoos is upward sloping. An increase in the demand for schmoos (the demand curve shifts to the right) will lead to all but which one of the following?
    a. The price of schmoos increases.
    b. The marginal physical product of labor schedule shifts upward.
    c. The marginal revenue product of labor schedule shifts upward.
    d. The demand curve for labor to produce schmoos shifts upward.
    e. Employment and/or wages increase in the schmoo industry.

11. In recent years the income premium for college graduates as compared to high school graduates has
    a. narrowed.
    b. stayed about the same.
    c. increased.
    d. fluctuated with little trend.

12. The theory of human capital says that
    a. individuals can repair their own bodies with artificial parts, just like machines.
    b. soon all work will be done by robots.
    c. individual decisions to seek training and new skills can be modeled in the same way as ordinary investment decisions, involving present costs in the expectation of future returns.
    d. slavery in the United States was doomed because it was uneconomical.

13. Human capital theory explains the correlation between education and wages as the result of
    a. learning in school that enhances productivity.
    b. sorting by social class.
    c. the dual labor market.
    d. the growing influence of white-collar unions.

14. What percent of American workers belong to unions?
    a. 42 percent
    b. 23 percent
    c. 13 percent
    d. 7 percent

15. In contrast with experience in Europe and Japan, unions in America
    a. are much more political.
    b. have resulted in almost twice the level of strike activity found in any other country.
    c. involve a smaller percentage of the labor force than in most countries.
    d. have been less adversarial than unions in Japan.

16. A single union that controls the supply of labor to many small firms is a
    a. socialist.
    b. monopsonist.
    c. oligopolist.
    d. monopolist.

17. If one company is the sole employer of labor, it is called a(n)
    a. arbitrator.
    b. monopolist.
    c. oligopolist.
    d. monopsonist.

18. According to Joseph Schumpeter, an innovative entrepreneur earns
    a. zero economic profit in the short-run.
    b. monopoly profit in the short-run.
    c. excess profit in the long-run.
    d. monopoly profit in the long-run.

19. Which of the following are the attributes of innovation?
    a. Fixed cost and public good
    b. Fixed cost and private good
    c. Variable cost and public good
    d. Variable cost and private good

262

20. A firm sells a product to one group of customers at a lower price than it sells it to another, even though it costs exactly the same to serve the two groups. The prices that are charged are called
    a. predatory.
    b. dumping.
    c. discriminatory.
    d. bundling.

TEST B

Circle T or F for true or false.

T F 1. Information on the marginal revenue product of labor can be used to derive a firm's demand for labor.

T F 2. The law of diminishing returns implies that the demand curve for labor will have a negative slope.

T F 3. The income effect of higher wages suggests that the supply of labor schedule may have a positively sloped portion.

T F 4. An increase in wages that increases the quantity of labor supplied is represented as a shift in the supply curve.

T F 5. If a labor union has complete control over the supply of a particular type of labor, it is a monopsonist.

T F 6. A market with a single buyer and a single seller is called an oligopoly.

T F 7. In general there is no conflict between union attempts to maximize wages for current union members and attempts to provide employment for the largest possible number of workers.

T F 8. A labor union faces a demand curve that is perfectly elastic.

T F 9. Price of an innovative product will initially be high and then will gradually be driven down by competition.

T F 10. Fixed costs and public good attributes in invention implies that invention will be successful financially if the price is set equal to marginal cost.

SUPPLEMENTARY EXERCISES

1. **Wages and Employment Under Monopsony**

   This problem is designed to show how monopoly elements in labor markets, either a monopsonist firm or a monopolist union, can affect wages and employment.

   Assume that Bearpaw Boots (the subject of the Basic Exercise for the chapter) is located in a small, isolated town in northern Maine and is the sole employer of bootmakers. Tony still sells his boots in a competitive market for a net price of $80. **Table 20-2** (on the next page) contains data on what wages Tony must pay to get various numbers of employees.

a. Use the data in the first two columns of Table 20-2 to plot the supply curve of labor in Figure 20-2. Use the data on the marginal revenue product computed in Table 20-1 to plot the demand curve for labor in Figure 20-2. These curves intersect where wages are $ _____ and the number of employees is

_____ .

b. Will Tony pay the wage determined by the intersection in question a? Remember, Tony is the only employer of bootmakers in town. As he employs additional workers, he must pay a higher wage not only to each new employee but also to all existing employees. Thus the marginal cost of an additional worker is (greater/less) than the wage. Fill in the remaining columns of Table 20-2 to compute Tony's marginal labor costs.

c. Plot the figures on marginal labor costs in **Figure 20-2**.

d. Tony should increase employment as long as the marginal revenue of additional workers exceeds the marginal cost. Using this logic, Tony's profit-maximizing level of employment is _____ workers.

e. While the curve of marginal labor cost is critical for Tony's calculation of the profit-maximizing level of employment, it is the supply curve for labor that tells Tony how much he must offer workers. What is the lowest wage that Tony must offer in order to attract the profit-maximizing number of workers? $ _____

Table 20-2

Supply of Bootmakers in a Small, Isolated Town

Number of Bootmakers	Monthly Wage (dollars)	Total Labor Cost[a] (dollars)	Marginal Labor Cost[b] (dollars)
1	600	_____	_____
2	800	_____	_____
3	1,000	_____	_____
4	1,200	_____	_____
5	1,400	_____	_____
6	1,600	_____	_____
7	1,800	_____	_____
8	2,000	_____	_____
9	2,200	_____	_____
10	2,400	_____	_____

[a] Total Labor Cost = (Number of bootmakers) × (Monthly Wage)

[b] Marginal Labor Cost = change in Total Labor Cost. For example, when employing 2 workers rather than 1, Total Labor Cost changes by $1,000.

Figure 20-2

Demand and Supply: Bootmakers

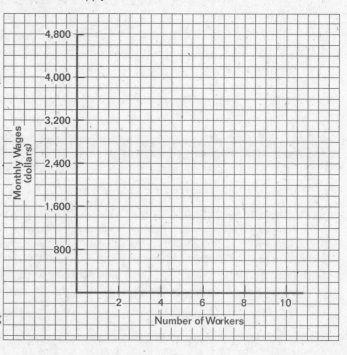

f. What are Tony's profits (net revenue minus total wages)? _____
g. If Tony must pay a minimun wage of $2,200 a month and can hire as many workers as he wants at the minimum wage, what would happen to wages and employment?
h. Would a union necessarily force the minimum wage solution to question g on Tony? Why or why not?

STUDY QUESTIONS

1. Why does the income effect of an increase in wages tend to reduce the supply of labor when wages increase?

2. Why does the substitution effect of an increase in wages tend to increase the supply of labor when wages increase?

3. What explains the demand for labor?

4. Demand and supply analysis seems to suggest that there should be a single wage, yet there is significant variation in the wages individuals receive. What other factors explain the difference in wages among individuals? Which of these factors can be seen as factors affecting the demand and supply curves and which cannot?

5. What is human capital theory and how might it explain differences in wages? How do theories of sorting and dual labor markets differ from human capital theory?

6. Economists often argue that a union can only raise wages by accepting a reduction in employment. When a union faces this sort of trade-off, what might it do to try and increase both employment and wages?

8. Is the introduction of labor-saving technological innovations good or bad for workers? for the economy? Why?

10. What are the implications of fixed-cost and public good attributes in invention?

ECONOMICS ONLINE

The Bureau of Labor Statistics offers a wealth of data and information about labor markets.

http://www.bls.gov

What's up at the AFL-CIO? Find out by checking their homepage.

http://www.aflcio.org

Does it pay to go to college? This web site has historical data on income and educational attainment for men, women, Blacks, Whites, and Hispanics. See for yourself by checking the data in Tables P-16 through P-35.

http://www.census.gov/hhes/income/histinc/incperdet.html

Poverty, Inequality, and Discrimination

21

Important Terms and Concepts

Poverty line

Absolute concept of poverty

Relative concept of poverty

Economic discrimination

Temporary Assistance to Needy Families (TANF)

Food stamps

Negative income tax (NIT)

Earned Income Tax Credit (EITC)

Affirmative action

Learning Objectives

After completing this chapter, you should be able to:

- discuss some of the facts of poverty and income distribution.

- describe the implications of the use of absolute or relative concepts of poverty.

- describe what factors account for differences in incomes, which of these factors reflect voluntary choices, and why these factors make identifying economic discrimination so difficult.

- explain why the trade-off between equality and efficiency implies that the optimal distribution of income will involve some inequality.

- explain the concept of a negative income tax and how it affects work incentives.

- explain why, if implementing a negative income tax program, policy makers can only choose two of the following three parameters: guaranteed level of income, tax rate, and break-even level of income.

- describe the controversy surrounding programs for affirmative action.

CHAPTER REVIEW

Discussions of poverty in America usually focus on the number of households below the poverty line. In 2009

(1) this dividing line was about $_____ a year for a household of four. It is adjusted every year for changes in prices. Since the yearly adjustment reflects only the change in prices and not general increases in real income, the poverty line is a(n) (<u>absolute/relative</u>) concept of poverty rather than a(n) _____ concept.

U.S. income data show that in 2009, households with incomes above $100,000 were in the top 20 percent of

(2) the income distribution. The top 20 percent of households received _____ percent of income while the bottom 20 percent received _____ percent.

Why do incomes differ? The list of reasons is long and includes differences in abilities, intensity of work, risk taking, wage differentials for unpleasant or hazardous tasks, schooling and training, work experience, inherited wealth, luck, and discrimination. Some of the reasons for differences in incomes represent voluntary choices by individuals to work harder, take more risks, or accept unpleasant work in order to earn higher incomes.

Economic discrimination is defined as a situation in which equivalent factors of production receive

(3) _____ payments for equal contributions to output. Average differences in income between large social groups, such as men and women or blacks and whites, (<u>are/are not</u>) sufficient proof of economic discrimination. These average differences tend to (<u>overstate/understate</u>) the amount of economic discrimination. To accurately measure the impact of possible discrimination, we must first correct for the factors listed above that could create differences in income without implying economic discrimination. Some factors, such as schooling, are tricky. For instance, differences in wages associated with differences in schooling would not imply any discrimination if everyone has had an equal opportunity for the same amount of schooling. But it is unclear whether observed differences in schooling represent voluntary choices or another form of discrimination.

Measures to equalize incomes may adversely affect the work effort of these individuals. In more technical

(4) terms, efforts for greater equality may reduce _____. This important trade-off does not mean that all efforts to increase equality should be abandoned. It does mean that efforts to increase equality have a price and should not be pushed beyond the point where the marginal gains from further equality are worth less than the marginal loss from reduced efficiency. Exactly where this point is reached is the subject of continuing political debate.

The trade-off between equality and efficiency also suggests that in the fight for greater equality one should choose policies with small rather than large effects on efficiency. Economists argue that many welfare programs have been inefficient. One important reason is the relatively large reduction in benefits for each additional dol-

(5) lar of earned income. These high implicit marginal tax rates (<u>increase/decrease</u>) the incentive for increased work effort on the part of welfare recipients who are able to work.

Many economists favor replacing the current welfare system with a negative income tax, that is, a system of direct cash grants tied to income levels and linked to the tax system. These schemes usually start with a minimum guaranteed level of income and a tax rate that specifies the decrease in the cash grant for every dollar increase in income. A low tax rate will retain significant work incentives; however, a low tax rate also means that grants continue until income is quite high. The point where payments from the government stop and payments to the government start is called the

_____ level of income.   (6)

A negative income tax with a low marginal tax rate can offer significantly better work incentives to those currently receiving welfare, but there will be (<u>positive/negative</u>) work incentives for those not now on welfare   (7) but who become eligible for grants. Experiments with versions of a negative income tax have investigated the size of these negative work incentives and found them to be (<u>large/small</u>). Food Stamps and the Earned Income Tax Credit resemble a negative income tax.

IMPORTANT TERMS AND CONCEPTS QUIZ

Choose the most appropriate definition for each of the following terms.

1. _____ Poverty line
2. _____ Economic discrimination
3. _____ TANF
4. _____ Food stamps
5. _____ Negative income tax
6. _____ Earned Income Tax Credit
7. _____ Affirmative action

a. Amount of income below which a family is considered "poor"
b. Active efforts to recruit and hire members of underrepresented groups
c. Tax credits that are linked to wage or salary income
d. Income share of poorest quartile of income distribution
e. Time limited welfare assistance
f. Income-conditioned cash grants available to all families
g. Equivalent factors of production receive unequal pay for equal contributions to output
h. Stamps that allow families to buy food at subsidized prices

BASIC EXERCISES

This problem illustrates the high marginal tax rates that often result from combining welfare programs. The numbers in this problem do not come from any specific welfare program but illustrate how the combination of separate and well intended programs can produce unintended consequences.

Imagine a welfare system that offers a family of four the following forms of public support.

- Food stamps that offer the family $450 a month or $5,400 a year but require payments equal to 25 percent of income above $500 a month or $6,000 a year.

- Housing subsidy that gives the family an apartment worth $600 a month or $7,200 a year. The family must contribute 30 percent of its net income toward rent. Net income is determined as 80 percent of gross income.

- A TANF grant of $6,000 a year that is reduced by one-third of any family income.

1. Fill in column 7 of **Table 21-1** by computing net income after taxes and after welfare payments for the different levels of earned income.

Table 21-1

Subsidy Programs

(1) Earned Income	(2) Social Security and Income Taxes*	(3) Earned Income Taxed Credit	(4) Food Stamps	(5) Housing Subsidy	(6) TANF Grant	(7) Net Income (1) − (2) + (3) + (4) + (5) + (6)
$ 0	$ 0	$ 0	$5,400	$7,200	$6,000	_____
6,000	372	2,410	5,400	5,760	4,000	_____
9,700	601	3,890	5,075	4,872	2,767	_____
12,700	787	4,204	4,325	4,152	1,767	_____
18,000	1,116	3,510	3,000	2,880	0	_____
18,550	1,150	3,405	2,863	2,748	0	_____
30,000	2,690	993	0	0	0	_____
31,175	2,880	741	0	0	0	_____
35,000	3,500	0	0	0	0	_____

2. Use the data in columns 1 and 7 to plot net income against earned income in **Figure 21-1**. Plot each pair of points and then connect successive pairs with a straight line. What does the graph suggest about work incentives under these programs?

3. Use the data in Table 21-1 to complete **Table 21-2**, computing the implicit marginal tax rates that this family faces as it earns income. What is the relationship between the implicit marginal tax rates you computed in Table 21-2 and the slope of the graph in Figure 21-1? How do these marginal rates compare with the statutory marginal tax rates under the positive portion of federal income taxes, which ranged from 10 percent to 35 percent in 2007? (Note that in 2007 the highest rate applied only to taxable incomes above $349,701. In 2007 the Social Security tax rate of 6.2 percent applied to wage and salary income up to $97,500. The Medicare Hospitalization Insurance rate of 1.45 percent applied to all wage and salary income.)

Figure 21-1

Income Before and After Subsidy Program

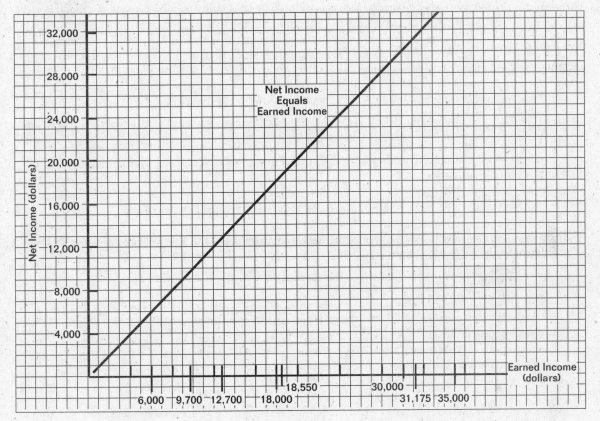

Table 21-2

Income and Implicit Tax Rates after Subsidies

(1) Earned Income	(2) Net Income Column (7) from Table 21-1	(3) Change in Earned Income	(4) Change in Net Income	(5) Implicit Taxes (3) – (4)	(6) Implicit Marginal Tax Rate (5) ÷ (3)
$0	_____				
$6,000	_____	$6,000	_____	_____	_____
$9,700	_____	$3,700	_____	_____	_____
$12,700	_____	$3,000	_____	_____	_____
$18,000	_____	$5,300	_____	_____	_____
$18,550	_____	$550	_____	_____	_____
$30,000	_____	$11,450	_____	_____	_____
$31,175	_____	$1,175	_____	_____	_____
$35,000	_____	$3,825	_____	_____	_____

4. One could reduce the implicit marginal tax rate by lowering the rate at which benefits are reduced under any of the programs. To investigate the impact of such reductions, construct a new version of Table 21-1 in which TANF payments are reduced by 25 percent rather than 33 percent, the food stamp subsidy is reduced by 10 percent rather than 25 percent, and the housing subsidy is reduced by 20 percent instead of 30 percent. What happens to the magnitude of the subsidy payments at each level of income? What happens to the break-even level of income for each program? What would happen to total public outlays for these programs?

SELF-TESTS FOR UNDERSTANDING

TEST A

Circle the most appropriate answer.

1. The facts on income distribution in the United States show
   a. a substantial move toward equality during the last 30 years.
   b. that the richest 20 percent of families receive about 80 percent of the total income.
   c. that the poorest 20 percent of families receive less than 2 percent of income.
   d. increased inequality during the past 20 years.

2. The poverty line computed by the government, estimated to be $22,000 in 2009, is an example of
   a. statistical discrimination.
   b. a relative concept of poverty.
   c. an absolute concept of poverty.
   d. economic discrimination.

3. Defining poor people as those who fall in the bottom 20 percent of the income distribution
   a. is an absolute concept of poverty.
   b. is a relative concept of poverty.
   c. means that continued economic growth will eliminate poverty.
   d. implies that all of above all correct.

4. Economic growth is likely to be most effective when poverty is measured as a(n) _____ concept.
   a. aggregate
   b. absolute
   c. proportional
   d. relative

5. Since 1975, the proportion of people below the official poverty line
   a. increased and decreased with little trend.
   b. decreased significantly.
   c. rose substantially.
   d. has stayed constant.

6. If the United States adopted the European definition of poverty of one-half average income, the number of families considered poor would likely
   a. be smaller.
   b. show no change.
   c. increase.

7. Compared with other industrial countries, data on the distribution of income in the United States show
   a. more inequality than most other countries.
   b. about the same degree of inequality.
   c. much more equality.

8. In 2009, the richest 20 percent of families received about _____ percent of total income.
   a. 23
   b. 32
   c. 50
   d. 57

9. In 2009, the poorest 20 percent of families received _____ percent of total income.
   a. less than 2
   b. between 3 and 4
   c. slightly more than 10
   d. 20

10. In 2009, families with an income above _____ were in the top 20 percent of the income distribution.
    a. $57,000
    b. $73,000
    c. $100,000
    d. $108,000

11. Consider a negative income tax scheme with a guaranteed minimum income of $8,000 for a family of four and a tax rate of 50 percent. The break-even level of income would be
    a. $4,000.
    b. $8,000.
    c. $12,000.
    d. $16,000.

12. If the Vincents earn $8,000 in wages, their total income after including the negative income tax would be
    a. $4,000.
    b. $8,000.
    c. $12,000.
    d. $16,000.

13. Reducing the tax rate while retaining the same minimum guarantee will
    a. reduce the break-even level of income.
    b. leave the break-even level of income unchanged.
    c. increase the break-even level of income.
    d. There's too little information to know.

14. If a negative income tax system is to be financed within a given budget, then a reduction in the negative tax rate to increase work incentives
    a. must be offset by a reduction in the minimum guaranteed level of income.
    b. needs no change in the minimum guaranteed level of income.
    c. must be offset by an increase in the minimum guaranteed level of income.

15. Which of the following work like a negative income tax? (There may be more than one correct answer.)
    a. food stamps
    b. Social Security taxes
    c. estate taxes
    d. Earned Income Tax Credit

16. When evaluated as a whole, taxes in the United States
    a. actually increase income inequality.
    b. have little impact on the distribution of income.
    c. make a small contribution toward a more equal distribution of income.
    d. dramatically increase the equality of after-tax income as compared to before-tax income.

17. If two individuals with similar productivity receive different pay for the same work, an economist would call this evidence of
    a. economic discrimination.
    b. poverty.
    c. statistical discrimination.
    d. luck.

18. All but which one of the following could give rise to differences in income without implying discrimination?
    a. schooling
    b. ability
    c. compensating wage differential for night work
    d. intensity of work effort

19. Which of the following would be an example of economic discrimination?
    a. Census data show that, on average, women earn less than men.
    b. Nurses earn less than doctors.
    c. Over the period 1990 to 2000, plumbers and electricians received larger percentage wage increases than did college professors.
    d. A careful study showing that among blacks and whites with identical education, work experience, productivity, and motivation, blacks earn less than whites.

20. The study of economics shows that the optimal amount of income inequality would result in the richest 10 percent of the population receiving
   a. 10 percent of total income.
   b. 25 percent of total income.
   c. 50 percent of total income.
   d. None of the above.

TEST B

Circle T or F for true or false.

T   F   1. It is easier for economic growth to eliminate poverty as measured by an absolute standard, but not as measured by a relative standard.

T   F   2. U.S. data show no change in poverty since 1960 as measured by the proportion of persons below the poverty line.

T   F   3. In the United States, the incidence of poverty is about the same for all social groups, e.g., men – women, black – whites.

T   F   4. Including in-kind income, e.g., public housing, health care and food stamps, means that poverty in the United States has been eliminated.

T   F   5. In the United States, the 20 percent of families that are poorest receive about 20 percent of total income.

T   F   6. The optimal amount of inequality is a poverty rate of 10 percent.

T   F   7. The fact that women, white or black, have lower average incomes than white men, is sufficient proof of economic discrimination.

T   F   8. In the absence of monopolies, unregulated markets would result in an equal distribution of income.

T   F   9. Some differences in income reflect voluntary choices, such as decisions to work more hours or to take early retirement.

T   F   10. The federal personal income tax system has substantially reduced the degree of income inequality in the United States.

|Appendix | *The Economic Theory*

The Appendix to Chapter 21 analyzes two forms of economic discrimination, discrimination by employers and discrimination by employees. For which form of economic discrimination can competitive market forces be expected to help minimize discrimination and why? Why would one expect market forces to not be effective in fighting the other form of discrimination?

SUPPLEMENTARY EXERCISES

1. **Table 21-3** reports data from the World Bank on the distribution of income for nine countries. Use **Figure 21-2** to compare the distribution of income by plotting the cumulative proportion of income against the cumulative proportion of population. Note that your line will start in the lower left-hand column of the graph as 0 percent of the population receives 0 percent of the income and it will end at the upper right-hand corner where 100 percent of the population receives 100 percent of the income. Which countries show the greatest equality in the distribution of income? Which show the greatest inequality?

   Note: Each column shows the proportion of total income received by that corresponding percentage of the population. For example, the first column shows the proportion of income received by the poorest 10 percent of the population; the second column shows the proportion of income received by the poorest 20 percent of the population; the last column shows the proportion of income received by the richest 10 percent of the population.

- *Table 21-3*

Data on Income Distribution for Selected Countries

	Year	Lowest 10%	Lowest 20%	Second 20%	Third 20%	Fourth 20%	Highest 20%	Highest 10%
Finland	2000	4.0%	9.6%	14.1%	17.5%	22.1%	36.7%	22.6%
Germany	2000	3.2%	8.5%	13.7%	17.8%	23.1%	36.9%	22.1%
Italy	2000	2.3%	6.5%	12.0%	16.8%	22.8%	42.0%	26.8%
South Korea	1998	2.9%	7.9%	13.6%	18.0%	23.1%	37.5%	22.5%
Mexico	2000	1.0%	3.1%	7.2%	11.7%	19.0%	59.1%	43.1%
Norway	2000	3.9%	9.6%	14.0%	17.2%	22.0%	37.2%	23.4%
Sweden	2000	3.6%	9.1%	14.0%	17.6%	22.7%	36.6%	22.2%
United Kingdom	1999	2.1%	6.1%	11.4%	16.0%	22.5%	44.0%	28.5%
United States	2000	1.9%	5.4%	10.7%	15.7%	22.4%	45.8%	29.9%

Source: World Bank, 2004 World Development Indicators, Table 2.7

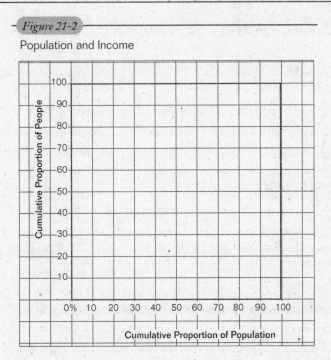

Figure 21-2

Population and Income

2. In 2006 median household income in the United States was $48,200 while mean household income was $59,067. Which measure, the median or the mean, is a better measure of income equality? Why?

3. Following is a suggested list of additional readings on three important topics covered in this chapter.

   On the general issue of trade-offs between increased equality and reduced efficiency, read Arthur Okun's *Equality and Efficiency: The Big Trade-off*, published by the Brookings Institution, 1975. This important book is the source of the "leaky bucket" analogy used in the text.

   The taxation of estates is a topic where the ratio of political rhetoric to economic analysis is very high. Find out more about estate taxes by reading "Ancestor Worthship: Everything you always wanted to know about estate taxes," *The Milken Institute Review*, Third Quarter 2000, pp. 36-49, by economists William Gale and Joel Slemrod.

   Women now account for about 49 percent of the American labor force. Economic issues concerning the role of women in the labor force are examined by Claudia Goldin in *Understanding the Gender Gap: An Economic History of American Women*, Oxford University Press, 1990.

4. Investigate the details of welfare programs in the city or county in which you live. Use this information to construct your own version of Table 21-1.

ECONOMICS IN ACTION

INCREASING INEQUALITY

The facts about increasing income inequality are quite clear as documented in Table 21-2 in the text. Economist Edward Wolff notes that between 1983 and 1998, 47 percent of the growth in real income in the United States went to the top 1 percent of the income distribution. The top 20 percent received 89 percent. While changes in other countries may not have been quite so dramatic, most industrialized countries have seen similar trends toward increasing inequality.

What is less clear is why there has been an increase in income inequality and whether anything should be done about it.

What explains the increase in inequality? Economists Robert Frank and Philip Cook argue that in many fields, the economy now offers ever greater and greater rewards to those at the very top. They have termed this the "winner-take-all society." While a key player on a professional sports team or a hot pop star has had the ability to command astronomical salaries, modern technology and an increasing global marketplace now allows those in other fields to exercise similar market power. For example, Frank and Cook argue that the ability to create national and international brands now allows successful business executives to command similar eye-popping compensation.

Increased returns to education have also been cited by many as an important factor helping to explain the increase in income inequality. Economist Marvin Kosters notes that the income advantage for college graduates over high school graduates has doubled since the early 1970s.

Should anything be done about the increase in income inequality? A number of economists would say no. To the extent that the market is rewarding particular skills or education, these economists would be concerned that any attempt to interfere with the market outcome could produce important unintended consequences.

Others are not quite as sure. Economist David Ellwood notes that a host of problems like drug use, teenage pregnancy, and reduced life expectancy are associated with low incomes. Increasing inequality will make these problems worse for those at the bottom of income distribution. Economist James Heckman is quoted in *The New York Times* as saying, "Never has the accident of birth mattered more
... this is a case of market failure: children don't get to 'buy' their parents, and so there has to be some kind of intervention to make up for these environmental differences."

1. What do you think explains the trend toward increasing income inequality? What if anything would you advocate to resist or reverse this trend?

Sources: Robert H. Frank, "Talent and the Winner-Take-All Society," *The American Prospect*, Vol 5, Issue 17, March 21, 1994. Alexander Stille, "Grounded by an income gap," *The New York Times*, December 15, 2001.

STUDY QUESTIONS

1. Which is the most meaningful measure of poverty, an absolute standard or a relative standard? Why?

2. If one defines poverty as the poorest 20 percent of the population, then the poor will always be with us. What if one defines poverty as incomes that are less than 50 percent of median income? Under this definition is it necessarily true that the poor will always be with us? If not, what would it take to eliminate poverty?

3. When looking for a measure of average income, one might consider mean income or median income. The Census Bureau reports information on both. What is the difference between the mean and the median as a measure of average tendency? Which do you think is a better measure of average incomes?

4. Differences in income may be related to a number of factors. What factors reflect voluntary choices and what factors might reflect economic discrimination?

5. How does a negative income tax improve work incentives as compared with a system of overlapping poverty programs?

ECONOMICS ONLINE

The United States Census Bureau has a wealth of data available on the web about American income distribution. You can access this data at

> http://www.census.gov/hhes/www/income.html

Information on how the Census Bureau measures poverty as well as detailed data on poverty measures is available at

> www.census.gov/hhes/www/poverty.html

Emmanuel Saez, Professor of Economics at the University of California, Berkeley, studies income distribution. You can access his data on changes in income distribution in the United States during the twentieth century from his web site at

> http://elsa.berkeley.edu/~saez/index.html.

International Trade and Comparative Advantage

Important Terms and Concepts

Specialization	Tariff	Infant-industry argument
Absolute advantage	Quota	Strategic argument for protection
Comparative advantage	Export subsidy	Dumping
Mercantilism	Trade adjustment assistance	

Learning Objectives

After completing this chapter, you should be able to:

- list the important factors that lead countries to trade with one another.

- explain how voluntary trade, even if it does not increase total production, can be mutually beneficial to the trading partners.

- explain in what ways international and intranational trade are similar and dissimilar.

- distinguish between absolute and comparative advantage.

- explain how absolute advantage and comparative advantage are related to the location and slope of a country's per capita production possibilities frontier.

- explain how trade means that a country's consumption possibilities can exceed its production possibilities.

- compare the advantages and disadvantages of tariffs and quotas.

- analyze the arguments used to advocate trade restrictions.

- explain the role of adjustment assistance in a country favoring free trade.

- explain the fallacy in the "cheap foreign labor" argument.

CHAPTER REVIEW

The material in this chapter discusses the basic economic forces that influence the international division of labor in the production of goods and services and the resulting pattern of international trade. Trade between cities or states within a single country is, in principle, no different than trade between nations. Economists and others spend more time studying international trade rather than intranational trade for several reasons: International trade involves more than one government with a resulting host of political concerns; it usually involves more than one currency; and the mobility of labor and capital between nations is typically more difficult than within nations.

Exchange rates—that is, how much of one country's currency it takes to buy one unit of another country's currency—are an important determinant of international trade and will be discussed in the next chapter. However, the real terms of trade—how many import goods a country can get indirectly through export production rather than through direct domestic production—are the important measure of the benefits of trade, and they are considered here in some detail.

Individual countries can try to meet the consumption needs of their citizens without trade by producing everything their populations need. Alternatively, they can specialize in the production of fewer commodities and trade for commodities they do not produce. Even if there were no differences between countries, special-
(1) izing and trading would still make sense if there were important economies of _____— in production.

An important reason for trade is that differences in climate, oil deposits, minerals, and other natural resources, as well as differences in labor inputs and productive capital, will affect the efficiency with which countries
(2) can produce different goods. It is the law of (<u>absolute/comparative</u>) advantage that then indicates where countries should concentrate their production to maximize the potential gains from trade.

Assume country A can produce 80,000 bushels of wheat if it produces one less car, while country B can produce only 70,000 bushels of wheat. For the same world production of cars, world production of wheat will in-
(3) crease if country (<u>A/B</u>) produced ten fewer cars and country _____ produced ten more cars. (World wheat production would increase by _____ bushels.) In this case country A has a comparative advantage in the production of _____.[1]

Looking only at its own domestic production, the opportunity cost of one more car in country A is
(4) _____ bushels of wheat. Country B can produce one more car by giving up only _____ bushels of wheat. Thus it should not be surprising if country B concentrates on the production of _____ and trades with country A, which concentrates on the production of _____.[2]

---

[1]Note that we have said nothing so far about absolute advantage. For example, if it takes 300 labor hours to produce one car or 70,000 bushels of wheat in country B and 600 labor hours to produce 1 car or 80,000 bushels of wheat in country A, country B has an absolute advantage in the production of both goods while country A still has a comparative advantage in the production of wheat.
[2]Does the law of comparative advantage imply that all countries should specialize in the production of just a few commodities? No, it does not, for several reasons. One important reason is that production possibilities frontiers are likely to be curved rather than straight lines. The implication of the curved

It is also important to realize that comparative advantage is not a static concept. The mix of industries that maximizes a country's comparative advantage is not something that can be determined once for all time. Rather, there will need to be continual adjustments in response to innovations and competition, both domestically and abroad. Countries that try to isolate themselves from foreign competition have usually ended up with stagnating industries and incomes.

As countries concentrate production on those goods in which they have a comparative advantage, equilibrium world prices and trade flows—that is, exports and imports—will be determined at the point where world demand equals world supply, not at the intersection of domestic demand and supply curves. Advanced courses in international trade show how prices derived under conditions of free trade will lead competitive, profit-maximizing firms to exploit the comparative advantage of individual countries and help to achieve an efficient allocation of resources.

Most countries do not have unrestricted free trade. Rather, imports are often restricted by the use of _____ and _____, and exports are often promoted through the use of export (5) _____. Tariffs reduce the quantity of imports by raising their _____ while quotas raise the price of imports by restricting _____. Either a tariff or a quota could be used to achieve the same reduction in imports, but the choice between the two has other consequences.

Tariff revenues accrue directly to the _____ while the benefits of higher prices under a (6) quota are likely to accrue to private producers, both foreign and domestic. (The government might be able to capture some of these profits by auctioning import licenses, but this is not usually done.)

Tariffs still require foreign suppliers to compete among themselves. This competition will favor the survival of (high/low) -cost foreign suppliers. What about domestic firms? They (do/do not) have to pay the tariff, so (7) high-cost domestic suppliers (can/cannot) continue in business. Quotas are apt to be distributed on almost any grounds except economic efficiency and thus have no automatic mechanism that works in favor of low-cost foreign suppliers.

Why do countries impose tariffs and quotas? Many trade restrictions reflect the successful pleadings of high-cost domestic suppliers. Free trade and the associated reallocation of productive resources in line with the law of comparative advantage would call for the elimination of these firms in their traditional lines of business. It is not surprising that managers and workers resist these changes. If everyone is to benefit from the increased output opportunities offered by free trade, then a program of trade _____ assistance will be neces- (8) sary to help those most affected by the realignment of productive activities.

Other traditional justifications for trade restrictions include the national _____ argument (9) and the _____-industries argument. In both cases it is extremely difficult to separate firms with

---

frontier is that the opportunity cost of cars in terms of wheat for country B will rise as B produces more cars. Simultaneously, the opportunity cost of cars in terms of wheat for country A will fall as A concentrates on wheat. In equilibrium, the opportunity cost, or slope of the production possibilities frontier, in both countries will be equal. At this point neither country has an incentive for further specialization. Exactly where this point will occur will be determined by world demand and supply for cars and wheat.

legitimate claims from those looking for a public handout. In recent years some have argued that the threat of trade restrictions should be used in a strategic manner to convince others not to impose restrictions.

Much of the free trade fuss in the United States is concerned about competing with low-cost foreign producers who pay workers lower wages. Concerns about wages need to be joined with measures of productivity. A clear understanding of comparative advantages shows that the standard of living of workers in (the exporting/ (10) the importing/both) country(ies) can rise as a result of specialization and trade. Even countries with high wages can benefit from trade when high wages are associated with high productivity and trade induces adjustments in the structure of worldwide production consistent with the principle of _____ advantage.

IMPORTANT TERMS AND CONCEPTS QUIZ

Choose the most appropriate definition for each of the following terms.

1. _____ Imports
2. _____ Exports
3. _____ Specialization
4. _____ Absolute advantage
5. _____ Comparative advantage
6. _____ Mercantilism
7. _____ Tariff
8. _____ Quota
9. _____ Export subsidy
10. _____ Trade adjustment assistance
11. _____ Infant-industry argument
12. _____ Strategic trade policy
13. _____ Dumping

a. Maximum quantity that can be imported per unit of time
b. Threats to implement protectionist policies designed to promote free trade
c. Selling goods in a foreign market at higher prices than those charged at home
d. Domestically produced goods sold abroad
e. Selling goods in a foreign market at lower prices than those charged at home
f. Tax on imports
g. Decision by a country to emphasize production of particular commodities
h. Provision of special aid to those workers and firms harmed by foreign competition
i. Ability of one country to produce a good less inefficiently (relative to other goods) than another country
j. Foreign-produced goods purchased domestically
k. Tariff protection for new industries, giving them time to mature
l. Payment by the government that enables domestic firms to lower prices to foreign buyers
m. Ability of one country to produce a good using fewer resources than another country requires
n. Doctrine arguing that exports are good while imports are bad

BASIC EXERCISES

This exercise is designed to review the law of comparative advantage.

1. Assume that the hours of labor shown below are the only input necessary to produce calculators and backpacks in Canada and Japan.

	Calculators	Backpacks
Canada	4	5
Japan	2	3

   Which country has an absolute advantage in the production of calculators? _____

   Which country has an absolute advantage in the production of backpacks? _____

2. If labor in Canada is reallocated from the production of calculators to the production of backpacks, how many calculators must be given up in order to produce one more backpack? _____ What about Japan? How many calculators must it give up in order to produce one more backpack? _____ Which country has a comparative advantage in the production of backpacks? _____ Which country has a comparative advantage in the production of calculators? _____ According to the law of comparative advantage, _____ should concentrate on the production of backpacks while _____ concentrates on the production of calculators.

3. Assume each country has 12 million hours of labor input that initially is evenly distributed in both countries between the production of backpacks and calculators: 6 million for each. Fill in the following table of outputs.

	Output of Calculators	Output of Backpacks
Canada	_____	_____
Japan	_____	_____
Total	_____	_____

4. Assume that Canada now reallocates 2.4 million labor hours away from the production of calculators and into backpacks. The change in Canadian calculator output is –_____. The change in Canadian backpack output is +_____.

5. What reallocation of labor in Japan is necessary to be sure that world output of calculators (Japan plus Canada) remains unchanged? _____ labor hours. What are the changes in Japanese output from this reallocation? The change in Japanese calculator output is +_____. The change in Japanese backpack output is –_____.

6. By assumption, the world output of calculators has not changed, but the net change in the world output of backpacks is a(n) (increase/decrease) of _____ backpacks.

7. Questions 3 through 6 showed how specialization according to the law of comparative advantage could increase the output of backpacks without decreasing the output of calculators. This is just one possibility. Adjustments in line with the law of comparative advantage could increase the output of both goods. Suppose Japan had reallocated 1,350,000 labor hours to the production of calculators. Fill in the following table and compare total outputs with your answers to question 3.

Calculators

	Labor Input (millions of hours)	Output
Canada	3.60	_____
Japan	7.35	_____
Total		_____

Backpacks

	Labor Input (millions of hours)	Output
Canada	8.40	_____
Japan	4.65	_____
Total		_____

8. Work through questions 4 and 5 again, but assume this time that the initial reallocation of 2.4 million labor hours in Canada is away from backpacks and to the production of calculators. Calculate the reallocation in Japan necessary to maintain world backpack output. What happens to the total output of calculators? Why?

9. Assume that the production of backpacks in Canada requires 6 hours rather than 5 hours. Work through the original output levels in question 3 and the reallocation of labor in questions 4 and 5 to see what now happens to total output of calculators and backpacks. Does your answer to question 6 differ from your original answer? Why or why not??

SELF-TESTS FOR UNDERSTANDING

TEST A

Circle the most appropriate answer.

1. Even if there were no differences in natural resources, climate, labor skills, etc., nations would still find it advantageous to specialize production and trade
   a. because of differences in absolute advantage.
   b. to take advantage of economies of scale.
   c. to take advantage of differences in national currencies.
   d. when inflation rates differ.

2. International trade is different from intranational trade because of
   a. political issues that arise from different governments.
   b. limitations of the ability of labor and capital to move between countries compared to their ability to move within countries.
   c. the use of different currencies.
   d. all of the above.

3. Economists argue that
   a. efficiency in international trade requires countries to produce those goods in which they have an absolute advantage.
   b. efficiency in international trade requires countries to produce those goods in which they have a comparative advantage.
   c. efficiency in international trade requires countries that have an absolute advantage in the production of all goods to become self-sufficient.
   d. countries with export surpluses will have a comparative advantage in the production of all goods.

4. Using per capita production possibilities frontiers showing the production of clothes on the vertical axis and cars on the horizontal axis, the absolute advantage in the production of clothes would be determined by comparing
   a. the slope of the per capita production possibilities frontiers.
   b. where the per capita production possibilities frontiers cut the horizontal axis.
   c. the area under the per capita production possibilities frontiers.
   d. where the per capita production possibilities frontiers cut the vertical axis.

5. Using per capita production possibilities frontiers described above, the comparative advantage in the production of clothes would be determined by comparing
   a. the slope of the per capita production possibilities frontiers.
   b. where the per capita production possibilities frontiers cut the horizontal axis.
   c. the area under the per capita production possibilities frontiers.
   d. where the per capita production possibilities frontiers cut the vertical axis.

6. Which of the following is an example of comparative advantage?
   a. Wages of textile workers are lower in India than in America.
   b. The slope of the production possibilities frontier between tomatoes and airplanes differs for Mexico and the United States.
   c. American workers must work an average of only 500 hours to purchase a car, while Russian workers must work 4,000 hours.
   d. In recent years, Swedish income per capita has exceeded that of the United States.

7. Specialization and free trade consistent with the law of comparative advantage will enable
   a. increased world production of all traded goods.
   b. increases in the standard of living for workers in both exporting and importing countries.
   c. countries to consume at some point outside their production possibilities frontier.
   d. all of the above.

8. From a worldwide perspective, economic efficiency is enhanced if production and trade is organized according to the law of comparative advantage. Economic efficiency within a single country is enhanced if regional production and trade are organized according to
   a. absolute advantage.
   b. the political power of particular states or regions.
   c. which regions have the highest unemployment.
   d. comparative advantage.

9. If shoes can be produced with two hours of labor input in Italy and three hours of labor input in the United States, then it is correct to say that
   a. Italy has an absolute advantage in the production of shoes.
   b. Italy has a comparative advantage in the production of shoes.
   c. the United States has an absolute advantage in the production of shoes.
   d. the United States has a comparative advantage in the production of shoes.

10. Assuming that shoes are produced as in question 9 and shirts can be produced with four hours of labor in both countries, then it is correct to say that
    a. the United States has a comparative advantage in the production of shirts.
    b. Italy has a comparative advantage in the production of shirts.
    c. Italy has an absolute advantage in the production of shirts.
    d. the United States has an absolute advantage in the production of shirts.

11. Under free trade, world prices for exports and imports would be such that
    a. countries would specialize production along lines of absolute advantage.
    b. all countries would show a slight export surplus.
    c. the quantity supplied by exporters would just equal the quantity demanded by importers.
    d. every country would be self-sufficient in all goods.

12. Which one of the following is not intended to restrict trade?
    a. export subsidies
    b. tariffs
    c. quotas

13. A tariff affects trade by
    a. imposing a tax on imported goods.
    b. limiting the quantity of goods that can be imported.
    c. offering a subsidy to producers who export for foreign sales.
    d. the voluntary actions of foreign manufacturers to limit their exports.

14. A quota affects trade by
    a. imposing a tax on imported goods.
    b. limiting the quantity of goods that can be imported.
    c. offering a subsidy to producers who export for foreign sales.
    d. the voluntary action of foreign manufacturers to limit their exports.

15. Which of the following is an example of a tariff?
    a. Japanese car manufacturers agree to limit exports to the United States.
    b. U.S. law limits the imports of cotton shirts to 20 million.
    c. Television manufacturers outside Great Britain must pay a 10 percent duty on each set they ship to Great Britain.
    d. Foreign bicycle manufacturers receive a rebate of taxes from their own government for each bicycle they export.

16. One economic advantage of tariffs over quotas is that tariffs
    a. typically give preferential treatment to long-term suppliers.
    b. expose high-cost domestic producers to competition.
    c. force foreign suppliers to compete.
    d. help avoid destructive price wars.

17. The imposition of a tariff on steel will lead to all but which one of the following?
    a. a lower volume of steel imports
    b. higher domestic steel prices
    c. reduced domestic demand for steel
    d. a smaller market share for domestic producers

18. The imposition of a quota on steel will lead to all but which one of the following?
    a. a lower volume of steel imports
    b. increased domestic production of steel
    c. lower domestic steel prices
    d. reduced domestic demand for steel

19. A quota that limits the importation of foreign computer chips is likely to be in the interest of all but which of the following? (There may be more than one correct answer.)
    a. domestic chip manufacturers
    b. domestic computer manufacturers
    c. labor employed domestically in the production of computer chips
    d. consumers interested in buying computers

20. Which one of the following is a justification for fewer trade restrictions?
    a. Some industries would be so vital in times of war that we cannot rely on foreign suppliers.
    b. A temporary period of protection is necessary until an industry matures and is able to compete with foreign suppliers.
    c. Competition from foreign suppliers will help keep prices to consumers low.
    d. The threat of trade restrictions may prevent the adoption of restrictions by others.

TEST B

Circle T or F for true or false.

T F 1. A country with an absolute advantage in producing all goods is better off being self-sufficient than engaging in trade.

T F 2. A country with an absolute advantage in the production of all goods should only export commodities.

T F 3. The unequal distribution of natural resources among countries is one important reason why countries trade.

T F 4. Which of two countries has a comparative advantage in the production of wine rather than cloth can be determined by comparing the slopes of the production possibilities frontiers of both countries.

T F 5. It is possible for all countries to simultaneously expand exports and reduce imports.

T F 6. Tariffs act like a tax on imported goods and have no impact on the price of similar goods that are produced by domestic firms.

T F 7. A quota on shirts would reduce the volume of imported shirts by specifying the maximum quantity of shirts that can be imported.

T F 8. The infant-industry argument is used to justify protection for industries that are vital in times of war.

T F 9. Dumping of goods by the United States on Japanese markets would necessarily harm Japanese consumers.

T F 10. If foreign labor is paid less, foreign producers will always be able to undersell American producers.

| Appendix | *Supply, Demand, and Pricing in World Trade*

This exercise is designed to illustrate the material in the Appendix to Chapter 34 and give you practice in understanding how world prices are determined and in analyzing the impact of quotas and tariffs. To simplify the analysis, the question assumes that the world is composed of only two countries, the United States and India.

1. **Figure 22-1** shows the demand and supply for shirts in the United States and India. Prices in India are expressed in terms of American dollars. In the absence of international trade, what are the domestic price and quantity of shirts in India and the United States?

	Price	Quantity
India	_____	_____
United States	_____	_____

2. Assume now that India and the United States are free to trade without restrictions. What is the world price of shirts? _____. At this price what happens to domestic demand, production, exports, and imports?

	Price	Domestic Demand	Domestic Production	Exports	Imports
India	_____	_____	_____	_____	_____
United States	_____	_____	_____	_____	_____

Figure 22-1

Demand and Supply: Shirts

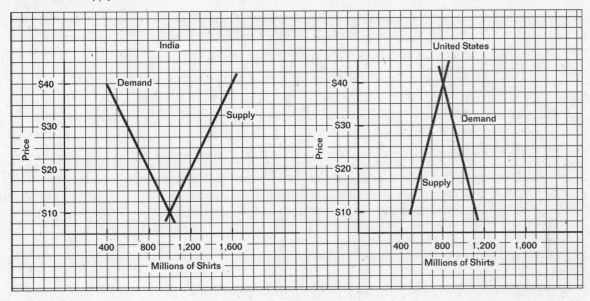

3. Assume that American producers are able to persuade the government to impose a quota limiting shirt imports to 200 million. Following imposition of the quota, what happens to prices, demand, production, and trade?

	Price	Domestic Demand	Domestic Production	Exports	Imports
India	_____	_____	_____	_____	_____
United States	_____	_____	_____	_____	_____

Compared to the free trade equilibrium described in question 2, shirt prices have increased in (India/the United States) and decreased in _____. The production of shirts has increased in _____ and decreased in _____.

4. What tariff would have yielded the same results as the quota of 200 million shirts? _____.

5. Discuss the reasons for choosing between a tariff and a quota.

SUPPLEMENTARY EXERCISES

1. Demand and supply for widgets in Baulmovia and Bilandia are as follows:

   Baulmovia
   Demand: $Q = 156 - 7P$
   Supply: $Q = -44 + 18P$

   Bilandia
   Demand: $Q = 320 - 10P$
   Supply: $Q = -20 + 10P$

   a. In the absence of trade, what are the price and quantity of widgets in Baulmovia? In Bilandia?
   b. With free trade, what is the one common world price for widgets? Which country exports widgets? Which country imports widgets? What is the volume of exports and imports?
   c. Manufacturers in the importing country have convinced the government to impose a tariff on widget imports of $4.50 a widget. What will happen to trade and the price of widgets in the two countries?
   d. What quota would have the same impact on trade?
   e. What factors might lead one to prefer a tariff over a quota?

2. This exercise offers another review of the law of comparative advantage.

Figure 22-2

Arcadia and Ricardia: Production Possibilities Frontiers

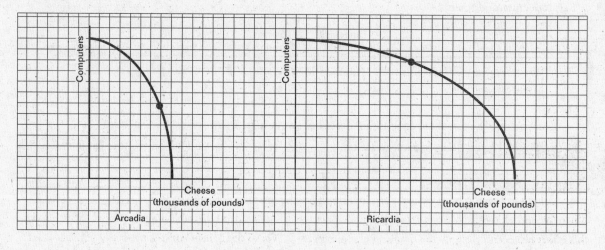

Figure 22-2 shows the production possibilities frontier for Arcadia and Ricardia. For every computer they buy, citizens of each country want to consume 1,000 pounds of cheese. As a result production and consumption in each country takes place at the dot on the frontier. Some have argued that citizens in both countries could consume more of both goods if each country concentrated production on the good in which it has a comparative advantage and traded for the other good.

In order to construct a numerical example, assume that at the dot the slope of the PPF for Arcadia is −2 while the slope of the PPF for Ricardia is −1/2. (Arcadia must give up two computers for an additional 1,000 pounds of cheese, while Ricardia can increase the production of cheese by 2,000 pounds at the cost of only one less computer.)

a. Which country has a comparative advantage in the production of computers? _____

b. Which country has a comparative advantage in the production of cheese? _____

c. Construct a numerical example that shows how what changes in production and what pattern of trade would allow both countries to consume outside their PPF.

3. Cimonoce is a small country that produces wine and cloth. The production possibilities frontier for Cimonoce is

$$W = 324 - C^2$$

where W = millions of barrels of wine and C = millions of bolts of cloth.

a. Use a piece of graph paper. Label the vertical axis "wine" and the horizontal axis "cloth." Draw the production possibilities frontier.

b. Since Cimonoce is a small country, it can export or import cloth or wine without affecting world prices. World prices are such that Cimonoce can export one million barrels of wine for 750,000 bolts of cloth or it can export 750,000 bolts of cloth for one million barrels of wine. The government's chief economist argues that regardless of consumption preferences, Cimonoce should produce 14.4 million bolts of cloth and 10.8 million barrels of wine. Do you agree? Why? (Hint: Consider what a graph of consumption possibilities looks like. For any production combination of wine and cloth, Cimonoce's consumption possibilities are given by a negatively sloped straight line through the production point. The slope of the consumption possibilities line reflects world prices. A movement up the straight line to the left of the production point would imply exporting cloth in order to import and consume more wine. A movement down the straight line to the right would reflect exporting wine in order to import and consume more cloth. Exactly where Cimonoce chooses to consume is a matter of preferences, but its choice is constrained by its consumption possibilities line, which in turn is determined by Cimonoce's production choice and world prices for cloth and wine. Why does the production point 10.8 million barrels of wine and 14.4 million bolts of cloth offer the greatest consumption possibilities?)

ECONOMICS IN ACTION

TRADE IN TEXTILES

Since the end of World War II there has been a conscious effort to lower barriers to international trade. Part of this effort has been driven by the intellectual arguments in favor of the benefits of free trade and part has been driven by a strong feeling that protectionist pressures in the 1930s added to the depth and severity of the Great Depression. Much of the advance to date has come in the form of reduced tariff barriers resulting from complicated, multinational negotiations and treaties.

Sensitive areas where tariff reductions have been more difficult include textiles and clothing along with trade in agricultural products. Other areas of concern include trade in steel, services, and intellectual property like books and movies. With tariffs in many developed countries now eliminated or very low, increasing attention is being paid to nontariff barriers that limit trade. Nontariff barriers include policies like quotas, excessively detailed and time-consuming processing at ports of entry, and the strict adherence to rules and regulations that serve only to protect domestic producers.

Reaching an agreement on freer trade in textiles in the mid-1990s was only possible when it was proposed that changes be made over a 10-year period of adjustment. Thus, a complicated system of tariffs and quotas that had evolved since 1950 was scheduled for elimination at the beginning of 2005. The production of textiles has been important to many developing countries and full implementation of the 1995 Multi-Fibre Agreement was seen as a major concession that would aid economic development. One estimate projected a gain of 27 million jobs in developing countries from the elimination of tariffs and quotas on textiles.

As January 2005 approached, a number of countries were having second thoughts. Developing countries that had secured preferential quota arrangements were now facing international competition. The big new competitor was China, which would be able to export textiles without limit. The rules allowed for "safeguard" tariffs against Chinese textile exports that would permit an additional three years of adjustment. At the end of 2004, there were cries in the United States and Europe to adopt safeguard tariffs to resist an expected surge in textile exports from China.

Other voices argued for restraint, pointing out that the magnitude of expected adjustments in 2005 was due in part to most countries waiting to the last moment to eliminate quotas. While it appears that bulk production of basic clothes may concentrate in Asia, primarily China, India, and Pakistan, there were those who expected production for the fashion industry to concentrate in Turkey and Latin America.

Textile production in Africa was of special concern as it did not appear that African producers had the efficiency of Asian production or the proximity of Turkey and Latin America to markets in Europe and the United States. The economic literature on international trade argues that benefits within a country should be sufficient to provide trade adjustment help to workers in industries that cannot compete following a move to freer trade. The same principle ought to apply internationally, but it is not clear how such help might be organized.

1. What has happened to trade in textiles? Who have been the winners and losers from the elimination of tariffs and quotas? How large is the increase in textile exports from China? What about exports from other countries? Have any countries adopted safeguard tariffs and if so, under what conditions?

Sources: "Textile and China," *The Washington Post*, December 16, 2004; "Textile producers weave a web to restrict China: Less efficient poor nations fear they will lose rich-world trade when the global quota system ends this year," *Financial Times of London*, October 22, 2004. "Textile and Clothing Summary," Global Trade Negotiations Home Page, Center for International Development, Harvard University, May 2004.

Trade data on U.S. imports of textiles and apparel are available online from the Office of Textiles and Apparel, U.S. Department of Commerce, International Trade Administration: http://otexa.ita.doc.gov/mrspoint.htm and from the U.S. Census Bureau: http://www.census.gov/foreign-trade/statistics/index.html. Data on exports and imports from different countries is available from the World Trade Organization at http://www.wto.org/english/res_e/statis_e/its2002_e/its02_bysector_e.htm.

STUDY QUESTIONS

1. Why do countries trade with each other? Why don't they try to be self-sufficient in the production of all goods?

2. What is the difference between absolute advantage and comparative advantage? (Use a per capita production possibilities frontier to illustrate your answer.)

3. Why do economists argue that a country with an absolute advantage in the production of all goods can still gain from trade if it specializes in a manner consistent with the law of comparative advantage? (Consider a two-good, two-country example.)

4. Why isn't it possible for all countries to improve their balance of trade by simultaneously increasing exports and decreasing imports?

5. Why aren't a country's consumption possibilities limited by its production possibilities?

6. It is often asserted that for every tariff there is a corresponding quota in the sense of having the same impact on prices and production. Is this statement correct and if so what difference(s) would one policy make over the other?

7. Since higher prices following the imposition of a tariff or a quota will reduce domestic demand, how can these policies ever be in the interest of domestic producers?

8. How do you evaluate the arguments supporting strategic trade policies?

9. What is the role of trade adjustment assistance and why do many think it a necessary element of a policy that favors free trade?

10. What is the infant-industry argument? Do you believe it is ever a compelling argument? Why or why not?

11. Some industries argue for trade protection on the grounds of national defense. Do you believe this is ever a compelling argument? Why or why not?

12. "In order to increase the consumption possibilities of Americans, the United States should never prohibit dumping by foreign manufacturers." Do you agree? Why or why not?

13. Why isn't it obvious to many economists that the United States should enact tariffs to level the playing field and protect American workers from unfair competition from low-wage foreign workers?

ECONOMICS ONLINE

Data on American international trade is reported by several U.S. government offices.
U.S. Census Bureau

http://www.census.gov/ftp/pub/foreign-trade/www

Office of Trade and Economic Analysis, International Trade Administration

http://www.ita.doc.gov/

Data on American international accounts is available online from the Bureau of Economic Analysis, U.S. Department of Commerce

http://www.bea.gov/

Information on international trade from the World Trade Organization can be found through the WTO homepage.

http://www.wto.org

Answer Key

Chapter 1

Chapter Review

(1) information; value

Important Terms and Concepts Quiz

1. e
2. a
3. d
4. b
5. f

Basic Exercises

1. C
2. G
3. B
4. E
5. A
6. I
7. H
8. J
9. D
10. F

Self-Tests for Understanding

Test A

1. c
2. b
3. d
4. a
5. c
6. a
7. b
8. d
9. c
10. b

Test B

1. F
2. F
3. T
4. T
5. F
6. F
7. F
8. F
9. F
10. F
11. F
12. F
13. F
14. F
15. F
16. F
17. F
18. F

Appendix

Chapter Review

(1) horizontal; vertical; origin

(2) vertical; horizontal; constant; positive; up; negative; no

(3) ray; 45-degree

(4) tangent

(5) contour; production indifference

Important Terms and Concepts Quiz

1. d
2. h
3. g
4. b
5. f
6. c
7. e
8. i

Basic Exercises

1. a. 400
   b. increase; 800
   c. 600
   d. −50
   e. Slope equals vertical change divided by horizontal change or the change in salary divided by the change in the quantity demanded. The change in the number of new Ph.D. economists demanded as salary changes is equal to the reciprocal of the slope: The demand curve implies that a $1,000 increase in salary will reduce the quantity demanded by 20.

2. a. 4
   b. 5

c. above

d. non-economics

Self-Tests for Understanding: Appendix

Test A

1. b
2. b
3. c
4. d
5. a
6. a
7. c; a; b; d
8. A&E; C; B&D; none
9. d   slope = vertical change/horizontal change; (16-10)/
(5-8) = 6/-3 = -2
10. c
11. b
12. b
13. b
14. d
15. c
16. a
17. d
18. a   slope = 2/5 = 0.4
19. b
20. b

Test B

1. F
2. F
3. T
4. T
5. F
6. T
7. F
8. T
9. T
10. F

Chapter 2

Chapter Review

(1) domestic product; GDP; productivity

(2) inputs; outputs; free; private

(3) open; closed; closed

(4) recessions

(5) factors

(6) labor; 15 cents; service

(7) small

Important Terms and Concepts Quiz

1. h
2. i
3. a
4. f
5. e
6. g
7. d
8. j
9. b

Basic Exercises

1. 1960: 13.7%; 39.6%; 46.7%
   2010: 10.5%; 17.5%; 66.9%

2. 1960: 49.4%; 2.9%; 25.0%; 9.7%; 13.0%
   2009: 19.3%; 25.6%; 33.8%; 7.3%; 14.0%

3. Men: 21.8%; 49.6%; 74.5%; 89.7%; 91.8%; 86.8%;
   70%; 22.1%
   Women: 23%; 48.6%; 68.2%; 74.7%; 75.1%; 75.7%;
   60.2%; 13.8%

Self-Tests for Understanding

Test A

1. a, d
2. c
3. b, c
4. d
5. a
6. c
7. a
8. d
9. d
10. c
11. d
12. d
13. b
14. d
15. d

16. a
17. c
18. d
19. c
20. a

Test B

1. T
2. F
3. F
4. T
5. T
6. F
7. F
8. F
9. F
10. T

Chapter 3

Chapter Review

(1) scarce
(2) opportunity cost
(3) scarce; specialized; slope
(4) increase; increasing; specialized
(5) inside; inefficient,
(6) will

Important Terms and Concepts Quiz

1. f
2. k
3. m
4. h
5. a
6. g
7. l
8. j
9. e
10. c
11. d
12. i

Basic Exercise

1. 560,000; 40,000; rises; 120,000; continue to rise; specialized

2. Point A is not attainable; point B is attainable; point C is attainable; on and inside; on

3. Point B is inefficient. You should be able to shade a small triangular area above and to the right of point B out to and including a small segment of the PPF.

4. Without additional information about the preferences of the citizens of Adirondack one cannot determine which point on the production possibilities frontier is best for a country.

Self-Tests for Understanding

Test A

1. c
2. c
3. d
4. d
5. a
6. b
7. c
8. b
9. d
10. d
11. b
12. c
13. c
14. a
15. b
16. c
17. c
18. a
19. b
20. d

Test B

1. F
2. F
3. T
4. F
5. F
6. F
7. T
8. T
9. F
10. F

Supplementary Exercises

2. a. 300,000 cars (set T = 0); 1,000 tanks (set C = 0)

   c. Yes, it bows out.

   d. $1/2C^*$, $1/2T^*$ should be on straight line connecting C^* and T^*. Combination is attainable, lies inside frontier; inefficient, not on frontier as frontier bows out.

   e. 6 cars; 30 cars; 120 cars

   f. Opportunity cost = $(0.6)T$ cars; yes, opportunity cost increases as the production of tanks increases.

Chapter 4

Chapter Review

(1) price; negative; more; movement along; shift in

(2) price; positive; more; shift in

(3) demand

(4) $300; 4,000; less; 6,000; 2,000; surplus; reduction; shortage; demanded; supplied; increase

(5) intersection; equilibrium

(6) demand; supply; movement along; supply; demand; demand

(7) maximum; minimum; above

(8) hard; auxiliary restrictions

(9) shortages; decrease

(10) high

Important Terms and Concepts Quiz

1. f
2. e
3. g
4. c
5. m
6. k
7. i
8. q
9. o
10. p
11. n
12. h
13. a
14. j
15. b

Basic Exercises

1. b. 60; 1,100

   c. increased; 70; increased; 1,200; less

   The impact of the change in price following the shift of the demand curve means that the change in the equilibrium quantity will be less than the horizontal shift in the demand curve.

   d. increase; decrease; 75; 1,100; less than

2. a. demand; right; rise; rise

   b. supply; right; fall; rise

   c. supply; left; rise; fall

   d. demand; left; fall; fall

3. a. 100; 100; neither, as ceiling exceeds equilibrium price

   b. 110; 80; shortage

   Price ceilings lead to shortages when they are less than the free market equilibrium price.

   c. 90; 120; surplus

   Price floors lead to surpluses when they are greater than the free market equilibrium price.

   d. 100; 100; neither, as floor is less than equilibrium price

Self-Tests for Understanding

Test A

1. c
2. a
3. d
4. c
5. c
6. b
7. a
8. a
9. d
10. b
11. c
12. a
13. b, d
14. b
15. b
16. c
17. b
18. a
19. d

20. b

Test B

1. F
2. T
3. T
4. F
5. F
6. T
7. T
8. F
9. F
10. F
11. T
12. F
13. T
14. F
15. F

Chapter 5

Chapter Review

(1) marginal; will; decrease; increase

(2) consumer's; price; greater; increase

(3) greater; marginal; more; up; negative; marginal

(4) shift in; utility; inferior; fewer

(5) horizontal; negative

Important Terms and Concepts Quiz

1. d
2. e
3. c
4. h
5. b
6. g
7. a
8. i

Basic Exercises

1. a. 110; 100; 80; 70; 50; 30; 20

   b. 2; 4; 5

   c. consumer's

   d. Col. 3: 20; 30; 20; 0; –40; –100; –170; 2
       Col. 5: 50; 90; 110; 120; 110; 80; 40; 4
       Col. 7: 70; 130; 170; 200; 210; 200; 180; 5

2; 4; 5; exactly the same

   e. at $P = \$90$, $Q_d = 2$, at $P = \$60$, $Q_d = 4$, at $P = \$40$, $Q_d = 5$

2. a. \$80 (\$270 - 190)

   b. \$ 135 (\$270 – 3 x \$45)

   c. consumer surplus up by \$15 (\$60 - \$45)

   d. 5

   e. \$155 (\$380 – 5 x \$45)

   f. 6; beyond this point price exceeds marginal utility.

Self-Tests for Understanding

Test A

1. b
2. a
3. d
4. a
5. d
6. c
7. c
8. d
9. c
10. c
11. a
12. b
13. c
14. b
15. b
16. d
17. c
18. d
19. d
20. a, c

Test B

1. F
2. T
3. T
4. F
5. T
6. F
7. T
8. F

9. F
10. F

Appendix

Appendix Review

(1) straight; negative; intercept; slope

(2) indifference; indifferent; are; never; negative

(3) in; more; substitution; decreases

(4) budget; indifference; highest; budget line

(5) budget line

Important Terms and Concepts Quiz: Appendix

1. c
2. d
3. a
4. e

Basic Exercise: Appendix

1. a. max hamburgers = 80; max books = 20
   b. 40; 10
   c. 6; 4
   d. At point W, Gloria has so many books that she would give up some for just a few more hamburgers as shown by the slope of the indifference curve. The budget allows Gloria a much better deal—she would get four hamburgers for each book she gives up. Choosing to move along the budget line increases Gloria's total utility as it allows her to move to higher indifference curves.
   e. equals the slope of the budget line

2. a. Z

   Neither is an inferior good as point Z shows an increase in the quantity demanded for both following the increase in income.

   b. Y

Self-Tests for Understanding: Appendix

Test A

1. c
2. c
3. d
4. c
5. b
6. d
7. c

8. b
9. b
10. c
11. d
12. b
13. a

Test B

1. F
2. T
3. F
4. F
5. F
6. T
7. F
8. F
9. T
10. T

Supplementary Exercise: Appendix

2. $F = (Y + 20P_C - 12P_F)/2P_F$

   $C = (Y - 20P_C + 12P_F)/2P_C$

   where P_F = price of food, P_C = price of clothing and Y = income.

   The demand curves come from solving the following two equations for F and C:

   Optimal purchases require that the marginal rate of substitution equals the ratio of market prices, or

   $(F + 12)/(C + 20) = P_C/P_F$

   The budget constraint requires that:

   $F P_F + C P_C = Y$

3. $F = 114$; $C = 43$
4. $F = 84$; $C = 44$
5. $F = 124$; $C = 48$; no

Chapter 6

Chapter Review

(1) elasticity; demand

(2) zero; infinite; changes

(3) elastic; inelastic; unit elastic

(4) will not; 1.0

(5) greater; decrease; increase; less; increase; decrease

(6) cross

303

(7) complements; negative; increase; right

(8) substitutes; positive; decrease; left

(9) shift in

Important Terms and Concepts Quiz

1. f
2. e
3. b
4. g
5. i
6. d
7. h
8. a
9. j

Basic Exercises

1. a. See diagrams below
   b. 1.0
   c. 1.0
   d. 1.0
      Do not be fooled by appearances.
2. a. straight
   b. %Δ price: 10.53%; 11.76%; 13.33%; 15.38%
      %Δ quantity: −18.18%; −15.38%; −13.33%; −11.76%
      elasticity: 1.73; 1.31; 1.00; 0.76; decreases

c. Total Revenue: $600,000; $648,000; $672,000; $672,000; $648,000.

Total revenue increases (decreases) as price declines if the elasticity of demand is greater (less) than 1.0. Total revenue increases (decreases) as price increases if the elasticity of demand is less (greater) than 1.0.

Self-Tests for Understanding

Test A

1. b
2. a
3. c
4. a
5. c
6. b
7. d
8. c
9. a
10. b
11. a
12. b
13. b
14. a
15. c
16. c
17. c

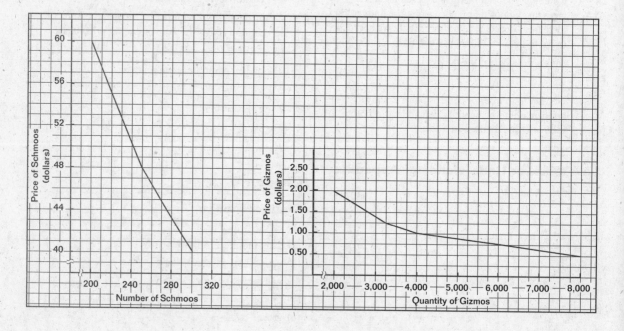

18. b

19. d

20. b

Test B

1. F

2. F

3. T

4. F

5. F

6. T

7. F

8. T

9. F

10. T

11. T

12. F

13. F

14. F

Appendix

Basic Exercises: Appendix

1. Not much; plotting historical data is an inappropriate way to estimate a demand curve.

2. a. 2005: $P = 22$; $Q = 380$

   2006: $P = 23$; $Q = 395$

   2007: $P = 24$; $Q = 410$

   When only the demand curve shifts, the historical data on price and quantity trace out the supply curve. If you connect the three points, you should have a graph of the supply curve. Each point comes from the intersection of the demand curve for the specific year with the unchanging supply curve. In this case, the points of market equilibrium provide no information about the demand curve.

   b. 2005: $P = 22.0$; $Q = 380$

   2006: $P = 20.5$; $Q = 407.5$

   2007: $P = 11.5$; $Q = 472.5$

   With shifts in both demand and supply curves, the points of market equilibrium trace out neither curve. Try drawing the demand and supply curves for each year on the same diagram. As both curves shift, a line connecting the successive points of market equilibrium gives no information about either curve.

Economics in Action

1. a. Elasticity of demand = $(3,570/1,997) \div (5.50/3.75) = 1.22$

   b. While the elasticity of demand is an indicator of the change in total revenue, a profit maximizing firm is interested in profits not revenues. Increased output may entail increased costs. In Mr. Grant's case, changing from first to second run movies dramatically cut the proportion of the ticket price claimed by movie distributors. The cut was so dramatic that net revenue before paying employees, utilities, etc., but after paying the admission tax and after paying the distributors, was unchanged at 61 cents a ticket.

2. a. If total revenue is to remain unchanged the price elasticity of demand would have to equal 1.0.

   b. Data on historical quantities is not a good way to measure demand. The relevant question is what would the demand for air travel in the summer of 1992 have been if fares had not been reduced. It is also relevant to note that some air travelers, those buying their tickets at the last minute, paid full fare and were not eligible for the discounted fares. At the same time it does appear that the fare war was a bonanza for travelers and not so good for airlines. A significant reduction in ticket prices appears to have induced only a modest increase in air travel.

3. The elasticity of demand must be greater than 1.0. Their statements imply that lower prices would increase sales enough to cover not only the lost revenue on existing sales when price declines but also any increase in cost from producing more books.

Chapter 7

Chapter Review

(1) increase; physical; revenue

(2) revenue; price

(3) more; less; reduce; increase

(4) reduce; less; more

(5) increasing; decreasing; constant

(6) short

(7) output; total

(8) long run; lower

(9) is unchanged; less; fall; more; rises

Important Terms and Concepts Quiz

1. k

2. d

3. b

4. h

5. f

6. g

7. i

8. e

9. c

Basic Exercises

1. 100 acres: increasing returns: 0 to 2 workers; decreasing returns: 2 to 4 workers; negative returns: 4 to 6 workers

2. 200 acres: increasing returns: 0 to 2 workers; decreasing returns: 2 to 5 workers; negative returns: 5 to 6 workers.

    300 acres: increasing returns: 0 to 2 workers; decreasing returns: 2 to 6 workers.

    The output-labor curve shifts up as land increases.

3. 100: 1; 3; 2; 1; –1; –2

    200: 2; 4; 3.5; 2.5; 1; –1

    300: 3; 4.5; 3.5; 3; 2; 1

4. Marginal returns to land generally decline.

5. increasing; increasing; constant; increasing; decreasing

    $10,000; $20,000; $17,500; $12,500; $5,000; –$5,000

    Hire 4 workers: (12,000 x $5) – ($8,000 x 4) = $28,000

    Hire 3 workers: (9,500 x $5) – ($8,000 x 3) = $23,500

    Hire 5 workers: (13,000 x $5) – ($8,000 x 5) = $25,000

Self-Tests for Understanding

Test A

1. d

2. c

3. d

4. b

5. d

6. b

7. c

8. c

9. d

10. a

11. b

12. a

13. a

14. d

15. c

16. c

17. b

18. d

19. b

20. d

Test B

1. F

2. T

3. F

4. F

5. T

6. F

7. F

8. F

9. T

10. F

Appendix

Appendix Review

(1) production indifference; more

(2) negative; will; diminishing marginal; do not

(3) straight

(4) lowest; less; more

(5) expansion

Important Terms and Concepts Quiz: Appendix

1. c

2. d

3. a

Basic Exercise: Appendix

1. 200; 2; 100; 3. Total costs are constant along a single budget line. Total costs are greater along higher budget lines.

2. $80

Self-Tests for Understanding: Appendix

Test A

1. d

2. b

3. c

4. c
5. c
6. b
7. c
8. d
9. d

Test B

1. F
2. T
3. T
4. F
5. F
6. F
7. T

Supplementary Exercises

1. See diagram. In order to graph the combinations of labor and machines that will achieve a production level of 500,000 widgets, create a table of possible combinations:

Table of inputs and output
(all units measured in thousands)

Labor	Machines	Widgets
250	1,000	500
500	500	500
750	333	500
1,000	250	500

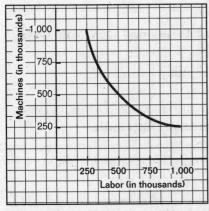

2. The slope of the production indifference curve = $-MPP_L/MPP_M$. The slope of the budget line = $-P_L/P_M$. The cost minimizing level of inputs is determined by finding where these two slopes are equal.

$MPP_L = 1/2 \ (M/L)^{1/2}$

$MPP_M = 1/2 \ (L/M)^{1/2}$

$MPP_L/MPP_M = M/L$; $P_L / P_M = 12/48$; at cost minimizing level of inputs $M/L = 12/48$ or $L = 4M$

When the price of labor hours is 12 and the price of machine hours is 48, the least costly combination of inputs requires that $L = 4M$.

From the production function

$W = L^{1/2} M^{1/2}$

Knowing that for the least-cost combination of inputs $L = 4M$, the equation for output can be rewritten as 500,000 =
$M^{1/2} (4M)^{1/2}$

$500,000 = (4M^2)^{1/2} = 2M$

$M = 250,000$ machine hours

$L = 1,000,000$ labor hours

3. a. Total output = $500 \ L^{1/2}$
   b. MPP of labor = $250/L^{1/2}$; the MPP of labor is the slope of the total product curve.
   c. For this production function, MPP of labor declines continuously, but is never negative.
   d. 1,085,069.45 labor hours; (Find the quantity of labor such that the MRP of labor is equal to the price of labor. $(250/L^{1/2}) \times 50 = 12$.)
      Output = 520,833.33 widgets.

4. For this production function, the expansion path is a straight line.

5. Constant: $(2M)^{1/2} (2L)^{1/2} = 2M^{1/2}L^{1/2} = 2W$. A doubling of inputs doubles output.

Chapter 8

Chapter Review

(1) average; marginal
(2) marginal; marginal; profits; revenue; cost
(3) total
(4) marginal; marginal; positive; zero; equals

Important Terms and Concepts Quiz

1. f
2. e
3. a
4. g
5. b
6. h
7. c

307

Basic Exercises

1. a. Total Profits: 1,500; 3,600; 5,200; 6,300; 6,600; 6,100; 5,000; 3,400; 1,300; –1,300; 5 widgets

    b. Marginal Revenue: 3,500; 3,100; 2,700; 2,300; 1,900; 1,500; 1,100; 700; 300; –100

    Marginal Cost: 2,000; 1,000; 1,100; 1,200; 1,600; 2,000; 2,200; 2,300; 2,400; 2,500, 5 widgets. The 5th widget adds 300 to profit: Increasing output to 6 widgets would lower profit by 500.

    c. profit; does not; does not; the difference between average revenue and average cost is greatest when output = 2. expanding output as long as MR > MC increases profits, but expanding output further, even if AR > AC, will reduce total profits.

    d. In the top panel of Fig 8-1, the total cost curve shifts up by $3,000. The total profit curve in the middle panel measures the difference between the two curves in the top panel; following the increase in fixed costs, the total profit curve shifts down by $3,000. In the bottom panel, neither curve shifts. The marginal revenue curve measures the slope of the total revenue curve and the marginal cost curve measures the slope of the total cost curve. Even though the total cost curve shifted up, there is no change in its slope.

2. a. is not; horizontal; vertical; horizontal

    b. $375,000

Self-Tests for Understanding

Test A

1. b
2. c
3. c
4. d
5. b
6. a
7. b
8. d
9. d
10. a
11. c
12. c
13. b
14. c
15. c
16. a
17. b
18. b
19. a
20. d

Test B

1. F
2. F
3. F
4. F
5. T
6. T
7. T
8. F
9. F
10. F

Appendix

1. a. yes

    b. yes; game 2 and game 10

    c. yes; game 3, game 4, game 6, game 7 and game 8

    d. yes; game 5 and game 9

2. a. The marginal profit curve should drop continuously and should equal zero where total profits are maximized not where total profits equal zero.

    b. The marginal cost curve should go through the minimum of the average cost curve. When average cost is falling, the marginal cost curve should be below the average cost curve, and when average cost is rising, the marginal cost curve should be above the average cost curve.

Supplementary Exercises

1. a. $16,000

    b. $AC = 16,000/Q + 120 - 0.4Q + 0.002Q^2$
        $MC = 120 - 0.8Q + 0.006Q^2$

    c. It should.

    d. $MR = 300 - 0.5Q$

    f. $Q = 200$

    g. Find the positive value of Q such that MC = MR; $120 - 0.8Q + 0.006Q^2 = 300 - 0.5Q$; $Q = 200$

    h. When $Q = 200$, P = $250; TR = $50,000; TC = $40,000; total profits = $10,000

    j. $AC = 20,000/Q + 120 - .04Q + 0.0002Q^2$ No change in profit maximizing level of output as the change in fixed costs does not change either marginal cost or marginal revenue; total profits = $6,000

2. a. Set MC = MR.

Marginal cost: when P_L = 12 and P_M = 48, the least cost combination of inputs uses four hours of labor input for each hour of machine time. (See Supplementary Exercise 2 in Chapter 7.) To produce one widget, a firm would use two hours of labor with a half-hour of machine time for a total cost of $48. As the production function exhibits constant returns to scale, average and marginal cost are equal at $48 per widget.

$W = 2,500,000 - 25,000 P_W$

Total Revenue = $100 W - .00004 W^2$

MR = $100 - .00008 W$

To find the profit maximizing level of output set MC = MR.

$48 = 100 - .00008 W$

$W = 650,000$

$L = 1,300,000$

$M = 325,000$

$P_W = \$74$

b. Output: $W = (200,000)^{1/2}L^{1/2}$

Labor Input: $L = W^2/200,000$

Total (labor) cost = $12W^2/200,000$

Marginal (labor) cost = $24W/200,000$

$= .00012W$

MR = $100 - .00008 W$

Set MC = MR

$.00012W = 100 - .0008 W$

$.0002 W = 100$

$W = 500,000$

$L = 1,250,000$

$P_W = \$80.$

3. We know that profit maximizing firms set MR = MC and MC = MR > 0. If MR > 0, total revenue increases if quantity increases and total revenue decreases if quantity decreases. That is the price elasticity of demand for a profit maximizing firm is > 1.

Chapter 9

Chapter Review

(1) limited

(2) stock; bonds; plowback (or retained earnings)

(3) are not; more; bonds; meet bond payments

(4) falls; loss; increase

(5) are not; riskiness

(6) higher; lower; insurance

(7) random walk

(8) reduce; insurance; derived; fell; recession

(9) borrowed; magnifies

Important Terms and Concepts Quiz

1. k
2. c
3. m
4. g
5. q
6. o
7. n
8. i
9. e
10. b
11. j
12. a
13. d
14. r
15. p
16. f
17. l

Basic Exercises

a.
$t = 1$	74.07407
$t = 2$	68.58711
$t = 3$	63.50658
$t = 4$	58.80239
$t = 5$	54.44666
$t = 6$	50.41357
$t = 7$	46.67923
$t = 8$	43.22151
$t = 9$	40.01992
$t = 10$	37.05548
PV principal	463.1935
sum	1000

b. $i = .07, P = 1070.236$

$i = .06, P = 1147.202$

$i = .09, P = 935.8234$

$i = .10, P = 877.1087$

c.
Years	P
t = 1	1018.868
t = 2	1036.668
t = 3	1053.46
t = 4	1069.302
t = 5	1084.247
t = 6	1098.346
t = 7	1111.648
t = 8	1124.196
t = 9	1136.034
t = 10	1147.202
t = 11	1157.737
t = 12	1167.677
t = 13	1177.054
t = 14	1185.9
t = 15	1194.245
t = 16	1202.118
t = 17	1209.545
t = 18	1216.552
t = 19	1223.162
t = 20	1229.398
t = 21	1235.282
t = 22	1240.832
t = 23	1246.068
t = 24	1251.007
t = 25	1255.667

Self-Tests for Understanding

Test A
1. b
2. b
3. c
4. b
5. a, d
6. d
7. c
8. d
9. a
10. d
11. b
12. c
13. c
14. e
15. c
16. a
17. b
18. b,c
19. d
20. c

Test B
1. T
2. T
3. F
4. T
5. F
6. F
7. F
8. F
9. F
10. F

Supplementary Exercises

1. The prices of bonds for all companies are likely to move together in response to changes in economy-wide interest rates. Stock prices are more heavily influenced by the fortunes and misfortunes of individual companies. As a result, changes in share prices are more likely to differ across companies.

2. The return on the diversified portfolio will be an average of the returns on individual stocks. The diversified portfolio misses the big gainers but minimizes the impact of the worst performers. The portfolio gross return in Table 9-1 is an average. Looking at the returns from Table 9-2, we see that if the individual put all $10,000 into Apple, he or she would have performed better than the portfolio. However, if the individual chose Home Depot, he or she would have received a lower return relative to the portfolio in Table 9-1. By investing in several different stocks, the individual is protected against poor returns (Home Depot and FedEx) for one company.

   The rate of return (gross return as a percentage of the initial share price) for these companies is as follows:

   Apple: $23,353.63, 133.54%

   Best Buy: $10,770.84, 7.71%

   Cisco: $9,904.91, -0.95%

   Exxon Mobil: $12,405.34, 24.05%

FedEx: $8,248.48, -17.52%

General Electric: $10,269.72, 2.70%

Home Depot: $6,932.16, -30.68%

Merck: $13,679.12, 36.79%

Microsoft: $12,059.75, 20.60%

Wal-Mart: $10,480.77, 4.81%

For the portfolio with the shares equally divided between the 10 companies, the investor would have earned a rate of return of 18.1%.

Chapter 10

Chapter Review

(1) Many; Identical; Easy; Perfect; do not; zero

(2) horizontal; marginal

(3) marginal; losses; variable; marginal cost; variable

(4) horizontal; demand; supply

(5) loss; two; better; opportunity; economic; accounting

(6) profits; (shaded rectangle should go from the y axis to the point where marginal cost equals 20, down to the average cost curve and then back to the Y axis); enter; right; fall; $15.00 (minimum long run average cost; see the Basic Exercise); long-run average

Important Terms and Concepts Quiz

1. d
2. f
3. e
4. a
5. g
6. b

Basic Exercise

1. 1,400; $5,544 = (P − AC)Q; $5,310; $5,330
2. 1,200; −$4;380 = (P − AC)Q; −$4,550; −$4,532; −$10,140 (fixed costs)
3. 0; price does not cover average variable cost.
4. Firm's short-run supply curve is the portion of its marginal cost curve above average variable cost.
5. While under perfect competition marginal revenue equals price, one also needs to consider how a change in output affects costs. That is, the relevant comparison is price with marginal cost.
6. $15.00; 1,300 widgets

Self-Tests for Understanding

Test A

1. b
2. c
3. a
4. d
5. c
6. c
7. b
8. c
9. b
10. b
11. c
12. d
13. d
14. b
15. c
16. c
17. b
18. d
19. c
20. d

Test B

1. F
2. F
3. F
4. F
5. F
6. F
7. F
8. T
9. F
10. F

Supplementary Exercises

1. a. Average Cost = $10{,}140/Q + 0.00001Q^2 - 0.02Q + 16.3$

   b. Average variable cost = $0.00001Q^2 - 0.02Q + 16.3$

   c. Marginal cost = $.00003Q^2 - .04Q116.3$

3. To find the minimum of either average cost curve sets its derivative equal to zero.

   At min AC, $Q = 1{,}300$; AC = 15.00; at $Q = 1{,}300$, MC = 15.00

At min AVC, Q = 1,000; AVC = 6.30; at Q = 1,000, MC = 6.30

4. Supply = 0 if P < 6.30

    Supply = $[0.4+(-0.000356 + 0.00012P)^{1/2}] / 0.00006$ if $P \geq 6.30$

Chapter 11

Chapter Review

(1) one; no

(2) natural; barriers; entry

(3) negative; lower; decrease

(4) marginal; marginal; price; is not

(5) average; less; below; above

(6) demand; greater; less; less; will not; higher; lower

(7) price; marginal revenue; less; greater; greater than

(8) down

(9) will not; does not; maker

Important Terms and Concepts Quiz

1. e
2. a
3. g
4. b
5. f
6. d

Basic Exercises

1. a.   14
    b.   Marginal revenue: $6,900; $6,500; $6,100; $5,700
         Marginal cost: $5,625; $6,075; $6,525; $6,975
         revenue; cost; 14
    c.   9,100
    d.   30,884
    e.   Marginal revenue: same as in b.
         Total cost: $96,816; $103,441; $110,516; $118,041; $126,016
         Marginal cost: $6,625; $7,075; $7,525; $7,975
         13 widgets; $9,300;
    f. $200; If Mario increased his price by $1,000, the quantity sold would not maximize profits.
    g. $17,459
    h.   No change in output = 14 widgets; no change in price = $9,100; profits down $13,000 to $17,884. No change in pollution as output is unchanged.

The differences between questions e and h reflect the differences between the effects of a change in marginal and fixed costs. In Question e marginal cost changed as the tax was imposed on each widget produced. In Question h marginal cost is unchanged as the pollution charge is independent of the number of widgets produced.

2. a.   Total Revenue: $2,400,000; $3,093,750; $3,675,000; $4,143,750; $4,500,000; $4,743,750; $4,875,000; $4,893,750

         Marginal Revenue: $37; $31; $25; $19; $13; $7; $1

         Price $33; Output 143,750; Profits $806,250

    b.   Centerville: Total Revenue: $480,000; $1,125,000; $1,680,000; $2,145,000; $2,520,000; $2,805,000; $3,000,000; $3,105,000

         Marginal Revenue: $43; $37; $31; $25; $19; $13; $7

         Price $30; Quantity 100,000

         Middletown: Total Revenue: $1,920,000; $1,968,750; $1,995,000; $1,998,750; $1,980,000; $1,938,750; $1,875,000; $1,788,750

         Marginal Revenue: $13, $7; $1; –$5; –$11; –$17; –$23

         Price $45; Quantity 43,750

         Profits: $1,031,250

    c.   Middletown; Centerville

Self-Tests for Understanding

Test A

1. d
2. c
3. b
4. d
5. c
6. c
7. a
8. c
9. a
10. d
11. c
12. c
13. c
14. b
15. c

16. c

17. b

18. c

19. b

20. a

Test B

1. F

2. T

3. F

4. F

5. T

6. F

7. T

8. F

9. F

10. F

Supplementary Exercises

1. a. Total revenue = $11,900Q - 200Q^2$

   Marginal revenue = $11,900 - 400Q$

   Average cost = $225Q + 52,416/Q$

   Marginal cost = $450Q$

   c. $11,900 - 400Q = 450Q; 850Q = 11,900; Q = 14$

   d. Per-unit charge:

   TC = $52,416 + 225Q^2 + 1,000Q$

   AC = $225Q + 52,416/Q + 1,000$

   MC = $450Q + 1,000$

   Fixed charge:

   TC = $65,416 + 225Q^2$

   AC = $225Q + 65,416/Q$

   MC = $450Q$

   Note that the addition of a fixed cost element does not change marginal cost.

2. If a monopolist is originally producing where demand is inelastic, then an increase in market price will increase profits. The increase in price reduces costs as quantity declines and increases revenue as the percentage decline in the quantity sold is more than offset by the percentage increase in price. Thus the initial point could not have been a point of profit maximization. Similar reasoning rules out b, the case of unit elastic demand, as a point of profit maximization: profits increase as the reduction in quantity from an increase in price reduces costs while revenue is unchanged from the assumption of unit elasticity of demand.

Chapter 12

Chapter Review

(1) monopolistic; negative; marginal revenue; marginal cost; zero; entry; average

(2) oligopoly; cartel; price leadership

(3) zero; lower; larger

(4) will; will not; marginal; cost

(5) payoff; strategy; dominant; maximin; Nash; zero-sum; reputation; credible

(6) entry; exit; opportunity cost; capital

Important Terms and Concepts Quiz

1. g

2. m

3. a

4. i

5. c

6. n

7. k

8. e

9. b

10. p

11. h

12. l

13. q

14. j

15. f

16. d

Basic Exercises

1. a. Profit-maximizing level of output = 1,000 meals

   b. Marginal revenue: $2,200; $1,400; $600; −$200

   Marginal cost: $1,000; $1,000; $1,000; $1,000

   Profit-maximizing level of output = 1,000 meals

   MC is less than MR at less than 1,000 meals

   MC exceeds MR at more than 1,000 meals

   See also the Supplementary Exercise to this chapter.

2. a. 1,000; $200; Marginal revenue exceeds marginal cost up to 1,000 sets and is less than marginal cost beyond 1,000 sets.

   b. No change in price or quantity. It is the kink in the demand curve that gives rise to the discontinuity in marginal revenue. Fluctuations of marginal cost within this discontinuity have no

313

impact on the profit maximizing level of output or price.

c. Marginal cost would have to rise above $150 a set.

d. Marginal cost would have to fall below $50 a set.

Self-Tests for Understanding

Test A

1. b
2. c
3. a
4. b
5. a
6. b
7. c
8. b
9. d
10. b
11. d
12. c
13. c
14. b
15. c
16. c
17. d
18. c
19. b
20. a

Test B

1. T
2. T
3. F
4. F
5. F
6. T
7. T
8. F
9. T
10. F

Supplementary Exercises

1. Total Revenue = $25Q - Q^2/100$

   Marginal Revenue = $25 - Q/50$

   Average Cost = $10,000/Q + 5$

   Marginal Cost = 5

Profit-maximizing level of output sets MC = MR:

$25 - Q/50 = 5$; $Q = 1000$

2. TR = $80Q - 0.005Q^2$

   AR = $80 - 0.005Q$

   MR = $80 - 0.01Q$

   AC = $0.00000015625Q^2 - 0.003125Q + 40.625$

   MC = $0.00000046875Q^2 - 0.00625Q + 40.625$

   a. Set MR = MC

      $Q = 6,000$; $P = 60$; profits = 135,000

   b. Set MR = 0

      $Q = 8,000$; $P = 40$; profits = 115,000

   c. yes

Chapter 13

Chapter Review

1. less; less
2. increasing; reduction; increase
3. predatory pricing; is not; variable
4. concentration; Herfindahl-Hirshman; little
5. scale; scope; is not; below; above
6. high
7. decline; less; losses
8. reduces;

Important Terms and Concepts Quiz

1. l
2. e
3. k
4. m
5. g
6. f
7. d
8. b
9. c
10. j
11. a
12. i

Basic Exercises

1. a. *Q*: 60; 90; 120; 150

   AC: 15¢; 11.7¢;10¢;9¢

   MC: 5¢;5¢; 5¢; 5¢

b. $6 million loss at all levels of output.

c. No; fixed costs are never covered.

2. a. 75¢ a pound

b. The admonition to shut down if price drops below average variable cost assumes that the acts of shutting down and restarting are themselves costless. If, in contrast, it is costly to shutdown and then restart production lines, a firm might continue with production for a short period of time even if price is less than average variable cost to avoid the costs of shutting down and restarting. In the case of predatory pricing, a firm would deliberately accept losses for a short period of time, if it gave the firm monopoly power and the ability to earn economic profits in the future sufficient to overcome the losses incurred while driving out rivals. Thus a price below average variable cost might be an indication of predatory pricing, but it might also be a rational response to changing market conditions and by itself is likely to be insufficient evidence of predatory pricing.

3. 80, 90, 90; 3,000; 2,075; 5,750

The Herfindahl-Hirshman Index gives greater weight to large firms because its squares market share.

Self-Tests for Understanding

Test A

1. b, d
2. a, b, d
3. a, d
4. b
5. d
6. c
7. b
8. b
9. b
10. a
11. c
12. d
13. b
14. b
15. d
16. a
17. c
18. c
19. c
20. d

Test B

1. F
2. F
3. F
4. T
5. T
6. F
7. F
8. F
9. F
10. F

Economics in Action

In June 2001, the Justice department's case was dismissed by Judge J. Thomas Marten who said, "There is no doubt that American may be a difficult, vigorous, even brutal competitor, but here, it engaged only in bare, but not brass, knuckle competition." In January 2002, the Justice Department appealed.

The government lost its appeal.

Chapter 14

Chapter Review

(1) are not

(2) selection; planning; distribution

(3) was not; efficient

(4) efficient; decreasing

(5) increase; cost; greater; is not; equals

(6) price; marginal cost; price; price

(7) utility; cost; equals

(8) maximize

(9) input; output

Important Terms and Concepts Quiz

1. c
2. e
3. b
4. d
5. f

Basic Exercise

1. $25; $15
2. $10; more
3. decrease; $3; fewer
4. $18

Self-Tests for Understanding

Test A
1. d
2. b
3. d
4. c
5. d
6. c
7. b
8. c
9. b
10. b
11. c
12. a
13. b
14. c
15. b
16. c

Test B
1. T
2. F
3. F
4. T
5. F
6. F
7. T
8. T
9. F
10. T

Supplementary Exercises
1. a. No
   b. increase; 1; increase; 2; inefficient
   c. Consumers respond to the same set of prices and consume so that marginal utility equals price.
2. a. 120; 1,200; 160; 800; +40; +400. Note that this reallocation of inputs should work to move the ratio of marginal physical products in the production of corn and tomatoes toward equality.
   b. In competitive markets, profit maximizing firms adjust the use of inputs until the ratio of marginal physical products is equal to the ratio of input prices. By adjusting to common prices, the ratio of marginal physical products is equated across alternative uses.

Chapter 15

Chapter Review
(1) opportunity
(2) marginal cost; marginal utility; on
(3) little
(4) externalities; detrimental; beneficial
(5) higher; higher
(6) private; inefficient; much; less
(7) depletability; excludability; public
(8) difficult; rider
(9) zero; zero
(10) does not; less
(11) irreversible
(12) limited

Important Terms and Concepts Quiz
1. q
2. h
3. b
4. i
5. n
6. e
7. d
8. f
9. k
10. p
11. l
12. g
13. m
14. r
15. o
16. s
17. c

Basic Exercise
1. Col. 1: $2,640,000; $11; $2,112,000; $10.56
2. Col. 2: 120; $2,640,000; $11; 100; $2,200,000; $11; cost of producing widgets unchanged; cost per hour of police service up 4.17 percent.
3. Col. 3: 80; $2,640,000; $11; 100; $3,300,000; $16.50; cost of producing widgets unchanged; cost per hour of police service up 50 percent over 10 years.

Self-Tests for Understanding
Test A
1. c
2. c
3. d
4. c

5. d   (and possibly b)
6. d
7. a
8. c
9. b
10. c
11. d
12. d
13. b
14. c
15. a, b, c, d
16. d
17. b
18. a
19. c
20. b

Test B

1. F
2. F
3. T
4. F
5. F
6. F
7. T
8. T
9. T
10. F

Supplementary Exercises

1. a.   See table and diagram below.
   b.   Widgets:
        MP(L) = 22.61
        AP(L)= 45.23
        Recitals:
        MP(L) = 50
        AP(L) = 50
   c.   Widgets:
        MP(L) = 25.63
        AP(L) = 51.26
        Recitals:
        MP(L) = 50
        AP(L) = 50

   Productivity of widget
   workers is up 13.3 percent.
   No increase in the productivity of musicians.

d.   Opportunity cost of recitals has risen 13.3 percent from 0.45 widgets to 0.51 widgets.
     PPF: Recitals = $50[40,000 - W^2/(3600K)]$

e.   Except for when all labor is allocated to playing recitals, the new production possibilities frontier is outside the original frontier.

Chapter 16

Chapter Review

(1) innovation
(2) invention; innovation; entrepreneurs; small entrepreneurial
(3) cost; entry
(4) ratchet
(5) externalities
(6) trading; licensing
(7) higher; lower

Important Terms and Concepts Quiz

1. r
2. g
3. c
4. p
5. i
6. n
7. s
8. a
9. d

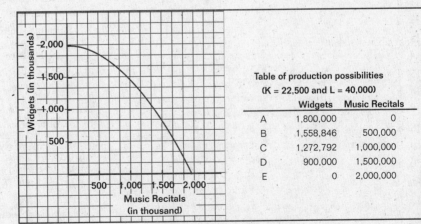

Table of production possibilities (K = 22,500 and L = 40,000)

	Widgets	Music Recitals
A	1,800,000	0
B	1,558,846	500,000
C	1,272,792	1,000,000
D	900,000	1,500,000
E	0	2,000,000

317

10. l

11. q

12. o

13. h

14. j

15. b

16. e

17. m

18. f

Basic Exercises

1. $31,000; $51,047; $83,849; $137,393; $224,584

    Note that although the growth rate increases by the same one-half of one percent, the difference in GDP per capita gets bigger and bigger.

2. 2 percent

Self-Tests for Understanding

Test A

1. b

2. c

3. b, d

4. d

5. a,b,c,d

6. b

7. a

8. c

9. b

10. d

11. d

12. a

13. d

14. c

15. d

16. b

17. c

18. b, d

19. b

20. b

Test B

1. F

2. F

3. T

4. T

5. T

6. T

7. F

8. T

9. T

10. T

Chapter 17

Chapter Review

(1) externality; decrease; taxes

(2) controls; inefficient; more

(3) marginal

(4) can never; price

(5) discourage; incentive; encourage; incentive; encouraging

Important Terms and Concepts Quiz

1. c

2. e

3. a

4. d

Basic Exercises

1. a. 15 cents; 10 million

    b. falls; rises; declines; shifts up by 5 cents; no change or falls to zero, i.e., some firms leave industry; declines.

    c. Since the tax is per bag, not per unit of pollution, the pollution control equipment will not reduce a firm's pollution tax.

    d. No. Since the equipment is only 75 percent effective, the total cost of using the equipment (4 cents plus the 1.25 cent emission tax per bag) is greater than the tax of 5 cents per bag.

    e. Less than 3.75 cents; more than 5.33 cents

    f. Price rises and industry output declines as some high-cost firms leave the industry.

2. a. Energy: 18.0; 17.8; 17.7; 17.4; 17.1; 16.7; 16.7; 16.4; 16.0; 15.6; 15.2; 14.4; 14.1; 13.5; 13.2; 12.6; 12.3; 12.2; 12.3; 12.2; 11.9; 11.9; 11.7; 11.6; 11.4; 11.4; 11.3; 10.9; 10.5; 10.2; 10.1; 9.7; 938; 9.6; 9.4; 9.1; 8.8

    b. Energy use rose during the late 1960s as the relative price of energy fell. The rise in energy prices following 1973 led to a significant decline in energy consumption per dollar of GDP. Energy consumption per thousand dollars of GDP has continued to decline throughout the 1980s even as relative energy prices have fallen. Patterns of energy consumption per thousand dollars of GDP up to 1981 could be interpreted as a movement along a demand curve in response to changes in relative price. The introduction of energy conservation practices, e.g., home insulation, energy-efficient machines and cars meant that one would not expect energy consumption to return to earlier levels even as relative energy prices declined. Changes in the structure of the economy, i.e., the increasing importance of services as compared to manufacturing, is also likely to have reduced the demand for energy. Energy prices were lower at the end of 2004 than they were in the early 1980s yet energy use is dramatically lower. In 2005 and 2006, energy use continued to all as energy prices started moving from lows touched in previous years.

Self-Tests for Understanding

Test A

1. b
2. e
3. c
4. b
5. d
6. b
7. a
8. b
9. b
10. b
11. a
12. d
13. c
14. b
15. d
16. b
17. a
18. c
19. c
20. d

Test B

1. F

2. F
3. F
4. F
5. F
6. F
7. F
8. F
9. T
10. T

Supplementary Exercise

1. MC = 15.

   $P = 65 - .025Q$; TR $= 65Q - 0.025Q^2$; MR $= 65 - 0.05Q$.

   Set MC = MR to solve for profit maximizing output: $15 = 65 - .05Q$; Q = 1,000; P = 40 cents; Profit = 25 cents on each of 1,000 million bags or $250 million.

2. If price rises by 5 cents, quantity demanded will decline to 800 million bags. At price of 45 cents, profit is 25 cents a bag or $200 million. Set MC = MR to determine profit maximizing level of output: $20 = 65 - 0.05Q$; Q = 900; P = 42.5 cents ; profits 22.5 cents a bag or $202.5 million.

3. Long-run equilibrium price equals minimum average cost = 15 cents. Market quantity = 2,000 million bags; 200 firms producing 10 million bags each.

4. Short run: For representative firm AC = $.4(Q - 10)^2 + 20$.

   TC $= 0.4Q^3 - 8Q^2 + 60Q$.

   MC $= 1.2Q^2 - 16Q + 60$.

   As each firm supplies 1/200 of the market, we can find the short-run profit maximizing position of each firm by setting MC equal to price.

   MC $= 65 - 0.025(Q \times 200)$, or

   $1.2Q^2 - 16Q + 60 = 65 - 5Q$.

   The mathematics of solving this equation for Q are a bit cumbersome. Rounding off, firm output = 9.6 million bags; industry output = 1,920 million bags; and price = 17 cents. Note that price is now less than average cost.

   Long run: Some firms leave in response to short-run losses. Long-run equilibrium occurs where remaining firms produce at minimum average cost.

   Price = 20 cents; market demand = 1,800; each of 180 firms produce 10 million bags.

The conditions in this problem—marginal cost for the monopolist equal to the minimum average cost of competitive firms, new firms can operate with the same cost curves, i.e., the long run industry supply curve is horizontal and the same demand curve under either market structure—imply the following: 1) by restricting output, the monopolist creates less pollution than the perfectly competitive industry; 2) the monopolist is unable to pass on the full extent of the pollution tax; and 3) in long-run equilibrium under perfect competition, consumers pay all of the pollution tax.

Economics in Action

1. Simon won the original bet and received a check for $567.07 from Ehrlich. You can read about the bet in John Tierney's article "Betting the Planet," *New York Times Magazine*, December 2, 1990.

    The United States Geological Survey publishes data on mineral prices. You might start with this Web site: http://minerals.usgs.gov/minerals/pubs/metal_prices/

Chapter 18

Chapter Review

(1) direct; indirect; personal income; payroll; corporate
(2) average; marginal; progressive; proportional; regressive; reduce
(3) payroll; regressive; do not; zero; are not
(4) sales; property; federalism
(5) equity; horizontal; vertical; vertical; benefits; benefits
(6) burden; greater; excess burden; does not; smallest
(7) higher; lower; smaller
(8) incidence; shifting
(9) demand; supply; inelastic; workers; firms

Important Terms and Concepts Quiz

1. b
2. p
3. i
4. n
5. r
6. g
7. s
8. v
9. a
10. j
11. u
12. w

13. x
14. k
15. y
16. f
17. m
18. h
19. t
20. o
21. c
22. z
23. d
24. q
25. e
26. l

Basic Exercises

2. $42; 50 million
3. $46; 44 million
4. $4; it is less than increase in tax.
5. All are likely to decline.
7. The first demand curve.
8. $50; 48 million; Figure 18-3; Figure 18-3; consumers

Self-Tests for Understanding

Test A
1. b
2. d
3. c
4. b, c
5. d
6. c
7. c
8. d As long as the marginal rate exceeds the average rate the average rate will increase whether the marginal rate increases, decreases or remains unchanged.
9. b
10. b
11. b
12. b
13. b
14. b
15. c
16. c
17. c
18. b

19. a
20. c
21. a

Test B

1. F
2. T
3. T
4. T
5. T
6. F
7. F
8. T
9. F
10. F

Supplementary Exercise

1. Taxes: 0; $2,000; $4,000; $6,000; $16,000; $46,000
   Average Tax Rate: 0; 0.0667; 0.10; 0.12; 0.16; 0.184
   Marginal Tax Rate: 0; 0.20; 0.20; 0.20; 0.20; 0.20

2. b. Revenue = TQ

   Harris: Revenue =
   $25.608\, T - 2.95\, T^2$
   T = $4.34 maximizes tax revenue; taxes = $55.57 billion

   Grossman: Revenue
   $= 27.5184\, T - 10.91\, T^2$
   T = $1.26 maximizes tax revenue; taxes = $17.35 billion

   c. Harris: ΔQ = -1.475; elasticity = 0.275
   Grossman: ΔQ = −5.455; elasticity = 1.107 When demand is more elastic, every increase in the tax leads to a larger reduction in the quantity demanded. As a result the revenue maximizing tax is lower.
   Harris did not solve for the revenue maximizing tax. Rather he analyzed the impact of $2 increase in cigarette taxes and estimated a net increase in revenue of $28 billion. The straight line approximation to the Harris demand curve for this exercise shows a gross increase in revenue of $37.56 billion following a $2 tax increase.

   d. When the supply curve is infinitely elastic (horizontal), consumers pay all of any increase in taxes. If the supply curve were perfectly inelastic (vertical), then producers would pay all of any increase in taxes and there would be no change in the quantity demanded regardless of the elasticity

of demand. If the supply curve has a positive slope, that is if the elasticity of supply is not infinite or zero, then the incidence of any increase in taxes will be divided between consumers and producers depending upon the elasticities of demand and supply.

Chapter 19

Chapter Review

(1) productivity; revenue
(2) negative; more; positive; higher; below
(3) discounting; fewer; lower
(4) is not; exceed
(5) all; no
(6) most; part; is
(7) higher; equal
(8) increase; increase; more
(9) greater; greater; greater

Important Terms and Concepts Quiz

1. g
2. c
3. l
4. d
5. j
6. m
7. e
8. h
9. a
10. i
11. n
12. f
13. k

Basic ExerciseS

1. Economic profit = Net revenue − opportunity cost of labor − cost of other inputs; Economic profit = $500 − ($10 × 40) − $60 = $500 − $460 = $40.

2. $60; The rent for the sunny plot should reflect the difference in the cost of production as compared to the marginal plot.

3. If the owner of the sunny plot tried charging a rent that exceeded the $60 difference in production costs, Darlene would make a greater profit by growing her flowers on the marginal plot. With a rent of $60 for the sunny plot she would be indifferent about using either plot.

321

Self-Tests for Understanding
Test A
1. d
2. a
3. c
4. b
5. c
6. c
7. a
8. c
9. d
10. d
11. a
12. b
13. c
14. a
15. c
16. b
17. b
18. b
19. c
20. a

Test B
1. F
2. T
3. T
4. T
5. F
6. T
7. F
8. F
9. T
10. F

Appendix

Important Terms and Concepts Quiz: Appendix
1. a

Basic Exercises: Appendix
1. a. $1,818.18; $2,066.12; $3,884.30; –$115.70
    b.   cost; no
    c. $1,904.76; $2,267.57; $4,172.33; $172.33
    d.   present value of returns; yes
    e.   5 percent: $200; $4,200; $2,200; $110; $2,310.
         10 percent: $400; $4,400; $2,400; $240; $2,640

f.   5 percent: $1,800; $90; $4,390; $190
     10 percent: $1,600; $160; $4,260; –$140

2. The contest sponsors could meet their payments to Mr. Calhoun by investing a smaller sum in 1993 and using both the initial investment along with the interest earnings to make the necessary future payments. Present value calculations show how much must be invested today to fund the future payments. Assuming the first payment was made right away, the sponsors need to invest a sum sufficient to fund 19 future payments of $50,000, or

$$\sum_{t=1}^{19} \frac{\$50,000}{(1+i)^t}$$

If the interest rate was 6.5%, the present value of the 19 future payments was only $557,906. Including the first payment to Mr. Calhoun brings the total cost of $1,000,000 to $607,906. A higher interest rate would mean higher interest earnings and result in a lower present value, while a lower interest rate would mean a higher present value and require a larger initial investment by the contest sponsors.

Supplementary Exercise
If dividends and future stock prices are known for sure, buying that stock should offer investors the risk adjusted market rate of return. If earnings and dividends reflect monopoly profits, the price of the stock will be high while the rate of return will still reflect the risk adjusted market rate of return. The biggest winners (the ones who will earn the highest rate of return), will be those who identified the potential for oil companies to generate higher future dividends before others in the market. These are the individuals who paid a low initial price and who therefore stand to gain the most.

Chapter 20

Chapter Review
(1) leisure; more; decrease; income
(2) more; substitution; increases; offset
(3) greater; revenue; negative
(4) demand; higher
(5) monopolist; monopsonist; lower; higher; two; bilateral
(6) Entrepreneurs, monoploy, reduces
(7) fixed, public, marginal

Important Terms and Concepts Quiz
1. i
2. f
3. h

4. a

5. c

6. e

7. g

8. d

9. j

10. k

Basic Exercises

1. 60; 55; 50; 45; 40; 35; 30; 25; 20; 15

2. $4,800; $4,400; $4,000; $3,600; $3,200; $2,800; $2,400; $2,000; $1,600; $1,200

3. 7; profits = $9,800

4. $2,000; 800; 8; $11,200; if 7 workers, profits also = $11,200 as MRP = wage for eighth worker.

5. a. $3,600

   b.   900 workers

   c. $2,800 and 600 workers, or $2,400 and 700 workers

Self-Tests for Understanding

Test A

1. d

2. a

3. b

4. c

5. b

6. c

7. b

8. a

9. d

10. b

11. c

12. c

13. a

14. c

15. c

16. d

17. d

18. b

19. a

20. c

Test B

1. T

2. T

3. F

4. F

5. F

6. F

7. F

8. F

9. T

10. F

Supplementary Exercises

a. $2,000; 8

b.   greater

Total labor cost: $600; $1,600; $3,000; $4,800; $7,000; $9,600; $12,600; $16,000; $19,800; $24,000

Marginal labor cost: $600; $1,000; $1,400; $1,800; $2,200; $2,600; $3,000; $3,400; $3,800; $4,200

d.   6 workers

e. $1,600

f. $13,200 = $80 × 285 − 6 × $1,600.

g.   Both wages and employment would increase. Tony would hire 7 workers at $2,200 a month. The "high" minimum wage increases employment because it changes Tony's marginal cost of labor schedule.

h.   No. If the union had more than 7 workers, it might want a lower wage to increase employment. If the union had 7 or fewer workers, it might be able to extract a higher wage by bargaining for some of Tony's profits.

Chapter 21

Chapter Review

(1) 22,000; absolute; relative

(2) 50.3%; 3.4%

(3) different; are not; overstate

(4) efficiency

(5) decrease

(6) break-even

(7) negative; small

Important Terms and Concepts Quiz

1. a

2. g

3. e

4. h

5. f

6. c

7. b

Basic Exercises

1. Col 7: 18,600; 23,198; 25,703; 26,361; 26,274; 26,416; 28,303; 29,036; 31,500

3. Col. 4: 4,598; 2,505; 658; -87; 142; 1,887; 733; 2,464

   Col. 5: 1,402; 1,195; 2,342; 5,387; 408; 9,563; 442; 1,361

   Col. 6: 23%; 32%; 78%; 102%; 74%; 84%; 38%; 36%

   The marginal tax rates in column 6 should be equivalent to the slopes of the line segments you graphed in Figure 21-1.

Self-Tests for Understanding

Test A

1. d
2. c
3. b
4. b
5. a
6. c
7. a
8. c
9. b
10. c
11. d
12. c
13. c
14. a
15. a,d
16. c
17. a
18. a Differences in schooling might reflect voluntary decisions or discrimination in access to schooling.
19. d
20. d

Test B

1. T
2. F
3. F
4. F
5. F
6. F
7. F

8. F

9. T

10. F

Appendix

Discrimination by employers; If some employers discriminate against particular workers, other employers should be able to hire these workers at lower wages and thus produce at lower cost than the first set of employers. Discrimination by employees does not give rise to a similar opportunity for a non-discriminator to operate at lower cost.

Supplementary Exercises

1. The graph is a Lorenz curve, named for American economist Max O. Lorenz who developed the graph in 1905 as a way to describe income distribution. If everyone received the same income, then the Lorenz curve for such a country would lie along the 45 degree line. Lorenz argued that the extent to which the line sags below the 45 degree line can be used as a measure of income inequality.

   For the three countries pictured in the graph, the line for Finland lies closest to the 45 degree line while the line for Mexico is furthest away. Plot the Lorenz curve for other countries to see how they compare to these three.

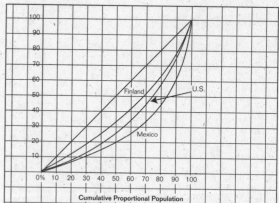

2. There are three interpretations of the word average: 1) the most frequent, measured by the mode, 2) the value that evenly divides a population, measured by the median, and 3) the sum of a variable of interest divided by the size of the population, measured by the arithmetic average or mean.

   The median income of $43,318 tells us that 50% of U.S. households earned more than $43,318 in 2003 and 50% of households earned less. The mean reports the arithmetic average income level. If a small number of households earn extremely high incomes, this will increase the average but leave the median unaffected. Many feel that the median income is a better measure of typical household income. The fact that the U.S. median is below the average implies that a small number of households have very high income levels.

4. Answers will vary.

Chapter 22

Chapter Review

(1) scale

(2) comparative

(3) A; B; 100,000; wheat

(4) 80,000; 70,000; cars; wheat

(5) tariffs; quotas; subsidies; price; quantity

(6) government

(7) low; do not; can

(8) adjustment

(9) defense; infant

(10) both; comparative

Important Terms and Concept Quiz

1. j
2. d
3. g
4. m
5. i
6. n
7. f
8. a
9. l
10. h
11. k
12. b
13. e

Basic Exercise

1. Japan; Japan
2. 1.25; 1.5; Canada; Japan; Canada; Japan
3. Calculators: 1,500,000; 3,000,000; 4,500,000
    Backpacks: 1,200,000; 2,000,000; 3,200,000
4. 600,000; 480,000

5. 1,200,000 hours; 600,000 calculators; 400,000 backpacks

6. increase; 80,000

7. Calculators: 900,000; 3,675,000; 4,575,000
    Backpacks: 1,680,000; 1,550,000; 3,230,000

    The output of both calculators and backpacks has increased as compared to the initial situation in Question c.

8. Canadian backpack output would fall to 720,000. Japan would need to reallocate 1,440,000 labor hours. Total calculator output would fall to 4,380,000. This reallocation is not in line with the principle of comparative advantage.

9. There will be no change in total world output. Neither country has a comparative advantage. The opportunity cost of increased calculator or backpack production is the same in both countries.

Self-Tests for Understanding

Test A

1. b
2. d
3. b
4. d
5. a
6. b
7. d
8. d
9. a
10. a
11. c
12. a
13. a
14. b
15. c
16. c
17. d
18. c
19. b, d
20. c

Test B

1. F
2. F

3. T

4. T

5. F

6. F

7. T

8. F

9. F

10. F

Appendix

1. India: $10; 1,000 United States: $40; 800

2. $20; India: 800; 1,200: 400; 0

   United States: 1,000; 600; 0; 400

3. India: 15; 900; 1,100; 200; 0

   United States: 30; 900; 700; 0; 200

   United States; India; United States; India

4. $15

Supplementary Exercises

1. a. Baulmovia: 8,100; Bilandia: 17,150

   b. 12; Baulmovia; Bilandia; 100

   c. Baulmovia: price = 10;

   Bilandia: price = 14.5;

   Trade = 50.

   d. 50

   Tariff revenues accrue to the government. Tariffs do not protect high-cost foreign producers.

2. a. Arcadia

   b. Ricardia

   c. Arcadia should increase the production of computers and export computers to Ricardia which should increase the production of cheese and export cheese to Arcadia. For example

   Change in Production

	Computers	Cheese
Arcadia	+ 4	− 2
Ricardia	− 2	+ 4
World	+ 2	+ 2

   Following the changes in production, both countries will be able to consume outside their PPF. If Arcadia exports up 3 computers for 3,000 pounds of cheese while Ricardia imports 3 computers for 3,000 pounds of cheese, both countries end up with 1

more computer and an additional 1000 pounds of cheese as compared to their pre-trade situation. Try locating these points of production and consumption to illustrate that adjustments of production in line with the law of comparative advantage allows both countries to consume outside their production possibilities frontier.

3. Production of 14.4 million bolts of cloth and 10.8 million barrels of wine allows Cimonoce to choose from the outermost consumption possibilities line. Note that to be on the outermost consumption possibilities line Cimonoce must choose to produce at the point where the slope of the production possibilities frontier equals the ratio of world prices.